JOE CANNING

MY STORY

JOE CANNING

MY STORY

CANNING

WITH VINCENT HOGAN

Gill Books

Gill Books
Hume Avenue
Park West
Dublin 12
www.gillbooks.ie

Gill Books is an imprint of M.H. Gill and Co.

978 18045 8083 7

Typeset by Typo•glyphix
Edited by Bernadette Kearns
Proofread by Noel O'Regan
Printed and bound in Great Britain by Clays Ltd, Elcograf S.p.A.

This book is typeset in 11.5/17 pt Sabon.

The paper used in this book comes from the wood pulp of sustainably managed forests.

A CIP catalogue record for this book is available from the British Library.

5 4 3 2 1

FSC
www.fsc.org

MIX
Paper | Supporting
responsible forestry
FSC® C018072

To Mam and Dad
for always giving me the opportunity
to be the best that I could be.

CONTENTS

PROLOGUE

I am a father. I am a father. I am a father!

Even now, less than half a year into the young life of Josie Canning, I still find myself staring at our daughter's tiny form with almost gormless wonder. She is – as every parent will tell you of their child – perfect. But Josie actually *is* perfect. Some day she will come to understand that. We'll make sure of it.

Meg and I became a mam and dad at precisely 11.06 a.m. on Tuesday, 28 May 2024 in Limerick's maternity hospital. That's when my old life ended in a way.

Until then, everything I'd chased and been measured by had an identifiable finish line. Success or failure. Light or dark. The only version of myself that really made sense – the version that was fully in sync with the world around me – was that of the hurler.

And then, almost in an eye-blink, that world tightened into something no metric could define. I'd say I heard the baby's cry within four minutes of stepping into the operating theatre. The magic of a Caesarean.

Meg had been kept in overnight just for monitoring of her blood pressure, the due date still thought to be two weeks away. But that morning, I was awoken to a 7.30 a.m. phone call.

'We're having a section at half 10!'

When Marguerite, the midwife, confirmed that we had a healthy baby girl, the emotion really hit me. We'd chosen not to know the baby's gender in advance, yet had long settled on a girl's name. If it was a boy, we were undecided.

Life's been hard for Dad since my mam, Josephine, passed, and I hope it meant a lot when he heard his new grandchild's name. He and a few of the brothers came over to Limerick to 'wet the baby's head', and that evening he said something really lovely.

'She's half a Galway girl and half a Limerick lady!'

Meg's from Limerick, you see. We first met in 2018 when I called into her café in Castletroy, No 13 The Factory, for a coffee, and the connection grew slowly over time. She's someone very private and understated. Hurling made little enough noise in her world before we met, and it's not exactly a deafening presence even now. I like it that way. We both do. For Meg, hurling has always been just something that I did, not the definition of who I was. I'm sure there have been days when just being among the Cannings has felt slightly overwhelming for her, given how the game resonates through just about every second family conversation.

No doubt she's occasionally found herself sitting in Gortanumera, thinking: 'Could we maybe talk about something else for once?'

You see, if anything, she comes from football people. Meg's grandfather, Paddy Hoare, hails from Mountbellew–Moylough and went to school in St Jarlath's with Seán Purcell. There's a photo in their Limerick kitchen today of himself and the great man sitting next to one another for a team picture. Married to a Milltown woman, Mary, Paddy has remained heavily involved with the Galway Association across the years. And Meg's brother, Jack, played football with Monaleen for a few years, winning three county championships.

There are now four generations of Paddy Hoares in the family, given Meg's dad is Pat, one of her brothers is Patrick and her nephew is Paddy.

Maybe the Galway connection made it easier for me to

assimilate into the family, but they have certainly been incredibly welcoming to me and all the Cannings.

Meg supports my hurling commitments without ever feeling pressured by them. Put it this way: when she asks how training has gone, it isn't exactly in pursuit of microscopic detail. Her day is as important as mine. Always will be.

Whenever I had a game on the horizon with Galway, it was never a case of her feeling compelled to be present. Sometimes it suited her to be there; sometimes it didn't. If she had something else already organised, there was never an expectation of cancelling that arrangement. For other players' wives and partners, maybe the match would always be the unquestioned priority. But it never bothered me if Meg wasn't there. Actually, when Portumna were going well in 2022, silly superstition had me actively discouraging her from going. Having won a few games in her absence, my fear was that any change might bring bad luck now.

Hand on heart, I've always been comfortable with the idea of life after hurling. I've never been afraid of who I'd be without it.

Yes, it was the focal point of my life for as long as I could remember, with everything else adjusted to work in harmony. Almost every single aspect of my life was geared towards one game after another. But I always felt able to step away from it too. I always had this thing that, off the field, I wanted to be in the position of working on my own terms. To a large degree, I've managed to achieve that.

For me, one thing never had to be irreconcilable with the other.

So even my commercial link-ups as an inter-county player were planned through a long lens. I was always preparing for life after hurling.

It never frightened me.

The first Galway game I went to after retiring from inter-county was a National Hurling League clash between Limerick and

Galway on a bitterly cold February night at the Gaelic Grounds in 2022. Just myself, Meg and her nephew, Paddy, sitting on the terrace; me with a hat pulled low and a snood pulled up for anonymity. I felt comfortable sitting outside the wire, though, being honest, I'm not sure I'd entirely closed the door on Galway at that point.

When you retire, there's what I would call a period of unreality that sets in. On some level, you're still thinking: *Jesus, maybe I could give it one last shot …?*

It takes time to rinse that from your system fully, and on the terrace that night, I can't honestly say I was fully reconciled with my new circumstances. There's still that voice in your head – your ego, essentially – declaring, 'I could still do a job out there!' It's not a realistic thought, but it's a stubborn one. Only time quietens it to the eventual point of silence. And that silence falls when you finally find yourself at a game one day, feeling glad that you're not out on the field. When you're thinking how you could be embarrassed now just trying to hurl at that intensity.

I can't say I'd reached that point in February 2022. In fact, I categorically hadn't.

Henry Shefflin's appointment as the new Galway manager muddied a lot of things inside my head. Just human nature. How could I not be tempted by the idea of working under a man of his calibre?

And that night in the Gaelic Grounds, Galway finished strong to inflict Limerick's first home National League defeat in three years. Reduced to 14 by Gearóid Hegarty's dismissal, the All-Ireland champions were held scoreless for the closing 10 minutes. Henry, thus, was two from two in the League. It seemed he had Galway flying.

But, deep down, I think you know when thoughts of a return are far-fetched. And over time, I slowly became increasingly comfortable just pitching up discreetly at games of all kinds in Limerick, young Paddy Hoare often by my side.

Josie's arrival this May has definitely made me even more settled and introspective. Funny how you can spend half your life seeking vindication with a hurl in your hand, only to realise that the emotions of winning and losing can't even begin to touch the stuff that matters most.

The Monday after she was born, Meg and I brought Josie to Mam's grave. A few neighbours came over to say hello.

'Meet Josie,' I said.

We both saw in their eyes an instant recognition of the significance of the name.

'That's just lovely,' one of them said.

And honestly, it felt it.

1.

THE KING AND I

'Joe, I can't play on Thursday. Something's after coming up at work ...'

The Tuesday evening text from Henry Shefflin began to make sense less than 24 hours later. We'd been due in Adare for a round of golf with a mutual friend, Alan Clancy, but an imminent Galway GAA announcement was about to spike our arrangement indefinitely.

When the best-kept secret in sport was revealed to a startled public the next day, Wednesday, 20 October 2021, I texted Henry a one-liner: 'No wonder you couldn't play!'

The moment I heard the news, I must admit that just one, single word came charging into my head: *Fuck!*

Meg and I went out to dinner that evening, and naturally, we were chatting about the identity of the new Galway hurling manager. 'Christ, I'd love another crack at it now,' I told her.

I'd retired in July 2021 from a conviction that Galway probably wouldn't be in the shake-up to win the MacCarthy Cup in 2022. Now I began to wonder if I'd just sabotaged my shot at going out in glory. In an ideal world, I'd have signed off on my inter-county career with an All-Ireland win in Croke Park. It's probably the most natural of conceits to have in your head, and the truth now was that I'd love to have seen how it might have worked out for me getting to play for Henry.

Meg may not be into hurling, but she could see straight away how conflicted the news had left me. If I wanted to return, I knew she would back me 100 per cent. And had I listened to my heart that evening, I'd have issued a statement immediately, declaring my retirement one of the shortest in GAA history.

But my head has pretty much always got its way in these matters, and of course, I was stubborn too. You make a decision; you stick to it. Deep down, I knew my body just really wasn't up to inter-county intensity anymore. Imagine if I went back only to discover I wasn't able to perform under the new management? I've dealt with pressure all my life, but that would have been an entirely different sort of pressure. Especially with the Henry angle.

For so much of my career, the media had me down as the prince to Henry's king. When Portumna and Ballyhale met in successive All-Ireland club championships – the 2009 semi-final and the 2010 final – it was as though we frequently found ourselves side by side in a convenient newspaper narrative, even though we barely knew each other as people.

This is a side to things that is all too frequently overlooked. People imagine that over the years you develop some kind of distant friendships with big rivals. That you all, somehow, get to know one another.

But you don't. I'd never really developed a relationship with old rivals from other counties, such as T.J. Reid or Patrick Horgan, even though our careers pretty much ran in parallel lines. While they're your opponents, a certain distance is maintained. It has to be.

With Henry, apart from sitting together – a little uncomfortably, it should be said – at the 2012 All-Stars function, we'd had pretty much zero opportunity to get to know one another across the years. Kilkenny became such frequent opponents once Galway were admitted to the Leinster Championship in 2009, it seemed as if we were always looking at one another from opposite sides.

But an offer to play golf at the venue which will host the 2027 Ryder Cup? For both of us, that was simply too good to turn down. At least, until Henry's itinerary dramatically changed.

Sometimes I wonder what might have happened had I not announced my retirement so quickly after Galway's championship defeat to Waterford in 2021. What if I had held off until Christmas, and in the meantime, taken a phone call from the new manager?

In other words, if my decision hadn't already gone out into the public domain, what would I have done? Honest answer? For better or for worse, I'd almost certainly have gone back.

It would have been an unmerciful gamble, no question. I was never the quickest, but with a stubborn hamstring issue in 2021, I was now aware of a haunting voice in my head declaring, 'Fuck, even that half yard of pace you once had seems to be gone now.' The body just never felt right, and I had absolutely no reason to believe that it ever would again.

And for the record, in time, Henry did ring me about returning. It was December and I was just after returning from Paudie O'Brien's stag do in Newcastle. I was lying on the couch as I answered the call, feeling more than a little brittle and with the added complication of a bout of Covid.

'Listen, I'm just checking that that's your final decision,' he said.

Feeling the way I felt now, I suppose the answer was an easy one. 'Henry, my head would love to, but my body is just saying I can't.'

To be fair, he didn't push it. Henry had been through enough wars with his own body to understand that there are a finite number of days you can reasonably take it to the front line.

I wished him and the team the best of luck and felt settled with my decision. But yes, there was still that niggling fascination about how it might have worked out between us if, for a change, we were on the same side.

How long did that fascination last? It's still there. Because when you retire, nothing else in your life is ever going to replace the adrenaline rush of running out in front of 80,000 people. There's nothing you can do to simulate the buzz of playing in a packed Thurles on some big championship day.

All in all, I've no regrets about having retired, but is there still that inkling that I'd have loved another shot at it under one of the greatest hurlers of all time? Absolutely. I know that sounds contradictory, but it's the truth. And I'm happy enough now living with that element of the unknown because there was a fair chance of me not being as good as I wanted to be, had I gone back in with Galway. Also, there's a selfish instinct about legacy that kicks in. A sense of what you've achieved in the game and how you've been looked at. It's human nature.

I always felt aware of how people viewed me, which is why I wanted to go out on my own terms. I didn't want to go out because I couldn't run five yards quick enough. If it was anybody else other than Henry Shefflin taking the Galway reins at the end of 2021, this conversation would never even have entered my head.

But it's human to wonder, isn't it?

It was probably a story the whole of hurling would have liked to see too. I get that. I still have people saying it to me now. 'Jesus, wouldn't it have been great to see yourself and Shefflin working on the one side?'

Even Dad keeps pressing the occasional button.

'Jesus, T.J. Reid's a fair detail all the same!'

And I know exactly what he's getting at. T.J. – a year older than me – was still hurling for Kilkenny three years after I'd waved the white flag with Galway. Patrick Horgan, five months older than me, was still soldiering with Cork.

But the truth is that T.J.'s and Patrick's early years in the game simply didn't carry the kind of mileage that mine carried. Remember, I was hurling senior championship at fifteen, which meant that everything in my life was instantly helter-skelter.

On some level too, we all probably want more than we can have, and for me, of course, the fairytale would have been winning another All-Ireland with Galway. But one thing I learned from 2017 is that winning that Celtic Cross doesn't change your life. Trust me, I loved winning it, but you realise over time that all the old stresses and headaches and worries are still there when the bedlam finally settles. You still have work to do and bills to pay.

Would I have retired when I did if I hadn't won an All-Ireland? I don't know. Maybe. Would I have retired if I honestly believed that there was another there to be won? Deep down? No.

That's the hold it has on you. The hardest thing is letting go.

2.

FAMILY

The butterfly was the gift.

That's how I saw it. Her way of being there for us. Reassuring us. Settling us. At first, I wondered if I was the only one who noticed it, fluttering around the altar of the church in Monaleen. On 25 November 2022 – our wedding day.

The moment the priest mentioned Mam, the butterfly stirred behind him. And to me, instantly, that was her. Just letting us know that she was with us. Even the priest momentarily stopped, realising that everyone's attention had been drawn to this tiny, winged creature. A butterfly in November. How often would you see that?

Maybe people will read this and think it silly. But I have faith, and if you ask me to explain that faith, that moment is where I'd go. Ten months after her passing, experiencing that profound sense of Mam's presence on our wedding day.

She was with us too for Meg's IVF treatment: three weeks of injections, and both of us acutely aware of a butterfly in the house. Then the moment Meg's pregnancy was confirmed, the butterfly was gone.

Maybe believing in an afterlife is the only real comfort available to us after losing somebody we love. And I believe we'll all see Mam again. I certainly hope so.

She had this deep equanimity about her. A calmness you never saw crumble. In many ways, I suspect that it fooled us into believing she was somehow unbreakable. The cancer coming back clearly wasn't good news, but you never got that sense from Mam. Even as she became increasingly unwell and experienced a few fainting episodes, I think we always believed that she would pull through.

I know I certainly did.

Call it naivety, but when someone is so strong, it's easy to underappreciate the seriousness of their predicament. Mam never really spoke about her cancer and certainly never betrayed any unease about the possibility of it being terminal. So it was all too easy to be fooled into believing that her condition was less serious than happened to be the case.

Even when she went into the Oncology Unit in St Joseph's University Hospital that Christmas of 2021, you couldn't detect even the tiniest sliver of self-pity. In hindsight, it was clear that she was very sick, and I don't doubt she probably knew herself that she was dying. But that knowledge could never be allowed weigh on us.

That was always her mentality: *my* problem, not theirs.

By then, she couldn't really eat as the cancer had moved to her stomach and, heavily medicated, she was sleeping a lot. But right up to the last few days, she could be extremely lucid too. It would almost fool you into believing that she was coming around and getting better.

Maybe on some level we all understood what was happening. I know for certain that my sister Deirdre did, but she'd only tell us as much as Mam would want us to know. And Mam was adamant that she didn't want to go to a hospice, because to her, that was where people went to die. It's not strictly true, of course. Often people go there for a period of convalescence and return home again.

But to Mam, I think going to a hospice would have registered as some kind of acknowledgement that she was giving up. And she would never countenance the idea of the rest of us seeing her accept defeat.

So maybe there was that element of denial in how most of us dealt with her final days.

Post-Covid restrictions were still in place, so we were confined to one visitor at a time. I'd bring her in a Calippo ice pop because she loved the cold sensation on her tongue.

And often, I'd come away faintly reassured that she was rallying a little; telling them all at home, 'She was good tonight.' I wanted to believe it. We all did.

About a week before her death, the doctors expressed a view that she might only have a day or two left. But it wasn't really until the very last 24 hours that she stopped talking. I had just arrived back in Limerick from the hospital when I got the call that they'd been told Mam was expected to pass that night. The doctors could see she was weakening.

We were all there at her bedside for the end: Dad and the seven of us, watching her breathing just getting slower, weaker and more laboured. Then it finally stopped, and we found ourselves looking at one another in silence. Mam was gone, and there was nothing that any of us could say to soften the realisation of what had just happened in our world.

There's this beautiful passage in a book called *The Five People You Meet in Heaven* by American author Mitch Albom that I think speaks to the heart of how those of us lucky in life are shaped by the people we call Mam and Dad. It goes:

Parents rarely let go of their children, so children let go of them. They move away. The moments that used to define them – a mother's approval, a father's nod – are covered by moments of their own accomplishments. It is not until much later, as the skin sags and the heart weakens, that children understand. Their stories and all their accomplishments sit atop the stories of their mothers and fathers, stones upon stones beneath the waters of their lives.

When Mam was first diagnosed with breast cancer around April 2015, she began losing her hair through the treatment. A few of us – me and my nephews, Nathan and Adam – decided to get our heads shaved in solidarity. There's actually a picture taken of Davy 'Darby' Glennon and me doing umpire at a Féile semi-final that my brother Seamus was refereeing, and we're both proud skinheads.

Until she got sick, Mam used cut everyone's hair at home, so she knew how finnicky we could be about it. Shaving it all off was a big thing for me then. Just my way of saying something.

As a family, we were always religious. Mam and Dad would say the rosary every night, and if you happened to be there at the time, the expectation was that you'd say it with them. This would involve kneeling on the ground and turning a chair around to lean on.

On Wednesday nights, Dad played cards up in Uncle Frankie's pub in Woodford and, on the way home, we'd say the rosary in the car. Often I'd pretend I was asleep in the back seat to avoid having to join in with 10 Hail Marys. It never felt especially heavy-handed or prescriptive, although – as with most families – Mass on Sundays was obligatory.

Today I'm not a regular Mass goer anymore, though there's still a certain comfort in getting to church the morning of a game. Even when I was living in Oranmore, Davy Burke and I would make a point of taking the two-minute walk to Mass that morning. An aunt of mine who lives nearby in Craughwell said she used hear of kids going to the church because they knew there was a fair chance that Burkey and I would be in the congregation.

To this day, I retain a faith. But if you asked me to articulate coherently what that faith is, I'd definitely struggle.

Every time I'm in Portumna, I go to Mam's grave and talk to her. I say a few prayers and always feel her presence. She died at quarter to midnight on 26 January 2022, but the headstone says 27 January, because that's what was written on the death certificate. We all still miss her terribly and believing in that 'next life' – whatever it may actually mean – probably helps with the process of grieving. When Josie was born this year, we all instantly noticed this tiny red mark between her eyebrows. And that's when I first heard the expression of a *stork*: a tiny birthmark some babies carry that is interpreted as a kiss from an angel.

Funny, the Clifford brothers in Kerry were interviewed in a newspaper a while back, talking about their late mother and the influence she'd had in their lives. And it struck me that if you just changed their surname to ours, the story would be identical. It was actually weird reading it, because to me, it was as if they were talking about my own mam. Someone endlessly quiet, someone understated, someone who did absolutely everything they could for their family. I remember getting Dad to read that article.

Maybe I was just more attuned to this stuff after her passing because I always had the tightest bond with my mother. Being the youngest in the family by some distance, and being named after her, I suppose I confided more in her than anyone. And, in a strange way, she in me.

She loved Ferrero Rocher chocolates, and even now, be it on her birthday or at Christmas, I still buy some to bring and leave at the grave. On some level, for me, just doing that brings her back, even if I find myself standing there eating one alone.

Just about all of my childhood days were spent around Mam

because she brought me everywhere. One of her jobs as a community nurse was to call to elderly neighbours in her role as 'home help'. She'd always bring along a newspaper, and the priest would get her to distribute envelopes for people to make their parish donations. The idea was that they would then bring the envelopes with money inside when attending Mass that Sunday.

Even though the religious structures in your life might slowly diminish over time, I sense there's still a comfort in just going to certain places like the church or graveyard. In that idea of death ending a life, but not a relationship. It's almost as if you can turn down the volume of the world and do some kind of psychological reset.

Within the GAA community, attending Mass the day of a match feels pretty natural too. Actually, it isn't entirely unusual for the presiding priest to reference that upcoming match while expressing a hope that it might produce the desired outcome.

In *Pride of the Parish*, the TV documentary filmed in 2008 on Portumna's rise to national prominence, there is one such scene in Gortanumera church the morning of our county final against Gort where Fr Brendan Lawless tells the congregation, 'It takes a great team to do back-to-back.' I suppose there's always something a little perverse in any idea of the Almighty taking one side or another in any kind of sporting battle. When I hear athletes thanking God for a victory, I'm struck by the temptation to ask: 'Using that logic, does it mean that God wanted your opponent to lose?' But the GAA is so tightly bound up in community, the concept of a man of the cloth wishing his local team well feels entirely reasonable.

That church has always been our meeting spot before getting on the bus for big Portumna games, sliotars fizzing around the car park as a kind of loosening-up process before we head to the game. I'm not sure there's a more quintessential GAA image, is there? Of a community bound together by one thing? We may be a small infinity of different human puzzles in Portumna, but we are, first and foremost, hurling people too.

The game is the glue that binds us all together.

3.

THE FARM

It starts with a wall, always a wall.

In my case, maybe a small multiple of them. From the beginning, our farm in Gortanumera crackled like some military firing-range: sliotars ricocheting off concrete, hurleys forever windmilling. Every shape, every surface had its use as a target. A tyre pilfered from the sileage pit hanging on a hook in the barn. An oil tank erected across the top of two panels of concrete blocks. A low wall at one end of the front lawn, and a slightly taller one at the other, sectioning off the yard. The big corrugated shed snapping violently every time a ball hit it.

Routinely, I'd stand in front of the bungalow, striking blind and waiting for that sound. The sound of a bullseye. But sometimes the noise igniting would instead be of glass breaking. An outside light.

And a cry from the yard: 'Jesus Christ, Joe!'

But we were hurling people, breakages a part of life. Glass one day, bones the next. I have no real memory of a day when the game didn't pulse through every family conversation.

Seán Canning first hurled as a juvenile in 1958 and played his last game – aged forty-two – as a junior 29 years later. He won little if anything beyond a couple of junior medals and an enduring pride of place. Portumna never had a senior team in his time, and when the club was temporarily disbanded shortly after an East Galway defeat by Mullagh, he hurled with Killimor – less than a mile up the road – winning a county junior medal in 1973. He could have hurled senior had he been open to overtures from Eyrecourt at the time and has often said that it's a real regret of his that he didn't.

Accordingly, his Killimor connection holds a kind of jaundiced place in his hurling history now. Recently, someone was asking him about it over a pint in Curley's.

'How come you played with Killimor?' he was asked.

'They gave me the most money,' he replied, happily stirring the pot.

Anyway, five sons and a daughter still bought unequivocally into his passion before – almost as an after-thought – Seán and Josephine welcomed their seventh child in October of 1988. Both now in their forties, my mother admitted that they'd got the shock of their lives on discovering her pregnancy.

There would be a 19-year gap between me and the eldest, Seamus; seven between me and the previous youngest, Ivan. They wouldn't have known it then, but they had all just inherited a shadow.

The age gap was a curse in one sense, a small blessing in another. I was way too small and brittle to be of much value in family matches – Ivan did take it upon himself to double-check with occasional games of three-goals-in, with my mother mopping up the inevitable tears – but I grew up in a house where hurling stories were already being written.

And the family genes were favourable.

Dad's brother, Frankie, was a Galway minor for three years in the 1960s before emigrating to London, where he won a multiple of senior hurling championships with St Gabriel's and was once named the UK's Hurler of the Year. He came home around 1980, opening a pub in Gurteeny, near Woodford, and was part of the Galway senior panel beaten in the 1981 All-Ireland final by Offaly.

The untold story about Frankie is that he actually never intended emigrating at all. He'd gone to London in 1967 to stand as godfather for a child of one of Dad's sisters, and with the outbreak of foot-and-mouth disease over there was advised not to come home. So having gone for a weekend, he ended up staying 13 years. It was easier to find work in the UK than at home and, having started out as a barman in the Britannia in Hackney, Frankie ended up working on building sites for nearly a decade.

He was considered a Galway star in the making at the time, having hurled for the county minors, under-21s, intermediates and seniors while still only eighteen. In 1967, he'd marked Justin McCarthy in a National League game against Cork in Ballinasloe and was said to have been 'well able for him'. To this day, he reckons it was a mistake not to bring him on in that 1981 All-Ireland final, but then I suppose that wouldn't be an uncommon view from anyone left sitting on the bench.

Mam was a Lynch from Kiltormer. Her brother Kieran won an All-Ireland club title in 1992, while two others, Tom and P.J., were senior county medallists. Because of that family connection, Kiltormer games were big events in our house. When I hear the old stories, it's clear that they're talking about very different, definitely safer times. Dad once left Ollie behind at a game in Kiltormer and was sitting having a pint in Killimor without even realising the oversight when his then-youngest son came marching into the pub, tears in his eyes.

'You're a lovely father, forgetting me like that,' said Ollie.

He'd been brought home by Bernie Forde, the All-Ireland-winning Galway corner forward of 1980.

Another day, the whole family was in Ballinasloe for a big championship game between Kiltormer and Gort. Ollie seemingly announced that he was going to the toilet and disappeared without anyone giving it a second thought.

23

Next thing, this big row erupted on the field, Uncle Kieran going at it hammer and tongs with Mattie Murphy. As the fists flew, Dad noticed a child rolling around on the grass, practically beneath the feet of the protagonists.

'That young lad's going to get killed down there,' he declared, not realising that Ollie had actually climbed under the pitch-side wire and was now in perilous danger of being trampled.

Anyway, as you will gather, hurling was in our blood from both sides, and I suppose it quickly showed.

Seamus, Frank, Davy, Ollie, Ivan and Deirdre all represented Galway at different levels, the story being that they and our parents would gather in the field once milking was done and engage in fierce family battles, my father in one goal, my mother in the other. So no surprise then that I was destined to hurl too, wanting – above all – to be a part of what had such a profound hold on everyone else in the family.

It wasn't just the Cannings who followed that rainbow in Gortanumera – a small crossroads in East Galway about two miles outside Portumna, boasting just a church and a two-teacher national school. It was the Hayes family too. And the Muldoons.

Damien Hayes would be a Portumna and Galway teammate of mine for most of my career. John Muldoon, who captained Connacht to the Guinness Pro12 title at Murrayfield in 2016, won minor A and B hurling titles with Portumna, and in 2000, an All-Ireland minor medal with Galway before committing full-time to a rugby career.

A childhood in Gortanumera put no limit on our dreams.

Probably my fondest memory of winning the 2017 All-Ireland would be a Friday trip to that tiny national school in the company of Martin Dolphin and my nephew Jack, who'd just won an All-Ireland minor medal. It was beautiful: a journey back to the intimacy of family, neighbours and old teachers who shaped so many of us into the men we are today. Maybe just 30 people gathered in this most rural of settings for a simple ceremony, Mam and Dad among them. That school is where it began for me, where I first put on a jersey to play a hurling match. The old school field is just across the road. So that was very special, seeing people who had contributed so much to my upbringing and basically saying thank you. I found myself getting emotional when it came to my turn to speak.

Because Gortanumera is what and who I am. Always will be.

It was from there I was ferried by an assortment of family members to training sessions, be they for Galway minors and seniors with Ollie; under-21s and seniors with Davy, or the camogie juniors with Deirdre. With Dad busy on the farm and Mam working as a public health nurse, I suppose it passed as a convenient form of babysitting.

When I think back now, I never had to seek lifts from other parents to training or games because there was always someone in my own family making themselves available.

By the age of six or seven, I even had a specific usefulness: pucking balls back out from behind the goals with sufficient aplomb not to become annoying. By then, I could strike a sliotar maybe 50 yards off left or right. Better still, I could do it consistently.

Children acquire an early self-awareness, and I recognised pretty quickly that I was good. I was also obsessive. I'd been the club mascot when Portumna won an intermediate crown in 1992 and would be in Croke Park two years later to see Ollie named Man of the Match as he collected an All-Ireland minor medal.

Galway beat Cork in that final, but the day will always be remembered for what followed: Offaly breaking Limerick's hearts at the death in a senior game that would forever more be remembered as 'the six-minute final'.

If I watched that game once on the old VHS player we had in the kitchen at home, I must have watched it a thousand times. The Johnny Dooley and Pat O'Connor goals, Billy Dooley's late flurry of Hill-end points – all running on an endless loop. I'd been in Croke Park that day and already considered myself more than familiar with the geography of the place. So, the day of the 1999 final, I remember assuring Mam and Dad that there'd be no issue with them sitting together and leaving me to a single Hogan Stand seat in a nearby section.

'Sure I know this place like the back of my hand,' I told them.

My bravery lasted maybe five minutes, the intensity of All-Ireland final voices just a little too ferocious for this ten-year-old. Honestly? I was afraid of my life, quickly settling back onto a step beside Seán and Josephine.

After Galway's minor win in 1994, we'd got down to meet Ollie in the Canal End corner where the old dressing rooms were at the time. The quiet pride of parents has a compelling beauty in those moments, and witnessing the tight hugs for Ollie then, I was well and truly hooked.

Not long before this, Davy had come striding up through the fields one day, a sheepdog pup in his arms. He'd made the purchase from a neighbour, and without realising it at the time, I'd just acquired my closest hurling ally. Ross would faithfully retrieve any ball I drove down into the fields. Whenever the others sought the same obedience, he'd just look back at them with eyes of boredom.

Ross became *my* dog, you see. Maybe my best friend.

When he was pretty much on his last legs, with old age taking its toll, it was decided to get a new sheepdog for the farm. We all felt that Ross had little enough time left, but lo and behold, the arrival of Prince into his world seemed to give him a new lease of life, and he actually thrived for another few years. In some strange way, I always took Ross's revival as proof of what a positive mind could do for a body.

I was six when Portumna made the 1995 county final, Paddy O'Meara training the team. The buzz and novelty of it all seemed to me completely addictive. I was at every training session no matter how bleak the night and in the dressing room before every game. Frank apparently signed himself out of hospital to play in that final, having spent most of the week on a drip for blood-poisoning in his shin.

I had the exact same predicament before the 2014 All-Ireland club final against Mount Leinster Rangers. Unable to train for 10 days, I was actually on antibiotics going into that final.

For Frank in 1995, it was a daft thing to do. But he was Portumna's scorer-in-chief, and I suppose those were days when it wasn't entirely unusual to put pride of place before any concerns about personal safety. We lost, but the emotional power of it all felt wonderful.

Back then, every night seemed a Galway training night. In Davy's case, that meant the Corrs up full blast – he seemed to only have a single tape – for the drive to and from Ballinasloe, Athenry or Salthill. I'll always have fond memories of the old Galway hurling secretary, Phelim Murphy, routinely rewarding me with a bottle of Lucozade for my ball-retrieval services when Ollie and Davy were in with the seniors. On a good night, I might even get a sliotar.

The quality of my ball-striking often drew complimentary remarks, and from the age of maybe eight, I'd been given a regular goalkeeping job at Galway junior camogie training with Deirdre. It was obvious I could play.

Gortanumera national school played in under-10 seven-a-side competitions, winning two titles during my time there. Actually, long before I arrived on the scene, Seamus scored five goals in a 1980 schools final played in Tynagh when Dad was in charge of the team. So I wasn't exactly breaking new ground here. But in my second last year, we won a final against Ballyturn from Kilbeacanty by 6–7 to 1–1 on a day that Tony Keady was doing umpire.

Tony's nephew, Colin Nevin, was our captain that day, and I scored 4–6 out of the team's 6–7 total. It was a real thrill to do it in front of one of Galway's greatest men. But I had this habit when running of dragging the hurley along the grass behind me, as if almost too lazy to carry it. Dad, Ollie and Ivan would be going ballistic when they'd see it.

'What the fuck is that about?'

At games, theirs were the voices I always heard. I was never the fastest, but my body language now implied some kind of ambivalence maybe bordering on arrogance even. I was still getting out in front of my marker, still winning ball and scoring freely. It just didn't look as if I was working as hard as the others.

Where did that habit come from? No idea. Sometimes I wonder was it something to do with how I'd become so used to Ross bringing the sliotar back to me that I was inclined to wait for the right ball. Was that embedded somewhere in my psyche? The idea that I wouldn't ever have to work really hard to get possession?

I'm honestly not sure.

I did like to wait in behind my man sometimes, something Eugene Cloonan did so effectively at the time with Galway and Athenry. The trouble with doing that, though, was it looked awful if the defender just came away with uncontested ball.

Anyway, people were noticing me. I felt that. At seven, I was Portumna's under-10 free-taker, and in one club final I scored the entire 1–12 of our team's total. Mam and Deirdre were ferrying me everywhere, something, at the time, I absolutely took for granted.

They often heard stuff that I was mercifully deaf to.

There was one under-14 game in Killimor against Kiltormer when my granny Maisie was still alive. I'd have been maybe ten at the time and Mam and Maisie watched from a car parked by the side of the pitch. At one point, apparently, as I was running with the ball, a Kiltormer supporter howled, 'Cut the fucking legs from under him!'

He didn't know who was in the car beside him and was never subsequently alerted to their identity either. But being from Kiltormer herself, Mam was absolutely disgusted. She never forgot it, never forgave it. She did tell the story to my father, of course, because the same Kiltormer man would have hurled with my uncles at one stage, and at one point, even played with Galway.

It was years later before I heard the story, and I always made a point after that of completely blanking this fella whenever he'd approach me. I did so out of respect for Mam.

To her, the idea of someone roaring something like that during an under-14 game was simply unforgiveable. Funny, the day of her funeral in January 2022, this fella turned up to pay his respects, shaking all of our hands. Dad and I just looked at one another with knowing smiles as he did so. Smiles that said she'd kill us for doing that, wouldn't she?

It's probably only with the gift of hindsight that you come to understand the time and energy parents invest in your childhood. An example? When I was 12, I was down at the Gaeltacht in Spiddal the week of an under-14 East Galway trial in Ahascragh. This was pre-motorway Galway, so Spiddal was a good two-hour drive from home.

Mam and Dad came down to collect me, brought me back another two hours' drive to Ahascragh, watched the trial game, then back to Spiddal that evening. Thinking about it now, I reckon they probably spent eight hours in the car that day just so that I wouldn't lose out. The kind of commitment that always went completely over my head at the time.

My attitude was: 'Sure what else would they do? I had a trial game to play.'

Most parents, even with the convenience of today's roads, would simply go, 'Joe's away at the Gaeltacht, he won't make the trial.' But not mine. Dad actually laughs about arriving back in Spiddal that evening, both in serious need of a quick trip to the toilet. A polite request to use the facilities was coldly rejected, the bean an tí flatly refusing to let them in.

It was frowned upon to take you out of the Gaeltacht for any reason, and they certainly wouldn't have told her it was for a hurling trial. It would have been equally frowned upon for anyone other than the children to be allowed beyond her front door.

So the refusal was unequivocal, Dad and Mam having to hop a gate into a field before commencing the long journey home.

On reflection now, my early days as a hurler pitched me into two parallel worlds. I only ever won two underage medals with Portumna – an under-12 thirteen-a-side competition in 2000, and subsequently, an under-21 B county title. But life in the maroon of Galway just took me to another place.

Actually, the only medal that would elude me at inter-county level was a Tony Forristal (under-14). I was on Galway squads that came up short in 2001 and 2002 and have a particularly painful memory of us failing to make the knock-out stages one of those years when we were awarded a last-minute free that could have got us through.

I'd been taking the frees all day and was hitting them well, so instinctively ran out to get the ball only to hear the manager's voice, 'No, Joe, leave it!'

His nephew had just come on the field, and for some reason, the decision was now made that the nephew would take the free.

He missed. The memory of that moment still annoys me, which I suppose, is ultimately a selfish thing. Like I could have missed too, but when you're hitting frees well, I suppose you feel you have a certain control over things. I never asked why that control was taken from me, and to be fair, the manager was hardly under any obligation to explain himself now to a child. But to this day that memory stings.

One of our trainers during my time hurling with Galway under-14s was the great Pete Finnerty. For a guy who never wore a helmet in his life, Pete was a stickler for making sure that nobody else ever went on the field without theirs already on. If even just one fella failed to meet this stipulation, Pete would punish the whole group with laps. His message wasn't slow in gaining traction.

My mother was always the unofficial medic with those teams. She carried a first aid kit – I can still see the green plastic box with a white cross on the lid – in the boot of her car for work as a public health nurse, so all of my teammates would have known her essentially as the team doc.

It was around this time that I started taking sideline 'cuts', having always tried to mimic the action of my brother Davy who was fairly handy at the art. I have a vivid memory of one day in Loughrea especially and being down in a corner on the stand side when he hit a line cut almost to the far 21. I was mesmerised.

Finnerty had one bottom-line piece of advice for those taking line cuts. 'Always concentrate on a point between the ball and the grass,' he'd say. That's stuck with me to this day.

Portumna lost a Féile B county final to Sarsfields in 2001 and then lost a Féile A semi-final to Tommy Larkin's in Ballindereen a year later. I struck the post with a late shot for goal in that game – which we lost by two points – and I'll always remember Seán Treacy, our coach, flaking the spare hurleys off the dressing-room table in frustration afterwards. Even at under-14 level, the margins were so fine.

But my national profile really took off then when Galway won the 2003 Nenagh Co-Op All-Ireland under-16 crown, beating a Liam Griffin-managed Wexford in a final replay. Over five games, my scoring tally in the tournament was 7–31.

I remember we faced Tipperary up in Dr Morris Park behind Semple Stadium, Shane Long – the future Ireland soccer international – playing in the blue and gold. After the game, James Skehill, our keeper, was giving him plenty of lip, singing, 'It's a long, long way to Tipperary'.

You could tell Long was a class hurler and he would play for Tipp minors later before committing to a professional life across the Irish Sea.

We successfully retained the title in 2004, this time beating Cork in a final replay. I had a really poor day in the drawn game, something my Rebel marker was only too happy to let me know. 'You're in me pocket, Joe!'

He was right too. It was just one of those games that pretty much passed me by, but his mouthing really riled me. From what I remember, there was plenty of lip in general coming from that Cork team, and we had something like 10 weeks to stew before the replay in Nenagh. I spent that entire stretch thinking to myself: *We'll see if I'm in your pocket the next day!*

And I wasn't. I scored 2–8.

That was enough to put me directly into Mattie Murphy's plans with Galway's minors for their All-Ireland semi-final against Cork. I'd been training with them all year but had gone to Lanzarote with Deirdre and her family the week of the quarter-final against Antrim. Mattie wasn't happy and duly let me know it.

'It's up to you, Joe. But if you go, you won't be playing.'

Why did I go? Maybe naivety? Maybe a little arrogance even, given I knew I'd had a decent chance of being in the first 15. We arrived home the day before that game in Parnell Park, and on some level, I suspect, I was still hoping that Mattie might start me. You're young, your head is all over the shop at that age, and in fairness, it was reasonably commonplace for minors to miss out on occasion because of pre-booked family holidays.

But then I suppose we were always going to beat Antrim too, so Mattie was never going to waver on this point of principle. When I think back on it now, he was 100 per cent right. It would have been absolute madness to let me swan straight back in in such circumstances.

Given I was still just fifteen, there was some surprise expressed locally when I was then named in the team to play Cork. Alongside me in the full forward line were two budding super-stars: Sarsfields' Keril Wade and Barry Hanley from Carnmore. Keril was our main man and would score 1–9 in a five-points win. I got 1–1.

Kilkenny, our final opponents, were going for three in a row with a star-studded team, the marquee name being Richie Hogan. Everybody was talking about this diminutive wizard who was D.J. Carey's cousin. And it's fair to say Richie didn't disappoint. We had looked in control with Hanley (2–3) and Wade (1–5) on fire, only to concede the last three scores of the game, Hogan nailing the equaliser a minute into injury time. He was just two months older than me, but already a big-game player.

The replay was held in Tullamore, O'Connor Park absolutely thronged. It felt a far more natural setting than the big, gaunt arena of Croke Park and the din of conversation humming in expectation of the senior final between Kilkenny and Cork.

Ten seconds in, I scored a point on the turn. Just controlled the ball with one hand, turned to my right and swept it over. That same day I nailed two line cuts as well. We won by a point. I was in heaven.

It was Galway's fifth All-Ireland minor crown in just over a decade, and I suppose it's fair to say that, with the benefit of hindsight, not everybody in the county regarded this necessarily as a healthy thing for our senior prospects. The feeling of some was – and to some degree remains – that maybe too much has been made of underage success in Galway, meaning that generations of young hurlers acquired a certain sense of entitlement.

To be fair to Mattie Murphy, he was fully aware of the danger of that happening. I'll always remember him making the point at one of my first minor training sessions that if lads weren't already playing senior hurling with their clubs, they'd be of little enough use to him in a Galway jersey. Mattie knew the pitfalls. He understood the traps. He also had a sense of loyalty to his own team that could, on occasion, catch you off guard.

In 2004, at the age of fifteen, I had already been eased into a Portumna senior squad that had delivered the club's first ever senior county title the year before. The very kind of introduction that Mattie had been recommending.

You grew up pretty fast in that environment, hurling against neighbouring clubs like Kiltormer, Mullagh and Meelick–Eyrecourt. Many of those games would be played before passionate, tightly packed crowds in Killimor. If you came through them in one piece, there was little enough fear of you.

One of my earliest games was against Carnmore, sent in for the last five minutes against Murty Killilea – a real, no-nonsense Sylvie Linnane-type corner back. I was smart enough to stay out of his way, but if I'm honest, physical fear never really felt a problem for me.

I was big for my age, you see, already touching six feet tall. It never struck me that exposure to adult hurling would in any way be dangerous.

In 2002, aged thirteen, I'd played in goals for Portumna under-21s after it was decided to play Ivan – the team's regular keeper – out the field. Our first-round championship game was against Athenry in Ballinasloe, and I was wearing Ivan's top, which, you can imagine, was like a heavy duvet on me.

Athenry had this big, stocky full forward – Cormac Cloonan, younger brother of Eugene and Diarmuid. At one point, he caught the ball and turned to shoot, but I'd read his intentions, throwing my body across to make what looked a really brave, dramatic block.

It seemed as if the ball had hit me a terrible belt, but in reality, it just died on contact with the huge folds of Ivan's jersey. In other words, I didn't feel a thing, bouncing straight back up and clearing back down the field. The save was painted as something heroic, and I remained a fixture between the posts for the rest of that campaign.

This put me on the same team-sheet now as men like Damien Hayes, Andy Smith and Eoin Lynch, lads who were at least five years older. Grown men, in other words. I loved that; loved the idea too that I was now actually hurling alongside one of my brothers.

Former Offaly All-Ireland winner Joachim Kelly was over Portumna seniors at the time, and I became aware the following February of some gossip about including me – as a fourteen-year-old – in the extended squad for the All-Ireland club semi-final against Dunloy. I was training with them the odd time, and honestly, if it was up to me, I'd have gone in a heartbeat.

It wasn't though, Mam and Dad wisely putting their foot down. Fourteen was too young. But fifteen? That was another matter!

So it would be the 2004 county campaign in which I made the

leap to senior, Portumna making it back to another county final, only to get beaten by Athenry. That was an ageing Athenry team, but they still carried the sting of a dying wasp. We had to play the final without Davy because of a suspension after being sent off in the semi-final against Turloughmore.

In many ways, I was still a relative innocent in that environment.

I made my debut on a Saturday, coming on as a late substitute against Abbeyknockmoy in Loughrea that May. At training before that match, the juniors were held back for a chat about their upcoming game on the Sunday. I knew there was a certain expectation that I might get a run with the seniors, but didn't want to be seen to be disrespectful. So I stayed back for the chat, and sitting there, one of the lads actually asked me, 'What are you doing here?'

I hated the idea of lads thinking, 'He's fifteen and he thinks he's a fucking senior hurler!'

But I never played with those juniors, that few minutes against Abbeyknockmoy disqualifying me from doing so. If I'm honest, I was already on a private mission now involving my own family. You see, Frankie was the Portumna free-taker and I knew that my elevation to the senior ranks would effectively – in due course – place us in direct opposition to one another.

Dad reckons that Frankie could have been even better than he was but for a bad fall off a hay shed when about sixteen. Mam had just come home from Portumna and was handing him up an ice cream when he lost his footing and went tumbling onto his back into a bed of nettles. They had to put him into a cold bath to calm the stings, and every time Dad watched Frankie bend to take a free after that, he felt he could detect a certain stiffness as some legacy from that fall.

Anyway, I had this image in my head of going home one day to announce to my father, 'Frankie's been dropped for me!'

It wasn't going to happen that year, but the truth is that I settled fairly quickly into the senior dressing room. A performance that really got me noticed came in late July when I scored 2–5 from play in the opening half hour of a group game against Gort in Loughrea. This came on the back of a Sunday roast and a big bowl of jelly and ice cream at home, which probably tells you something about my general state of mind.

The older I got, the more nerves came into play for me on a hurling field. But at fifteen, I just wanted to be out there.

I turned sixteen the day of the semi-final against Turloughmore, and as long as I live, I'll never forget the abuse their manager kept giving me throughout.

At one point, I went out to take a free near the sideline and what he didn't say about me wasn't really worth saying. Every ball I got, this man was roaring. His name? Mattie Murphy.

Over time, I came to recognise this as the essential Mattie. If he was with you, he'd back you 100 per cent. He'd have your back from first minute to last, go to war on your behalf. But if he was against you, everything flipped 180 degrees. And that day, Mattie was a Turloughmore man.

Portumna and Joe Canning? Completely uncomplicated. We were the enemy.

I've always respected that kind of tunnelled approach to hurling. Like, Mattie was a huge figure in the hurling lives of Ollie and Davy and would be my minor manager with Galway not just that year, but for 2005 and 2006 as well. He would have known me from the age of five or six from going in to county training. Ollie says he often commented on me at those training sessions in terms of the hurler I might become.

So shouting abuse at me now in that 2004 semi-final? I was grand with it. I mean Davy 'Fitzy' Fitzgerald is exactly the same kind of personality: a man who would have done anything for his players when we were hurling for the Fitzgibbon Cup for Limerick Institute of Technology (LIT). You just knew he'd back you to the hilt.

But when he was in the opposite corner for Clare, Wexford or Waterford in subsequent years, and I was wearing the maroon of Galway, old friendships were well and truly parked for the day. I remember in his last game as Clare manager in 2016, he sent on his namesake – David Fitzgerald – to do a man-marking job on me.

And Fitzy, being Fitzy, was more than a little animated barking out his instructions – a finger jabbing aggressively in my direction, the language raw. Standing on the line alongside Dónal Óg Cusack, I knew he was trying to put me off. And I just looked over at them, laughing. Knowing that nothing would irritate him more.

Bottom line, you always knew what you got from men like Mattie and Davy. When they were with you, they had your back 100 per cent. When against you, they had no intention of being nice to you. I respected that absolutely. They were there for their team, pure and simple. But I always knew that once the game was over, the respect would still be there. There would always be a handshake.

When playing in goals for Portumna under-21s, I used one of Ivan's hurleys, but I'll never forget the thrill of getting my first Mike Conroy hurl as an under-12. Mike's sticks were coveted: hand-shaved to perfection in a cowshed up the road in Abbey. My brother Davy always used a Conroy hurley, and the sense of something special was amplified by the fact that Mike's was a small, part-time business. You could be waiting weeks for the stick you ordered, and I'll always remember Michael Ryan, our under-12 manager, bringing mine out to me the Friday before our under-12 county final. It was a big hurley: a size 34 – I'd been using a size 30 until then – but that was immaterial to me. If he'd made me a 36, I'd have still used it. After all, it was a Mike Conroy hurley.

For me, almost a stamp of manhood.

I won an under-12 long puck at Mosney with that 34, beating Brian Whelahan's son – Aaron. One of my father's tips that helped me win was to drive the ball a small bit lower so that it bounced forward on contact with the ground. Sounds simple, but you'd be amazed by how many yards can be lost in the air. A high ball will usually bounce just once or twice before coming to a stop. A lower strike gets far more purchase from contact with the ground.

I still have that medal and hurley at home. Actually, I still have almost all the hurleys from All-Ireland finals I played in – under-16, minor, under-21 and senior – their significance written on the bas. That's a habit I picked up from Ollie. His hurley from the 1994 minor final is in his old bedroom at home, hanging up on the equivalent of a gun rack.

There would also be a pet hurley I used for those under-16 All-Irelands – a stick that was probably repaired 10 times, band over band. You can actually track the repair lines, each one carrying its own history.

Maybe we're a bit odd like that in Gortanumera, but those old hurleys have always spoken louder to us than medals.

4.

THE CLUB

Around Portumna we've always carried the wounded sense of an independent republic, the reason being a mix of geography and hard lessons.

No question, our close proximity to Tipperary gives us a faint sense of isolation from the rest of Galway. But there's routinely been the impression too of a latent hostility towards us from those in GAA authority within our own county, not to mention some of our closest neighbours.

The fall-out from the 2006 county final would be the most luminous example of that, but it told us nothing we didn't already know.

If you said we had a chip-on-the-shoulder approach to our hurling lives, I don't think we'd contradict you too loudly.

Portumna spent so long regarded as nobodies in the game – be that within Galway itself or from our blue and gold 'friends' across the Shannon – it's fair to say we built up a suspicion of people looking down their noses at what we were trying to do. Sometimes legitimately, sometimes not.

Mostly, I escaped the energies feeding that suspicion, but my family certainly didn't.

To a man, my father and brothers talk about a not-so-distant past when Portumna hurlers experienced what they came to read as condescension from all sides. The geography part is easily explained.

As a child, I remember a lot of our most important games being played in Ballinasloe, meaning we drove a straight line through places like Tynagh, Killimor, Eyrecourt and Kiltormer. A straight line that is from the toes of the Tipperary border.

We were outsiders and we knew it.

East Galway was strong hurling country throughout my brothers' formative years, but Portumna mostly wasn't a part of that strength. We were a junior club in the early '80s; Eyrecourt, Kiltormer and Tynagh all senior.

At one point in the 1960s, Portumna had six representatives on a Galway minor squad, but every one of those players emigrated, my uncle Frankie among them. Behind them, they left a club on life support. It took a lot of great men and women to build what we have today after the club's temporary disbandment, first in 1969 and then once again in 1973.

The club my father remembers from that time is one endlessly struggling to field full teams. But having played for and won a junior county title with Killimor, he returned to Portumna in 1974, winning an east county junior title almost immediately.

What followed over time would have been unimaginable throughout his childhood.

Dad's view is that Portumna would have had great teams over the years if only they could have kept people from leaving. He actually hurled intermediate for Galway in 1969 against Cork in a Munster final in Charleville – Galway teams played in Munster at the time – and remembers playing one senior challenge against Gus Lohan's Clare in Ennis 'because they had no one else to play'.

The childhood he describes is one with lots of love, but few enough privileges.

His father, Jimmy, was married twice; the first time to a woman twenty years older than him. After she died, he married Maisie. He was fifty and she was twenty-nine. They had five children

42

together, so Jimmy would have been fifty-six by the time Dad arrived on the scene and eighty-four when Mam and Dad got married in 1973.

Grandad died suddenly in 1978, after which Maisie came to live permanently with Mam and Dad until her own sudden death, sitting by the range in the kitchen, in 1999. One remarkable quirk to their story is that both Jimmy and Maisie died on the same date (27 March); both at the age of eighty-eight – just 21 years apart.

It was really farming or nothing in Gortanumera back then. Of the six boys in Dad's national school class of ten, not one of them went on to secondary school, the assumption being that sons simply went straight to the land. In the Cannings' case, that land amounted to 30 acres.

The way Dad remembers it, the family had little enough money, yet he can't remember a single day of being left hungry either.

They were the first family in the area to own a car, a Volkswagen Beetle bought for £400 from Spooners garage in Roscrea that my grandfather never actually drove. Mostly, the family used it as a tool in the fields, pulling trailers, and with the engine being in the rear, using the front boot as a trough for feeding livestock.

Hurling-wise, Portumna began to change profoundly with that 1982 junior county win when Dad was thirty-seven, a day he remembers thinking that he could 'die happy now'.

As sons of his, I suppose we were always destined to inherit that kind of passion.

My brothers Frank and Davy were on a team that won an under-12 B county title in 1984, the same year we lost an under-14 B final. In 1985, Portumna lost an under-14 A final, then won that crown in 1986 and 1987.

Little acorns …

Roughly the same group of players would win two county under-14s, two under-16s and two minors. Frank and Davy were on the first of those minor teams in 1990, Ollie and Davy on the second in 1991.

When Seán Treacy made the Galway minors in 1983, apparently it was a huge thing around Portumna because Seán, essentially, was breaking the mould. But by 1990 the club had four representatives on the county minor squad, our place in the game beginning to change.

We lost an intermediate final replay in 1989 and were beaten again in the final a year later. Eventually, in 1992, we became a senior club, winning the intermediate title in a replayed final against Kilconieron.

My brothers Seamus, Frankie and Davy were all starters on that team; Frankie actually playing his fifth (because of replays) intermediate final at the age of twenty.

Even though I was just four at the time, I had an acute sense of something important stirring. We were always a big family for watching games back on old VHS tapes, Dad happy behind his own front door to deliver the kind of coldly forensic assessment he'd have spared the lads when stopping for a pint on the way home from a big game. The Canning boys always knew that the living room was where they'd encounter honesty. But with any kind of audience, Dad's words were reliably gentle.

I grew up in love with this environment, besotted with the idea of games that almost seemed to matter more than anything else in our world. Those tapes became my window into the brothers' lives, and I'd have them on endless rewind in the kitchen, swept up on the wild rhythms of the commentary. Out on the front lawn, I'd do my own Mícheál Ó Muircheartaigh, the boys always entertained to hear me roar, 'And it's Joe Dolan on the ball ...!' Joe Dolan? Apparently, he was centre back on the Kilconieron team we beat in that 1992 final, his name somehow anchored in my head.

To me, hurling was everything and everywhere. Seamus had won a vocational schools All-Ireland with Galway and Deirdre an All-Ireland minor in camogie. Frankie and Davy had made Galway Tony Forristal teams, as – in time – would Ollie and Ivan.

Davy won an All-Ireland under-21 medal in 1992, the same year Ollie first made Galway's minor panel. Hurling-wise, I was in a high-achieving house, and with Portumna now a senior club, that house hummed with endless possibility.

I was mascot for that 1992 intermediate final, and we then made our first senior county final in 1995, by which time Davy and Ollie were both in with the Galway seniors.

Frankie didn't start that final against Sarsfields, having spent the week in Portiuncula Hospital being treated for a septic shin. Club chairman at the time despite being only twenty-three, he signed himself out to play, coming on as a second-half substitute in a 1–9 to 0–17 defeat. He would finish that season as the championship's top scorer from both play and frees, but it was eight long years before Portumna got to play on that stage again.

Through those eight years, we were always considered contenders, only to come up short with knock-out game defeats, a kind of delusion carrying us through the subsequent winters. If the team that beat us – usually Sarsfields or Athenry – went on to win the title, didn't that then make us the second-best team in Galway? Of course, it didn't. But you cling to these consolations.

If anything, our proximity to Tipp deepened the sense of isolation. By the late 1980s, Tipperary and Galway had hurling's biggest rivalry: Babs Keating against Cyril Farrell.

Prior to 1987, Tipp went almost a decade without winning a single championship game. Yet in Portumna, it was as if they saw themselves as some kind of superior beings. The view in the town was you'd always see Tipp lads drinking in Portumna if they'd won a game. When they lost, you wouldn't see them for dust.

They had this attitude built up from a distant past, and we had a routine sense of that attitude being pushed in our faces.

So you will gather we pretty much felt we were being looked down upon from all sides. Barely accepted in our own county by the clubs immediately around us, and over the road in Lorrha, sensing a perception of Galway as nobodies.

The 'Keady Affair' in 1989 served only to deepen cross-border spites, and Frank (a Galway minor that year) remembers being back in the Ashling Hotel after that All-Ireland semi-final loss to Tipp, a brooding Sylvie Linnane sitting on a table across the way, speaking to no one.

Sylvie had been sent off after an incident with Nicky English, and the same day Hopper McGrath got his marching orders too. The atmosphere between Galway and Tipp felt absolutely raw at the time, and in Portumna, we were immersed in the crossfire.

It was burning us up that we couldn't win a county senior title, and maybe too often, there was an inclination to look for excuses in our disappointments. I suspect there was a certain paranoia in this too, the sense of believing other clubs to be only too delighted that we couldn't make the breakthrough. You might think I was too young to absorb this, but in hurling your family's prejudices tend to become your own.

Like, one of the sweetest victories of my career would be a county under-21 B final defeat of Killimor that ended with me getting a red card and a patchwork of stitches. Killimor is just a mile up the road from us, and for much of my brothers' hurling lives, they'd have sensed only derision coming at us from that direction.

This particular final took place not long after Portumna had hit the national headlines with All-Ireland club glory in 2008 and at a time when Killimor were hurling intermediate.

We understood implicitly just how much they wanted to beat us that evening, and it's fair to say that the feeling was absolutely reciprocated. I was already on a yellow card and ended up tangling on the ground with someone, when out of the corner of my eye, I saw the butt of a hurley coming through my face guard. It belonged to a lad I'd gone to school with in Portumna and caught me just under my left eye, opening a gash that would require three or four stitches.

Christy Helebert – who hurled for Galway – was referee that day and duly sent me off for a second yellow. I was due at the Galway Sports Awards that night and had to get stitched in Salthill by Dr Dan Murphy on my way.

I still have a small scar to remind me of that day, but beating Killimor offered more than sufficient consolation. They didn't like us; we didn't like them. It's never much more complicated than that.

For years, Seán Treacy was Portumna's marquee player, having played in the 1993 senior All-Ireland final against Kilkenny. Funny, his brothers, Vincent and Stephen, were Secretary and Treasurer of the club respectively at a time when there were four Cannings and four Treacys in the starting 15.

After every setback, a story would do the rounds that the Treacys and Cannings had fallen out. It was always bullshit. Not alone were the families staunch teammates, between them they had the three key officer positions in the club. But I suppose that when you're not winning, there's always a rumour.

The harsh truth was that we consistently failed to back up big victories. Every year, before the start of the senior championship, the *Connacht Tribune* would rate every club from one to sixteen, with Portumna invariably in the top three or four. But the gap to number one was becoming a bit of a chasm psychologically.

Maybe the worst defeat I remember arrived in a 2002 semi-final against Sarsfields in Ballinasloe.

Joachim Kelly, a dual All-Ireland winner and All-Star with

Offaly, had taken over as Portumna coach, and we duly dethroned the county champions, Clarinbridge, in a tight quarter-final. A lightning start put us nine points clear against Sarsfields, but then white-line fever seemed to kick in and the lead began to dwindle.

With the game in injury time, Portumna led 3–12 to 2–13 only for referee Michael Conway to penalise Davy for picking the sliotar off the ground. What followed comes back to me almost in slow motion now. With maybe 10 Portumna players camped on our goal line, Joe Cooney duly roofed the 21-yard free for Sarsfields to knock us out of the championship. Joe might have been one of Galway's best-loved hurling sons and a real hero of mine growing up, but I honestly hated him for that moment. I remember crying my eyes out in the dressing room after and always subsequently carried a quiet resentment towards Joe when he'd referee schools games that I played in.

To be honest, it was a sensational finish that nobody but Cooney could have produced, but Portumna were better than a declining Sarsfields in 2002 and we knew it. Trouble was, we'd never beaten them in championship.

That psychological gulf was weighing heavily on our hurling lives.

Worse, I suspect there was a sense too that many of our near neighbours had come to relish our torment. We'd passed out clubs like Killimor and Eyrecourt largely through the arrival of an exceptional group of minor players, including Damien Hayes, Aidan O'Donnell, Eoin Lynch, Kevin Hayes, Leo, Peter and Andy Smith and my own brother, Ivan.

Portumna won a county minor B title in 1998 and minor A in 1999. The undoubted star of that B-winning group was Keith Hayes, older brother of Damien and a clear superstar in the making. Keith was Man of the Match in the 1997 All-Ireland minor final and was Galway's captain the following year when he was also a part of a Portumna team that won the All-Ireland Sevens tournament in Kilmacud. He made the county under-21 squad in 1999, but tragically, died within a mile of home on 10 April of that year, killed at just nineteen in a road accident on his way to pick up playing gear for a challenge game.

The shock at losing Keith was seismic around Portumna – one of those moments when life almost seems to come to a standstill. He'd scored 2–9 from play in the county minor B final replay against Kiltormer, and there was a real sense that he'd be the next big thing in Galway hurling.

I remember it as a strange, almost eerie time in the town because there was something like half a dozen deaths in close enough proximity, including that of my own grandmother, Maisie.

Keith's death seemed to set Damien on a personal crusade to honour his brother's memory in the years to come, and I think it's fair to say he more than managed to achieve that. For some, the emotion of trying to do that could have been overwhelming. But it always seemed to me that Damien took huge energy from love for his lost brother, a powerful thing to see.

When the big breakthrough came and Portumna finally won that senior title in 2003, I remember vaulting over the old dugouts in Pearse Stadium at the final whistle and just running blindly onto the field. I'd say, all any of us felt that day was absolute relief.

My brother Frank was Portumna's oldest player at thirty-three. Davy the second oldest at thirty-one. To see Ollie then go up those steps to collect the Tom Callanan Cup on a day in which Ivan, Davy and Frank all started against Loughrea, and Seamus was on the bench, just felt like the day all of us had been waiting our entire lives to witness.

My memory of that night is a blur of bonfires and moist eyes and grown men hugging one another like survivors of a shipwreck.

Journey's end was John Pardy's Shannon Oaks Hotel, where Frank spent the entire night sipping mineral water, determined not to allow alcohol blur his memory of a single second of the celebrations.

Little did we realise this journey was only beginning.

5.

COULD HAVE BEEN SOMEONE

Around Christmas of 2023, I was sent a screen grab from a past I thought I knew, but didn't.

It's of a rugby team-sheet from late January 2006: Portumna Community School against Gowerton. An old teacher of mine reckoned I might be startled by one name in particular on the host's squad list, especially as we ended up in direct opposition that evening.

He wasn't wrong.

You see, I was Portumna's out-half for that trip to Wales. And the man wearing 10 for Gowerton? Dan Biggar.

Actually, another name to catch the eye from that screen grab is that of Ben Whitehouse, now a top professional referee. Needless to say, neither had any great status in my head that Friday night on a field a few miles north of Swansea.

Thinking back on it now, that would probably have been one of the last games of rugby I ever played before hurling slowly squeezed it out of my life. Portumna were building towards an All-Ireland club semi-final against James Stephens, and I was headed into my third year of involvement with the Galway minors.

I was also soon to embark on third level college life in Limerick and the pursuit of a Fitzgibbon Cup medal under the management of Davy Fitzgerald.

But rugby at the time was the number one sport in our school, passionately promoted by the principal, David Leahy, and in time, his successor, Derry Long. As a result, a good number of us would play up through all of the underage grades with Ballinasloe RFC. I was still in national school when Kevin 'Chunky' Hayes and Andy Smith played in the 2001 Connacht Schools final against Garbally in the Sportsground.

Chunky's dad, Enda, brought me to the game in his Pajero jeep on a day a first cousin of mine, Jonathan Kenny, would captain Garbally to victory.

I was on an under-12 team that got to a Community Games Connacht final with Willie Burke – a councillor in Galway – as manager, but we never did it make it to the rarefied air of Mosney.

I loved the game, and over time, became half decent at it too. A lot of us did. Eoin Lynch and Andy Smith were both in Irish youth squads, Eoin playing up to Ireland A level.

For a Portumna kid, the club options were narrow and pretty uncomplicated: Ballinasloe or Nenagh. As Ballinasloe had a minibus picking up some of the older lads for training on Friday nights and a game on Sunday, that was where I went.

How good could I have been? Well, I could kick off either foot and sometimes I think I might have played for Connacht had I stayed within the game. On what basis do I think that? Nothing concrete.

I did go to under-16 Connacht trials one day in Athlone, Ollie driving me in in his Toyota Corolla hatchback. I think both of us anticipated that everything would be done and dusted within an hour or 90 minutes, but how wrong we were. The trials dragged on for nearly four hours, and accordingly, I never went back.

There were plenty of calls made after to try and get me back in, but honestly, that day put me off completely. I was used to high-intensity hurling training at this stage, so the idea of what felt like an interminable, stop-start session holding my attention – never mind my enthusiasm – was just never going to work.

And, of course, pretty soon Portumna's hurling story flew into this wild orbit that meant rugby never really got a hold on me again.

Our involvement in that 2006 All-Ireland hurling club championship meant that I missed the under-18s All-Ireland with Ballinasloe. And despite plenty of gossip to the contrary, I was never seriously courted by any All-Ireland League (AIL) rugby clubs when moving to Limerick that autumn.

Plenty of the lads played both games. James Skehill, who had already been a year at LIT, was playing rugby with UL Bohemians; Paul 'Dumper' Loughnane was in with Shannon, as was Stanley Hayes.

All those lads had played under-18s rugby with Ballinasloe.

Deep down, I suspect it would have broken my father's heart had I ever chosen to pursue a future in the game. He'd never have articulated it; I know that. Actually, I'm sure he'd have said, 'Fair enough, if that's what you want to do.' But I'd have known too that it was hurting him.

Dad had no real interest in the sport, though himself and Mam sometimes came to those Ballinasloe games, partly for the novelty value, partly – I suspect – in quiet dread that I might pick up a bad injury.

Funny, I have just a single jersey hanging up in my house in Castletroy today, and it's a rugby jersey. It's the number 10 shirt worn by Jonathan Sexton during Ireland's 2018 Autumn Internationals defeat of the All Blacks in Dublin. I've never really been into keeping stuff like that, but this was an exception.

One thing that always stuck in my head about Sexton was

a presentation that Paul O'Connell made to the Galway squad coming up to the 2017 All-Ireland final. We were staying in the Radisson Blu in Dublin city centre and one of the boys asked O'Connell to name the best Irish player he had played with.

Instinctively, I presumed he was going to pick one of two: Brian O'Driscoll or Ronan O'Gara.

So I was genuinely shocked then to hear him say 'Johnny Sexton'.

O'Connell's explanation was that Sexton didn't simply know his own job on the field, he knew everyone else's too. And with that knowledge, he'd basically micromanage everyone's position. It's an aspect of his play that people probably became far more appreciative of towards the tail end of Sexton's career, but back in 2017, it felt like a revelation.

I had never met Johnny in person but then a brief exchange on Instagram in December 2018 led to us exchanging jerseys. I was actually heading to Dublin en route for a weekend in Edinburgh with some of my old buddies from college when Sexton suggested I call over to his house in Rathgar to make the exchange. He was getting the poor end of this deal, no question. My All-Ireland jersey had long since gone home to Gortanumera national school to be raffled, so all I really had to offer was a bog-standard signed Galway shirt.

Anyway, Johnny couldn't have been nicer when I called.

The next time I'd meet him was the following year in Japan when Shane Lowry and I were invited to the Irish team hotel for a question-and-answer session the day before their World Cup quarter-final against New Zealand.

Shane, a relatively newly crowned Open champion, was in Japan to play in the Zozo Championship. I was there as a rugby tourist, having just flown in with a group of friends.

We'd just settled in a bar around 2 p.m. on this Friday when I got a text from Conor Murray: 'Joe was wondering if you'd come along tonight with Shane?'

I'd met Joe Schmidt a couple of times and always found him very affable. I knew a good few of the Munster lads too and – through our Audi connections – the Leinster pair, Rob Kearney and Garry Ringrose.

So a few hours later, Shane and I were sitting in the team room, basically just exchanging war stories.

Typically, Sexton was last to arrive after a lengthy kicking session, and I have to say it was one of those pinch-me moments, sitting in such an intimate setting with this group of players that I'd just flown in to support.

On some level, I was conscious too that hurling wouldn't have been high in the interests of some of the players. Actually, in my head, I imagined some of them thinking: 'Who the fuck is this fella with Lowry?'

The questions from the floor naturally focused largely on Portrush that July, and frankly, I was only too happy to sit listening to Shane's stories. But then a voice from the floor announced, 'A question for Joe.'

And sitting there with a grin on his face was Connacht's Jack Carty. 'What's the story with this financial scandal in Galway GAA?' he asked. Ah, thanks, Jack!

Needless to say, my answer was a pretty short one.

To this day, Ronan O'Gara is probably my favourite Irish sports person, never mind rugby player. I love what I interpret to be a furiously independent mind, and it's quite incredible to see the courageous career choices he's made in a coaching capacity, not to mention the extraordinary success that has followed.

To be fair, Sexton seems fairly similar. You never feel that they're just spouting some kind of comfortable consensus when they speak. They'll happily go against the flow no matter whose feathers they manage to ruffle as a result.

The first time I saw O'Gara in action was in an AIL game for Cork Constitution against Buccaneers at Temple Hill. We'd have gone to a lot of Buccs games at the time when it was normal for them to draw huge attendances to Ballinasloe or Athlone.

My brother Davy went to agriculture college with a Buccs prop, Jimmy Screene, so we'd have been in Temple Hill that day to support him.

I'll always remember O'Gara, wearing these Adidas Predators, basically running the show without looking like he'd even got up a sweat. Because I was an out-half too, I couldn't take my eyes off him, particularly the way he'd spiral these kicks with incredible precision, left and right. Years later, it was a real thrill for me that he was the one presenting me with the 2005 *Irish Examiner* Young Hurler of the Year award. Never meet your heroes? Don't believe it.

6.

WHEN WE WERE KINGS

About seven months before we played Newtownshandrum in the 2006 All-Ireland Senior Club Championship final, we had a challenge game against them on their field that had to be abandoned.

It all exploded after a dangerously high pull by one of their players across the back of Andy Smith's head, the referee deciding almost instantly that the safest thing was to just end it there and then. There was a slightly surreal atmosphere immediately afterwards as we were treated to a fine spread of tea, sandwiches and cakes in their clubhouse while the Newtown players just went straight home. The club, in other words, couldn't have been more welcoming. The team? Much less so.

Not long afterwards, their manager, Bernie O'Connor, gave an interview to a local Cork newspaper, deriding us as 'soft'. To put it mildly, his tone offended us.

Around the same time, Loughrea had a challenge game against them abandoned too, so maybe the problem didn't lie entirely on the side of Newtown's opponents. But, at the time, that did seem Bernie's opinion.

Then the day we beat them in the All-Ireland final, nobody from their side came into our dressing room afterwards. In fact, they didn't come up to the players' lounge either, apparently choosing instead to go straight home again. I didn't even drink at the time, but still remember being struck by how ungracious that seemed.

It's funny how we'd meet Bernie O'Connor regularly at the Ploughing Championships in subsequent years, where, like us, the family would have a stand selling hurleys. And, in that environment, he couldn't have been friendlier. But when it came to the heat of battle, you could say we found Newtown a little short on basic class. If you can't even shake hands with your opponent at the end of an All-Ireland final, I think you probably need to take a long, hard look in the mirror.

It was a strange thing to be going into that final as favourites, especially against a team powered by the O'Connor twins – Bernie's sons, Ben and Jerry – who'd been so influential in Cork's successful All-Ireland title defence the previous September.

But we'd demolished the defending champions, James Stephens, by a dozen points in the semi-final whereas Newtown had just a single point to spare in their battle with Down champions, Ballygalget.

For me, the build-up to the final brought some clear reminders of my changed circumstance, with Marty Morrissey bringing an RTÉ camera crew down to Portumna Community School to film me in my Leaving Cert class.

Naturally, there was huge giddiness at the sight of the cameras – not to mention Marty himself, of course – but I already felt perfectly comfortable being interviewed by national media.

We were an emotional team the day of that final in Croke Park with pictures of Keith Hayes and Joe O'Meara pinned to the inside of our dressing-room door. Two young Portumna county minors who were tragically killed in separate road accidents.

I've already spoken of Keith's untimely death, while Joe, a best friend of our captain, Eugene McEntee, had been killed in a horrific accident way back in January of 1991. He was only seventeen and a Leaving Cert student at the time, and he died when a tree crashed down on the minibus in which he and Tommy McClearn were ferrying six Swiss tourists to a holiday home.

Everyone in the bus, apart from Tommy, died.

Not much needed to be said about having those pictures of Keith and Joe on the dressing-room door then. We all understood their significance: the enduring sense of loss their deaths still carried for so many.

There would be four sets of brothers on duty for Portumna that day, representing the Canning, Hayes, Smith and Treacy families. To say we were a tight dressing room would have been an understatement.

As often happens with St Patrick's Day, the weather on final day was rotten, with a bitterly cold wind whipping around Croke Park. To us, though, this was immaterial. Given our collective mindset, we'd have happily played Newtown in a blizzard.

Within eight minutes, we'd hit them for two goals – myself and Niall Hayes both finding the net – and though they got the margin back down to three points by half-time, we were always just about able to keep them at arm's length in a hard-hitting, low-scoring game.

Ollie's move onto their danger man, Cathal Naughton, significantly diminished their attacking threat, and maybe there was an element of gamesmanship in Newtown leaving us a good five minutes out in the elements before they returned for the second half, especially with us now facing 30 minutes of playing into that strong wind.

But with McEntee having a towering game at full-back, we were able to withstand the storm, Newtown being reduced to 14 men late in the game when their All-Star defender, Pat Mulcahy, received a second yellow.

We didn't actually register a single score from play in the second half, but my brother Davy probably encapsulated our attitude best afterwards with his comment that 'Guys just threw their bodies on the line out there. They didn't care if the sliotar hit them on the leg, the hand, anywhere. It was all about stopping them from scoring.'

That win set in train an unimaginable run for us that would bring three more All-Irelands and a sense of inner confidence about our ability to match and beat anyone in the country.

We'd end up playing in seven consecutive county finals between 2003 and 2009, winning five. This gave us a momentum that, at times, made us feel almost impregnable.

Routinely, we'd play and beat county sides – Tipperary, Clare, Waterford – in challenge games without anyone being unduly surprised. I remember playing Tipp in Thurles in 2008 before their All-Ireland semi-final against Waterford. I had been away on a holiday in Santa Ponsa with my college buddies, Gavin O'Mahony, Eoin Forde and John Greene, Galway's season having been ended by defeat to Cork in Thurles.

I flew home the day of the game and went straight to Semple Stadium where I scored 4–2 from centre forward in a Portumna win.

That's how good we were. Yes, Tipp's starting 15 that evening was made up mainly of subs with a few first-team starters, but they were in serious mode too, getting ready for that All-Ireland semi-final.

I doubt too many club sides could routinely play and beat county teams, but it became the level we were operating at now.

We played Galway in early 2008 – Ger Loughnane's second year as manager – and beat them too. It was obvious that defeat really stung Ger, as well as some of the Galway players who duly gave us dog's abuse on the field.

Ollie was outstanding that day, and I suspect it was the game that convinced him to come back out of inter-county retirement, having missed all of 2007. He and Ger had a chat immediately after, and he was back in the Galway fold for that 2008 championship, my first as a county senior hurler.

In many ways, you would sometimes feel in a safer, more controlled environment hurling at county level than with the club. You certainly felt less likely to be blackguarded.

There's a scene in the *Pride of the Parish* documentary following Portumna's journey in 2008 where I'm filmed on the field immediately after we've beaten Clarinbridge in a county semi-final. It's been a typically aggressive, angry game, played right on the edge of control. And my tone communicates a sense of exasperation at what was commonly allowed pass for 'tough' hurling in the Galway championship.

'It's a load of bull,' I say to no one in particular. 'There's a line. We need fair play, like. We can't take it every day we go out. We'll be retired by the time we're twenty-seven or twenty-eight with broken legs and broken fingers and nothing said about it, you know!'

There was this kind of parallel world to my hurling life now. Within the Galway championship, there was always a sense – rightly or wrongly – that most within the county would quite like to have seen us beaten.

In that regard, it felt a massive thing to win that county title in 2008, beating a young Gort team in the final. This was Portumna's first time to win back-to-back crowns, and you'd probably get the gist of our collective mindset from my post-match quotes.

Describing the win as 'a big monkey off our backs', I reflected, 'It's sad to say how much we've won, and it's still not enough for the people in Galway.'

This was a sweeping statement, of course, as I'm sure there were plenty of non-Portumna people within the county who weren't entirely set against us. But sometimes it serves a purpose to carry that siege mentality. It sharpens the will to win.

I was held scoreless from play as we made it three-in-a-row when beating Loughrea in the 2009 final, Damien Hayes doing most of the damage with a personal tally of 3–3.

Between us we'd scored 3–17 in the 2005 final against the same opposition, and Damien and I certainly became a hugely effective double-act through those years, even though our personalities would be poles apart.

Hayesey is an open book, one of the least guarded people you could ever come across. A larger-than-life character who wears his heart on his sleeve. He could tell you straight after a match, not just what he'd scored, but how much he'd set up too. In fact, he'd invariably have a better idea of what I'd scored than I'd have myself.

Damien took some punishment over the years, but he had a ruthlessness in him too, a defiance that nobody was ever going to easily get the better of him. Sometimes he'd win a ball and I'd find myself wondering how the fuck he did that. For a small man, he had these huge, bucket-like hands that the ball would be drawn to like filings to a magnet.

There was a fearlessness in him too, and I learned a huge amount from just playing in the same forward line, specifically from the cleverness of his movement. As a young fella, my priority was often just making sure that I didn't get in his way.

Mind you, little did we think when that three-in-a-row win propelled us towards our fourth All-Ireland final in five years that we would not claim another county crown until 2013. But time just seemed to catch up with the group, miles in the legs taking a toll.

When my own brother Frank took the manager's job for 2013, hand on heart, I don't think any of us envisaged the glory days returning. He'd actually gone for the job the year before only to be beaten in a vote. When he then announced at home that he was going to try again, apparently my mother replied, 'Don't be such a fool. They didn't want you last year; don't give them the chance to turn you down again.'

Now, mostly, Mam's advice was heeded in our house, but for whatever reason, Frank believed there might be one last dance in the team. He made it clear that he was only taking the job on for that one year too. In other words, if there was anything left in us, it would have to be found immediately.

He brought Noel Larkin with him as coach, and Ollie was confirmed as captain, but Gort then duly beat us in our first League match. I was playing full forward the same day, and Frank instantly spotted how I'd unwittingly been indoctrinated into the defensive mindset now so prevalent at county level.

Having scored from a 21, I immediately went sprinting out the field.

'Where the fuck are you going?' he roared.

'Out to defend the puck-out,' I replied.

'And where are you playing?'

Point taken.

The two of us had more rows that year, I'd say, than any other because the smallest of things would set either one of us off. But I knew he was smart too.

I played midfield in both our county semi-final and final wins, as well as the All-Ireland semi-final against Na Piarsaigh. But when we played Offaly in a challenge in Birr before the final against Mount Leinster Rangers, he inexplicably stuck me in at full forward. Honestly, I was furious. To me, it made zero sense as I'd been going well in midfield and really enjoying the freedom. Actually, he made a number of switches that day that served only to confuse us. So much so, I wasn't the only Portumna player bulling with him that day, a few others making their feelings known too.

Most of us drove home from Birr a little pissed off that evening, but what Frank neglected to tell us was that the Mount Leinster Rangers' management team had been spotted at the game.

The Portumna side they 'spied' on that day was a lie.

Looking back, they were the best days of our lives, I suppose; days when we knew we could go toe-to-toe with any opposition. Seeds sewn by that first All-Ireland final win against Newtownshandrum had given us the psychological freedom to expect success once we'd escaped the attrition of Galway. But that attrition was never really far away. By the end of 2006, we were in Pearse Stadium for a county final against Loughrea that everyone expected was going to test our appetite for driving on again.

And, as history records, it well and truly did.

7.

LOOSE TIMBER

We had a sense of the heat coming our way that day, just maybe underestimated the intensity.

To say it was white-hot would be an understatement. Chasing their first senior county title for 65 years, it was always clear that Loughrea would be gunning for us. We'd beaten them in the finals of 2003 and 2005, the latter defeat – we knew all too well – still niggling them deeply.

They were a team inclined to hurl on the plainest of terms, but that day Loughrea's ferocity just flew to another place.

Were we ready for it? Given that we'd objected to Michael Conway's appointment as referee, I think it's fair to say that we anticipated trouble. The Portumna view was that Conway would be nowhere near strong enough for a game certain to be played close to the very edge. Our underlying fear was that it could get out of control. We weren't afraid of Loughrea, but we wanted a hurling match.

An added source of concern was that Conway was living in Loughrea. Fair to say we had a certain history with him too, given he'd been referee for the '02 semi-final against Sarsfields when the questionable awarding of that late free gave Joe Cooney the opportunity to break Portumna hearts.

In his match report for the *Connacht Tribune* the following week, John McIntyre referenced Portumna as having 'an understandable sense of outrage at Michael Conway's decision-making'.

My brother Frank was our club delegate to the Galway Hurling Board in 2006, and he had three separate conversations in the weeks before the county final with board secretary, John Fahey. Apparently, it was eventually proposed that Frank should send a fax outlining Portumna's concerns. Yet there was no subsequent evidence of any reference to that fax at a board meeting the Monday before the game. The word was simply that Conway and his match officials would be told to clamp down on any overly physical play.

Hot air, in other words.

Everything that unspooled the following Sunday duly backed up Portumna's concerns.

The day would acquire a certain infamy on the back of an extraordinary image snapped by renowned Galway photographer, Ray Ryan. An image that, in today's language, duly went viral.

The picture is a close-up of a Loughrea boot descending towards my face as I lay on my back after taking a heavy shunt from Greg Kennedy. The studs of the boot are about to pierce my face guard, leaving me in need of gluing just above the mouth.

At the time, I had no idea what hit me, just felt something across my face, and then that familiar sting that tells you you've been cut.

I remember putting my hand to my mouth, and instantly, just blood everywhere.

Ollie came over to check on me, and seeing the damage, wanted me to name the culprit. I hadn't a clue. Kennedy's hit had sent me tumbling, everything afterwards just a blur. Only on seeing the video afterwards could I identify the owner of the boot.

And the worst part of seeing that video was the clarity it delivered, not simply of an opponent stamping down on my face, but of someone actually changing the angle of their run to do so. Of the ball going one way, and the Loughrea player turning in the opposite direction towards me on the ground. In other words, of him committing a plainly deliberate act.

The linesman was standing no more than 10 yards away with a perfectly clear view of everything now happening directly in front of him, yet stood motionless. It seemed he might as well have had his eyes closed.

And Ollie?

'Calm down and get up to fuck,' he told me, grabbing my jersey. 'Let's fucking win this!'

Hand on heart, that was my one and only sentiment too. We'd anticipated plenty of timber that day and were more than primed to meet it, having been exposed to all the familiar shite-talk in the build-up. Talk about All-Ireland champions being brought back down to size. Talk about big shots getting a softening. Maybe, above all, talk about an eighteen-year-old boy wonder getting a lesson in the harsher ways of the world.

You expect the talk; that's never the issue. But when that talk is allowed to become reality? That's when those in charge have a duty of care to honour.

So nothing about that first half was a surprise to us: the clipping relentless, the sense of cheap shots being taken at every opportunity. If I'm honest, our attitude was 'bring it on!'

Tough hurling never spooked us. We weren't exactly altar boys ourselves, and if the need arose, we could play with some gunpowder of our own too.

And here's the thing. For all of Loughrea's hitting, we went in at the break 0–10 to 0–2 clear, their only scores coming from frees.

There was plenty of pushing and shoving – among mentors as well as players – as the half-time whistle blew, but my memory of our dressing room is one of absolute calm; voices low and resolute as I lay on a table, the cut on my face being tended.

And then? We went back out and duly folded.

When I think back on that day, that's what sickens me most. The fact we lost a game that had felt so comfortably under our control.

Not the dirt, not the weak refereeing, not even the pathetic Hurling Board grandstanding we were subjected to in the aftermath. No, the sickening thing is that, as a team, we pretty much went missing in a final quarter that Loughrea would win 0–9 to 0–2 to give an overall score of 1–13 to our final score of 0–15.

Their winning free arrived six minutes and fifteen seconds into injury time (despite the fourth official indicating just four additional minutes) and, needless to say, the final whistle triggered wild celebrations. In the midst of those celebrations, one of our players – Matt Ryan – actually had his leg broken by a swinging Loughrea hurley.

If I'm honest, my overriding emotion at the end of the day was that we had only ourselves to blame for losing to such a limited team. And your sole instinct when you lose a game like that is to gather your stuff as quickly as possible and get the hell out of Dodge.

But what followed became a bit of a media circus that would end, farcically, with Portumna hit by the brunt of suspensions handed out by a Games Administration Committee (GAC) investigation headed by Galway secretary, Bernie O'Connor.

In a hearing at the Quality Hotel in Oranmore, their only punishment for a Loughrea player was a four-week ban for their wing back, Johnny Dooley, meaning he would miss their Connacht final against Roscommon champions, Athleague.

O'Connor wasn't a man with too many admirers around Portumna, and fair to say this would diminish his reputation within the club further. Adding to our sense of hurt was the fact that Frank Burke – a long-serving county chairman at the time – was an Ardrahan man with strong Loughrea connections, having spent much of his life living and teaching in the town.

Our manager, Jimmy Heverin, and coach, Seán Treacy, had both been scathing of Loughrea's conduct in the immediate aftermath of the game, specifically referencing the treatment I'd been subjected to.

Jimmy spoke of me getting 'dog's abuse', while Seán, recently appointed a selector to incoming Galway manager, Ger Loughnane, gave an interview to the *Irish Independent* suggesting that he was now considering his future with the county.

'When you see a lad like Joe Canning being walloped all over the place, there's something seriously wrong,' he said. 'The way young Joe is feeling now, he may never play hurling again. And who can blame him? He was butchered from start to finish.'

Immediately after the game, the Hurling Board announced that they would be undertaking a full investigation of incidents in the final with chairman Miko Ryan declaring that they would go through the match video 'inch by inch'.

But whatever they thought they saw in that video is anybody's guess – even now, 18 years later. The two most highly publicised suspensions of two months each would be handed out afterwards to Jimmy and Seán for – apparently – 'bringing the game into disrepute'. Almost comically, they were invited to apologise to the GAC, an act that would presumably have lessened if not completely removed their punishments. Both declined.

My brother, Davy, got three months for an alleged strike with the hurley.

By comparison, in the Loughrea ranks, just Dooley was sanctioned with that four-week ban. And otherwise? A few gentle warnings for the new champions. One for a pitch encroachment. Another for someone standing in the team photo while suspended.

How perverse was that? The team that did the protesting hit with the lion's share of suspensions.

Maybe Billy Keane, son of legendary playwright, John B. Keane, put it best. Writing in the *Irish Independent*, Billy described the Galway Hurling Board as 'the champions of free speech who banned two men for voicing their opinions'.

And the lad who stamped on my face? Nothing.

Funny, the same fella never subsequently played a League game against Portumna afterwards. Never came near our place. He'd tog out in championship, right enough, because there'd be eyes on you then, but always went missing when we played them in the League.

I always felt that said everything about the type of character he was. He certainly knew he'd be a marked man if ever setting foot on our field.

Of course, the Loughrea manager, Pat O'Connor, welcomed those GAC sanctions, suggesting that everything in Salthill that day had simply been 'blown out of proportion'.

I lost all respect for the Hurling Board when the suspensions were handed out, and those feelings never really softened across the years. My relationship with most of them could, at best, be described as cold. Routinely, I'd just blank them if they came to me after games.

Mam always had this saying: 'Bite your lip; there's no point in going down to their level.' You'd always kind of hope that your silence got the message across because I was never a naturally confrontational person. But if I had no time for somebody, I wanted them to know it too.

That said, I wasn't exactly thrilled to be front and centre of that county final fall-out either. While Jimmy and Seán were cutting loose, supposedly on my behalf, no one really took the time to get my take on things.

Don't get me wrong, I knew that they were absolutely sincere in what they were doing. Their words reflected a genuine anger within the club, an anger that – in time – would persuade Jimmy to reverse his decision to step down as manager for 2007.

And Seán will rightly always be considered one of Galway's and Portumna's greatest hurling men. He's actually back coaching us this year, alongside Damien Hayes and Paddy Dolphin, after a spell on the Clare management team, and he would have been a constant hurling presence in the lives of the Canning family going right back to my father's playing days.

You see, when Dad won that county junior in 1982, Seán was a sixteen-year-old on the Portumna bench. Twenty-one years later, when we finally won that first senior title with Ollie as captain, he was on the bench aged thirty-seven. Over the years, Seán's trained or coached most Portumna teams, even serving for a time as club secretary. Twice an All-Star, during more than a decade hurling with Galway, he is as admirable a hurling man as you could hope to meet.

But in 2006, I just watched the fall-out to that county final unspool, feeling increasingly uncomfortable that people presumed I was now torn in some kind of conflict about whether or not I'd ever even hurl again.

As I was about to start a Construction Studies course at LIT, there were even suggestions that I had been approached by a couple of AIL clubs in the city to turn my full attention to rugby.

Little of this was actually true. It was just idle speculation arising from the fact that some of the lads I'd played rugby with in Ballinasloe were now involved with Limerick clubs, specifically Shannon. There might have been a few idle conversations on a night out between us at the time, but it was just lads tossing out a harmless bait. There was no formal conversation with any rugby club representative, absolutely nothing concrete along those lines. I did take a call after that county final on behalf of Shannon from Ger Casey, father of current Ireland international Craig, but nothing came of that.

I certainly had no intention of walking away from hurling anyway, but I did want a break from it now; needed one, actually.

I could take the Loughrea defeat on the chin too. The truth is most of us could. It might be a stretch to say we lost the game fair and square, but there was one spell in the second half in which they scored seven unanswered points.

That's why we lost the game. Not because some fella stamped on my face.

A bus-load of Portumna players even went over to Loughrea that Monday night, as is tradition, to share a drink with the new champions. And, if I'm honest, that's where I would have liked it to end.

The last thing I wanted was to be depicted as some kind of precious young fella who couldn't stand his ground when the temperature rose. Put yourself in my shoes. I was eighteen and didn't want anyone looking on me as a soft touch.

I didn't want a sob story then, and I still don't want it now.

Honestly, in our house, we just wanted to forget it. That was the attitude we always went home to: 'Get back up and get on with it!'

That said, a certain sense of paranoia was probably under-standable given both the referee and county chairman were living in Loughrea.

And the action – or maybe, more accurately – the *inaction* of the board suggested that what had happened in the game was somehow acceptable. For me, that was an eye-opener. I mean, even many of the local match reports alluded to Loughrea's conduct as being, at best, borderline in that final. The reporters weren't blind to what they had seen. All we wanted was some semblance of fairness from a board that seemed to imply that we were primarily to blame for what went on in Salthill that day.

Bearing in mind that this was just months after we'd brought an All-Ireland club title to the county, I thought they could have shown us a little more respect. But then that was to become a long-running story in my life as a Galway hurler.

8.

FATHERS

Becoming a father is the best and most terrifying thing I've done in life.

It's been more daunting than I imagined, yet less confusing – if that makes any sense. The instinct of protectiveness is all-consuming. The worry about tiny things. Meg has undoubtedly carried the heavier load, but I like to think I'm reasonably hands-on too.

I want to be good at it maybe even more than I ever wanted to be a good hurler, because it feels like this is the beginning of the rest of my life now.

If Mam's was the stronger parental presence in my own childhood, I've always known I've had the blessing of a great father too. And the more I see in the world, the more I come to realise that that's no small thing.

Dad's what you'd call an old-school father, someone with little enough interest in telling their own story. Everything is just a shrug and a chuckle, unless the talk is hurling talk. Then you see a change: the game lighting fires in him that nothing else can.

He hurled intermediate for Galway and, at thirty-seven, scored 1–2 in an 1982 county junior final win over Ardrahan. At the time, it was Portumna's biggest day since winning a junior title 68 years earlier.

By all accounts, he was half decent then – though you'd never get that sense off him.

Given all seven of his children wore maroon at different levels, I suppose he has always seen his own hurling history as something unremarkable.

One of his fondest days was lining out with Frank, then a fifteen-year-old, in goals for a junior championship game, albeit Dad says he only did it 'to make up the numbers'. Seamus hurled with the intermediates the same day, so maybe – on some level – that felt like passing on a baton.

Over time, our stories became his: our achievements the only ones he had any appetite for exploring. He has always loved his few pints in Curley's with friends the night of a Portumna or Galway win, especially so if someone in the family had a good day.

I've often felt guilty about how instinctively closed I would be whenever he'd ask how training might be going with Galway. 'Ah, it's grand' would be the extent of my reply, telling him nothing.

Why? Because that's how you become programmed within the modern inter-county bubble. It's as if you're protecting the very secrets of Fatima. There's a reflex paranoia in how the county player communicates with the outside world now that actually makes little sense. But we've all invested in it, promoted it even – the clichéd theory of 'us against the world'. You could call it a psychological security blanket.

I'm pretty sure that over the years Dad's friends would routinely fish for snippets from the Galway camp on the basis that two of his sons were so centrally involved. And I'm equally sure there were times he'd feel embarrassed at having absolutely zero to tell them. It's not as if he was ever going to be shooting his mouth off about anything I might disclose. That wouldn't be him at all. He's just a proud father. But I think the fact that Galway never really trained anywhere in or around Portumna, there was always this added curiosity in the town about how things might be shaping up at our sessions in Athenry and Salthill. And, of course, training eventually went behind closed doors, adding to the sense of mystery. So inevitably, he'd be getting 'How's Ollie?' or 'How's Joe?'

In hindsight, how hard would it have been for me to give him a line? I doubt I'm alone in thinking there's something faintly absurd about how closed the modern inter-county player feels compelled to become, even within their own family. Mostly, the secrets we keep aren't really worthy of being secrets at all.

Dad and Mam were always polar opposites at games. Mam had a kind of worldly-wise calm about her, a sense of adult perspective that I suppose hurling doesn't always foster. She'd spray us all with holy water going out the door to games, and that would be the extent of her visible anxiety.

Seán Canning and Josephine Lynch met in Kiltormer's Crystal Ballroom in 1964 and married five years later, having their reception in Athlone's Hudson Bay Hotel. That night, apparently, they drove to Dublin in the Volkswagen, and then spent the next week cruising all over the country to places like Tramore, Killarney, Lisdoonvarna and Salthill, with – as Dad now recalls –'the lights of the car like two candles'.

I think it's fair to say they remained genuine soulmates through over half a century of marriage – until Mam's death in 2022 left a gaping hole in all our worlds.

But talking about grief isn't easy, maybe for men especially. There's more unsaid between us than we have the capacity to recognise. It's probably easier that way.

I do know that Dad misses Mam hugely now. Sometimes he pulls out the Book of Condolences from her funeral and just reading some of the messages again brings immediate tears to his eyes. He makes no bones of the fact that hers was always the voice carrying the most weight in the house. She never had to raise it, though. If she was cross about something, everybody knew it instinctively.

Dad and Mam never really travelled abroad until Granny Maisie's death in 1999, but after that, Lanzarote became a favourite destination – sometimes twice a year. They went to Rome too. And to Lourdes and Fatima.

I'm told that Seán Canning can be hot-tempered in a hurling crowd, but given I'd almost always be playing in a game that might trigger him, I haven't honestly seen this for myself. Thinking about it logically, though, how could he be any other way? Just imagine the kind of comments he's heard across the years when we've been playing. Maybe about me, especially.

People assert some kind of public ownership over players, buying them licence to be intensely mean-spirited about people they often know little or nothing about. For a parent, that can make spectating an incredibly uncomfortable experience.

Something that's maybe all ahead of me now.

Anyway, Dad was never the type to leave cheap shots go unchallenged. He'd fight his corner. And not just for his children, but his grandchildren too.

To him, hurling is the only game that matters. He'd look at me with incredulity sometimes if I said I was going to play a game of soccer. 'Just lads falling around the place,' as he'd put it. He describes his time playing junior football as 'pure pull, drag and draw'. So his passion for hurling blocks out all other sports. Maybe if Ireland were playing a Six Nations game, he might sit down and watch. But he certainly wouldn't be planning his day around the fixture.

Humour has always been his default setting, and it makes him easy company. Once, when I was at under-14 training with Galway, a mother of one of the other players asked him if he was my grandfather. To be fair to her, it was an understandable question given he'd have been fifty-six when I was a thirteen-year-old. Most of the other parents there were in their mid-thirties, and the poor woman was absolutely mortified when Dad put her straight on his identity. But Dad being Dad, he just took a fit of laughing. It didn't bother him in the slightest. Anytime he was ever asked if he was my father, his reflex answer would be, 'Well, sure I'm married to his mother anyway!'

It wouldn't be quite as simple when Deirdre was occasionally asked if she was my mother. An understandable question again given the 18 years between us, but one seldom met with a welcoming smile.

Of course, we almost lost Dad the day of the 2005 All-Ireland hurling finals.

It was a monumental weekend for the family: me hurling with the minors against Limerick; Ollie on the senior team to play Cork. Mam and Dad appeared that Saturday night on RTÉ's *Up for the Match*, seated alongside the mothers of Cork players, Seán Óg Ó hAilpín and Diarmuid O'Sullivan. They were booked into the Citywest Hotel (where we all hoped there would be a double Sunday evening victory celebration) for two nights, dinner included. Everything was planned to a tee, including seats in the Hogan Stand lower tier so they could come to the side of the pitch as they'd done the year before after our drawn All-Ireland minor final against Kilkenny.

But on their way to Croke Park this time, he felt a pain down his arm and slight discomfort in his chest. It was something he'd experienced a few times previously out on the farm and simply filed it away as indigestion. This time, though, he sensed something more urgent about the symptoms.

His last memory of the minor game is of me scoring a goal, after which he took himself out under the stand and caught the attention of someone from St John's Ambulance. A doctor was beckoned, and within minutes, Dad was in the back of an ambulance headed for the nearby Mater Hospital. It was there he suffered a major heart attack, meaning instant admittance to the Intensive Care Unit.

Mam had stayed behind so that I wouldn't be spooked, but by the time I finally tracked the family down somewhere under the Hogan Stand – the senior game already underway – they'd just been told that his condition was extremely serious. Some of them were crying; others staring ghost-like from ashen faces.

It was the oddest sensation. You go from an absolute high to a kind of emotional numbness. Everyone was reassuring me that he'd be fine, but their expressions didn't exactly convey confidence. Hand on heart, I cannot remember a single thing from the second half of that All-Ireland final, other than that Cork broke Galway hearts. I was in a complete daze, the only thought in my head being, 'How the fuck are we going to tell Ollie?'

But here's the thing. If Dad had been at home on the farm that day of 11 September 2005, he'd have died. And probably alone too. If he'd had that heart attack down in the fields, who's to say how long it would have been before somebody found him? Instead, Croke Park was quite possibly the best place he could have been that day. It actually saved his life.

By evening, the word coming from the Mater was of an improving condition, so we all went through with our plans for the Citywest that night, the minors celebrating, the seniors cursing another spurned final opportunity. As a family, our heads were in a spin. You wake up that Sunday morning thinking this could be a day of days; you go to bed that night with that old saying in your head: 'God laughs at the man who makes plans!'

I'll always remember Mam making it back out to the hotel around 10 p.m. and us having this little family conference under the big staircase in the lobby.

The following morning, Ollie and I went in to visit, me with a cup in my hands. Dad was sitting up in bed, smiling as if everything had just been some kind of silly misunderstanding. His attitude was: 'What the hell are ye doing in here? Ye should be off out enjoying yourselves!'

He'd laugh at his own predicament at a moment like that, though it was all too clear that he'd just been incredibly lucky. There was no real history of heart trouble in his family, but he also knew that he'd become heavier than was advisable. That week in the Mater, he had a stent inserted before being discharged on the Friday. And over the next year or so, he managed to shed two stone.

I very much doubt that hurling would be a cardiologist's first choice for their patients, and certainly not patients burdened with a short fuse. My understanding of Dad is that he'd never ever instigate a row, and he'd certainly never come to blows with someone. But if he didn't like something that was said, he isn't one for just letting it go. I suspect the game has shaped his personality every bit as much as life on the farm.

He had another, less serious heart attack in February of 2008, this time after attending our All-Ireland club semi-final against Tipperary champions Loughmore–Castleiney in the Gaelic Grounds. His familiarity with the symptoms meant little time was wasted when, down on the field after the game, he began to experience mild chest pains. Mam drove them home, took him to the local doctor, and pretty quickly, he found himself in Ballinasloe Hospital.

The medical advice was that he should stay away from our subsequent All-Ireland final against Birr on St Patrick's Day. He ignored it. With four sons starting (plus Seamus, who was a sub), there was only one place he was ever going to be that day.

He remembers the doctor in Ballinasloe, a man who had little understanding of GAA passions, observing flatly that it would be unwise for him to go to the game. Dad's reply was, 'Well, doctor, it's like this. Five of my lads are involved with this team, and everyone else in the house will be going. Wouldn't I be better dying with the whole family in Croke Park than dying alone at home?'

Realising that he was fighting a losing battle here, the doctor just prescribed an extra Valium for the day.

Dad says he could have 'killed' he was so angry that day we were blackguarded in the 2006 county final against Loughrea. At one stage, seemingly, Olivia Muldoon (John's sister), expressed concern that his anger might bring on another heart attack. 'Will you stop and mind yourself,' she said to him.

It was Portumna's fourth senior county final in a row and, like a lot of us, he got the distinct impression that certain people in authority didn't especially want us to win.

An impression that hasn't ever really receded across the years.

9.

COLLEGE LIFE

G etting out of Galway wasn't just something I wanted to do in 2006 – I *needed* the escape.

There'd been a relentless, claustrophobic intensity to my hurling life between the three years chasing All-Ireland minor glory and what had become a rollercoaster ride with Portumna.

In the short term, college life would now turn the volume down significantly. I'd had the offer of a scholarship to one of the big Dublin universities, but a lot of friends found their way to Limerick. The vibe I got from them was primarily one of fun. It sounded exactly what I needed.

No question, the Fitzgibbon Cup – the top hurling champion-ship for universities and institutes of technology – was a pull too. LIT had won the competition for the first time in 2005 under the guidance of Clare's long-serving goalkeeper, Davy Fitzgerald. Tipperary's Eoin Kelly was the star of that team, and though he was now gone, core members of that side, such as Galway's Iarla 'Tan' Tannian, Kilkenny's Jackie Tyrrell and Tipperary pair, Shane McGrath and Conor O'Mahony, were still available for selection.

My perception of Davy would have been faithful to cliché. I suppose I saw him as a bit of a madman the way he'd flake advertising hoardings with his hurley as some kind of self-psyching gambit before the start of big Munster championship games.

Anecdotally, his training sessions were brutal, and I was braced for a fairly intense initiation on my arrival in Limerick. It never materialised, though. Fitzy pretty much left me to find my bearings until after Christmas. This meant I piled on the pounds, between frequent takeaways and my first real introduction to the pleasures of a pint.

Sharing a house with my old friend, James Skehill, as well as Limerick's Gavin O'Mahony, Clare's Bernard Gaffney and a Tipperary man, John Dwyer, it would be fair to say that our social lives gathered full steam. I wouldn't go so far as to liken our lodgings to what Americans call a 'frat house', but it wasn't that far removed either.

This brought a real lifestyle change for me. You see, I never really drank until just before my eighteenth birthday, having taken the pledge for my Confirmation. Even when we won that first club All-Ireland in March of 2006, I didn't break it. Drink just didn't really interest me.

It wasn't that I was a Holy Joe. I just had this stubbornness in me that you either committed to something or you didn't.

There was one night, late in 2005, when I sampled a few sips of cider. It was in the Lodge – a nightclub in the Kilmurry Lodge Hotel in Limerick. I was a fifth-year student pitching up for the afters of Portumna Community School's debs. Anyway, the cider did absolutely nothing for me. I put the pint down and stayed alcohol-free for another year.

I didn't even drink at my own debs in Birr in 2006, as Galway's All-Ireland minor quarter-final against Antrim was coming up in Mullingar. That night we had our final trial game, meaning the Portumna players involved actually missed our debs dinner. Worse, two or three of the lads were told immediately after that trial that they were being dropped from the panel.

It was only a couple of months later, the day after our

All-Ireland minor final loss to Tipperary, that I finally gave in to the temptation with a few bottles on the train home.

Mam and Dad would have been fairly easy-going about it, to be fair. I think they just didn't like the idea of fifteen- or sixteen-year-olds drinking. By eighteen, their view would have been that you were old enough to make your own decisions – and mistakes.

My changed lifestyle is self-evident in photographs of me taken during that 2007 Fitzgibbon campaign compared to how I looked in the county final just a few months earlier. Life was good in LIT. And it showed.

On some level, I suspect that Davy sensed I needed that blowout, that the fall-out to the Loughrea defeat on top of a heavy loss to Tipp in the All-Ireland minor final had, for me, left a bit of a sour taste after the high of Portumna's St Patrick's Day glory.

I'd been Galway captain in our bid for a minor three-in-a-row, much being made of the fact that I was trying now to emulate the achievement of Tipp great, Jimmy Doyle, who won his third on the bounce in 1957. None of this weighed heavily on me. In fact, I can honestly say I had no sense of carrying any undue pressure into that campaign because that kind of historical context always seemed to matter more to the media than those of us directly involved. You hear subsequently that other players, technically, won three-in-a-row too, just not always as members of a starting 15. So the perceived pressure on me was absolutely not a factor in our defeat by Tipp. They were simply much better than us, and I personally had one of those days where I probably ended up trying too hard to impact a game that always seemed under their control.

Pádraic Maher marked me in the first-half; Thomas Stapleton, in the second. I moved out, I moved around, I ended up chasing my tail. For example, I scored the grand total of 0–1 from four 21-yard frees, three of my shots being blocked. My radar was off with the general free-taking too, and we were just well beaten in the end. I don't remember the experience as anything I needed help processing in any way afterwards. I didn't feel too traumatised.

A fortnight earlier, Vincent Mullins – the Galway under-21 manager – had brought me in to train with them the week of their All-Ireland semi-final against Kilkenny in Tullamore. We'd been well beaten in that game too; though, my scoring return of 2–4 – having been introduced after about 21 minutes – had Mullins singing my praises. 'Without him, what would the score have been?' he mused to media afterwards.

But then the county final took the course it did, and I suppose I just felt I needed a small break from the game. Davy seemed to recognise this as we were almost into Christmas before he began to finally crack the whip. But once he did, the rhythms of college life changed fairly radically in our house.

LIT had an unbelievable team for that 2007 Fitzgibbon with Cork's 'Fraggy' Murphy our captain and other inter-county players like Alan Cadogan (Cork), Alan Byrne (Tipp), Austin Murphy (Kilkenny), Aonghus Callanan (Galway) and Limerick's Mossy O'Brien at Davy's disposal.

And the training was, as predicted, savage.

Fitzy's a great believer that team spirit is fostered by collective hardship, and over the next few years, those of us hurling for LIT would be introduced to the 'delights' of Cratloe Woods, Broadford sand track, the famous hill in Shannon and Kilworth army camp. Everything was a mental challenge in which you were only as strong as the weakest link within the group. In other words, nobody got left behind. It was routinely tortuous, but it helped build some of the closest friendships I have today.

Fitzgibbon, you see, was a different world to anything I knew. Above all, it introduced me to the idea that players from other counties didn't have to represent some kind of sworn enemy. It also turned into a whole new adventure for my family, particularly Dad and Uncle Frankie. You see, I was the first Canning to have a sustained Fitzgibbon Cup career (although Ollie played a little with both DIT and GMIT), and I know that Dad especially came to love how those games would be a melting pot of people from all over Ireland. To him, talking hurling with people from other counties has always been one of the great pleasures of life.

Himself and Uncle Frankie relished coming to midweek games, up through Broadford and Sixmilebridge and into the LIT campus off the Cratloe Road. Dad couldn't believe the crowds and the passion of mentors on the line.

Cratloe became my first experience of the torture chamber, with Davy getting us to do a warm-up run to a certain point in the woods where we would then face these one-kilometre time-trials. The rule was you had to cover that kilometre inside a certain time limit, otherwise you did it again. And Fitzy's time limits were invariably wild.

I remember Tan knew the trail off by heart and had a short-cut – only to be found out eventually. This, needless to say, helped none of us. If the weakest runner didn't cover the kilometre in a certain time, we all had to go again. You could, therefore, end up doing seven or eight runs in one session. It was Davy's way of getting everyone working together, encouraging one another – building unity, in other words.

Broadford followed the same principle. A horse training centre with a circular sand track that we'd run time-trials on. At the end of the run, you'd arrive at this steep gradient of maybe 150 yards and be timed running to the top, where Fitzy stood, roaring instructions. We might only do it four times, but I remember it as absolutely horrible, with plenty of stomachs being emptied of their contents afterwards.

This was never, I quickly came to realise, about physical fitness. It was always more a mental challenge, forcing people to work through pain together, building steel within.

Once, across a three-day span over Christmas, he got us to do Cratloe, Broadford and Shannon on consecutive days. We stayed in this small hotel, the Pier Hotel, in Limerick, and I'll always remember the expressions of mild disbelief at home when telling them I'd be training on Stephen's Day.

Sometimes you'd be doing this stuff, thinking: *If anyone sees us out here, they'll think we're fucking insane!*

One year, Richie McCarthy took a fit of laughing when we were at the army base in Kilworth. These soldiers had us standing to attention when the first sniggers became audible. Next thing, one of them was almost apoplectic, doing his best Joe Pesci in the movie *Goodfellas* as he roared, 'You think I'm fucking funny?' Trouble was, the more he roared, the funnier the whole scene became. Eventually, Richie was just fucked into a drain, and the rest of us punished with team-building exercises.

We spent another Christmas staying in holiday homes in Lisdoonvarna, the place a virtual ghost town. After a tough hurling session, Fitzy announced that we could go for a few pints that evening so long as everyone was in bed by midnight. I reckon it was around 4 a.m. when the bedroom doors swung open with roars of 'Get up!', and in minutes, we were running down through the village.

Everyone, that is, except Gavin O'Mahony, who'd locked himself in his room.

Sounds insane, I know, but I loved the bonds those hardships built. A lot of my family would have been in Carlow the day we beat NUI Galway in the 2007 final, and I will forever be grateful for what Fitzgibbon hurling brought into my life.

Put it this way, I meet the likes of Gavin, Paudie O'Brien

and Seán Collins for lunch almost every week now as they all live within 10 minutes of me in Limerick. For years, we've had a WhatsApp group called 'The LIT Stalwarts' that was only recently rechristened 'The Ventry Escape'.

I consider Willie Hyland one of my closest friends because of our Fitzgibbon connection. Willie was good enough to hurl for any county but, being a Laois man, never got the opportunities to challenge for the game's biggest prizes.

I'll always remember a 2008 group game against University of Limerick – John Greene (who, years later, would be my best man) racing through our defence for a late goal chance that would have knocked us out of the tournament. His shot snapped back off our crossbar, only for Tom Stapleton to collect the rebound and score a point that looked to have won them the game. UL's celebrations suggested that they certainly thought that to be the case, until Willie grabbed their puck-out and swung over a spectacular equaliser that brought us back from the dead. That was Willie Hyland all over. A big-game player, always present in the big moments.

Just before last Christmas, a crew of us stayed in Mick Galwey's house near the late Páidí Ó Sé's pub in Ventry. We always try to meet up somewhere before Christmas, and this one especially was brilliant fun because we were there in the week the RTÉ programme *Other Voices* was recording in the little church in Dingle. It was a fabulous few days, largely because we could all immerse ourselves anonymously into this creative, artistic community which had a zero recognition factor for GAA faces.

Willie has four girls now; Paudie O'Brien, two girls and a boy; Gavin has a girl and a boy; Seán's just had a baby boy, while Timmy Dalton and Mark Hayes both have baby girls. In 2024, with fatherhood on my own horizon, it suddenly felt natural to be talking about families, and I loved it.

If I hadn't played Fitzgibbon, I'd never have those friends in my life. Like, Gavin was captain of the Limerick team Galway beat in the 2005 All-Ireland minor final, and honestly, I couldn't stand him at the time. Why? Because you can just form a perception of an opponent that routinely bears little relation to their true personality. Timmy scored 1–3 for Tipp when they hammered us in that 2006 minor final. If I hadn't subsequently hurled with him in college, what would I know about him?

So looking back at my Fitzgibbon days, I feel only a deep gratitude. I learned a lot off Fitzy too. We'd have had plenty of disagreements over time, and there'd be loads of stuff I'd categorically disagree with him on. But he taught me a lot hurling-wise. He probably came into my life at just the right time too, and I can honestly say that when that man's in your corner you can rest assured he's in there unequivocally.

An example? In the 2008 Fitzgibbon, I pulled a hamstring while taking a line cut in that Willie Hyland game against UL. This would have been around two weeks before Portumna's All-Ireland club semi-final against Loughmore–Castleiney. Fitzy tried to get me an appointment with Gerard Hartmann, but word came back that he wouldn't see me. Apparently, he had an unpaid bill for the Galway County Board from the year before and had simply run out of patience waiting to be paid.

Hartmann is one of the most respected physical therapists in the world, and he'd been brought into the Galway set-up under Ger Loughnane. I've gotten to know him well since, and he's now a regular morning visitor to Meg's café in Castletroy.

Anyway, through no fault of his own, Davy Fitz couldn't get me that appointment. Instead, he organised access to the cryotherapy chamber in Whites Hotel in Wexford – the only one in Ireland at the time – where I spent a couple of days undergoing intensive treatment of the hamstring. He could easily have done nothing, as this essentially was my club's problem now. But Fitzy's attitude was: 'he got injured with us; it's our responsibility to look after him!' And because of that cryotherapy treatment, I made it back in time for the Loughmore game.

Maybe that's a side of Davy Fitz that goes unseen by those who don't really know him. It's as if they see only a cardboard cut-out. But, for me, he has a purer sense of loyalty than a hell of a lot of his critics.

10.

CASH COW

I understood quite quickly that I was in a position to monetise my status as a hurler to an entirely different level to any of my teammates. But how I did that led to a fantasy world of rumour and innuendo.

The idea seemed to take hold that the game was making me wealthy: imagined sponsorship figures conveniently exaggerated on almost every telling. I'd hear stories – second- and third-hand – of people having confirmation from 'well-informed sources' that I'd got some astronomical sum from one brand or another, my link-up in 2009 with Red Bull especially feeding the wildest of speculation.

It was a connection that I realised instantly carried a certain edge, given a perception of the energy drink in Ireland that was a good deal more contentious than most other places in Europe. For a lot of Irish parents, stories of teenagers going wild on Red Bull and vodka were too commonplace for comfort. Whereas elsewhere the drink was interpreted as doing exactly what it said on the tin, the Irish perception was broadly of something destructive and maybe even exploitative.

Did I worry about that? Absolutely, I worried about it massively.

This, after all, was happening in just my second year as a senior inter-county hurler. The optics, I knew, wouldn't be to everyone's taste, even though Dublin footballer Bernard Brogan had already signed up to the brand. But one of the instant attractions for me was that, as a Red Bull ambassador, I was granted access to world-class training feedback, specifically spending three days at their facility in Salzburg, where I underwent just about every physical and psychological test imaginable.

Maybe there was a certain naivety, even vanity, in my decision to take on the role. But all I saw was this worldwide brand linked with some of the biggest sports stars on the planet now wanting to be associated with an Irish hurler. Bottom line, I was hugely flattered.

The contact for the deal was Eamonn Seoige – brother of TV personalities, Gráinne and Síle – and one aspect of it was a feature article on me appearing in this glossy colour magazine they published called *The Red Bulletin*. So there I was, posing in the same pages as cliff divers and racing drivers – all extreme sports, which, essentially, is how they were bracketing hurling too.

One of the assessments I underwent in Salzburg concluded that there was a split-second delay in my decision-making, a fractional hesitation they reckoned had to be costly in elite sport. That conclusion actually made a lot of sense to me and set me thinking.

The more I reflected on how I'd been playing around that time, the more I sensed that I hadn't quite been trusting my instincts. In other words, I wasn't hurling with spontaneity.

It was never part of the deal that I would ever have to drink Red Bull, and there were plenty of perks on offer if I wanted to avail of them – stuff like VIP tickets to the Monaco Grand Prix or any Red Bull-sponsored event in the world, basically. I never did really avail of those perks, though my deal did require me pitching up at a couple of events in Ireland like the Red Bull Crushed Ice event in Stormont, and closer to home, cliff diving on Inis Mór.

I attended the latter twice, and it was a pretty cool event, which on the first year required me to stand on a platform 100 metres above Poll na bPéist – the so-called Serpent's Lair – pucking sliotars into the Atlantic Ocean.

The second year, Cork camogie star Ashling Thompson attended, and we had this long puck competition on the beach, involving the divers. The competitor who drove the ball furthest got to pick the sequence in which they wanted to dive. The diver with the worst puck was, in other words, left at the mercy of their opponents.

I loved the opportunity of meeting people from other sports, though I always felt conscious of not ever appearing overly familiar. To some degree, this wariness was rooted in my own experience of people latching onto me on the basis of a single meeting. On an idea that even the most superficial connection now amounted to some kind of friendship.

I hated people making assumptions after meeting me just once; assumptions implying that they now knew me and could, accordingly, expect access to me. Just because you might have spent an enjoyable day in somebody's company doesn't mean you're now buddies. I instinctively bristled at the idea of someone overstepping the mark like that, and accordingly, was maybe ultra-conscious of not being guilty of the same thing myself. On some level, this was undoubtedly rooted in a certain insecurity too. The sense of 'I'm only a GAA man …'.

That said, the marketability of big GAA names was now going to another level with the likes of Brogan and Cork hurler Seán Óg Ó hAilpín in huge demand for public appearances. Bernard especially seemed to change the terms of commercial engagement for inter-county GAA players. In terms of Red Bull, I can remember no real outbreak of negativity towards their GAA connection until the summer of 2018.

In other words, almost a decade after my initial link-up, it suddenly became a newspaper story that Galway hurlers were using towels and drinks bottles carrying Red Bull branding. It was highlighted that before taking a free, I'd wipe the sweat off my hands with a Red Bull towel. The hullaballoo was astonishing given that that very same branding had been all over our towels and drinks bottles in 2017 as Galway were crowned All-Ireland champions for the first time in 29 years.

It was as if the energy drink's involvement with Galway was hidden in plain sight up to that moment, despite a big Red Bull tank always being parked out the front of the Pearse Stadium stand for all our home games. Had nobody actually noticed it?

Maybe this is just the kind of sideshow that kicks off when you are All-Ireland champions, but I found it really bizarre that this suddenly became a media focus. Worse, I resented the way some almost presented it as a Joe Canning production, when the truth was it was a Galway County Board link-up that nobody had seemingly paid any heed to when we were on our way to winning the MacCarthy Cup.

One thing that I will admit did make me uncomfortable that summer of 2018 was when my face started appearing on Red Bull cans. I absolutely hated the timing of that launch, but when you sign up to certain commercial deals, I suppose you have to accept that not everything done is going to be entirely on your terms. In this case, the cans were launched the evening after our Saturday All-Ireland semi-final replay defeat of Clare in Dublin. Or, more precisely, at 6 p.m. that Sunday, at which point I had to post a video we'd recorded some weeks earlier.

To put it mildly, I was uncomfortable pressing the Send button on that video.

Given that we would lose the subsequent All-Ireland final to Limerick, some chose to question my focus going into that game, specifically in light of my commercial involvements. It was obvious what they were trying to get at here.

You just have to steel yourself to this kind of stuff: the appetite for culprit-chasing after any championship defeat. The truth was I'd been a Red Bull athlete for nine years at this stage, but it was the first time that that connection became the focus of media. Did it affect me in the build-up to that final or in the game itself? Categorically not!

Despite the loss to Limerick, 2018 would go down as one of my best years in a Galway jersey, bringing my fifth All-Star award. But history often gets written in subjective ways, and by now, I more than understood that. It might sound glib, but I always aspired to commercial partnerships that were long-term because I didn't like the thought of blithely jumping from one brand to another. My idea was that they would endure, that the connections would be real. And that was the case with brands like Bord Gáis Energy, Adidas, Opel, Red Bull and Audi. I will forever be grateful to all those brands for the support they gave me throughout my career because it always felt more to me than some kind of cold business alliance.

Most of those connections would have been set up through John Trainor of Onside. John hailed from Tuam and was someone I owed a great deal to across the years. I would describe him as a sponsorship genius. Apart from my brother Frank, there was simply nobody I trusted more in terms of making business decisions.

In fact, I'd say trust was the defining characteristic of his career, one in which Onside became a huge player in the world of marketing and sponsorship. On some level, I suspect that made him a unique figure in a world often dominated by brazen fronts and performative confidence.

When you think of the people you could absolutely trust 100

per cent in life, at best most of us have just a handful. There are your parents. Your wife or partner. After that? Maybe a couple of your closest friends. But you really are talking about a very small number of people. For me, John categorically existed in that group.

I still find it a little shocking that I'm now talking about John in the past tense, but he died in February 2024 from cancer. I knew he was struggling, having visited him a few weeks before he passed. He was confined to a wheelchair at the time, but his brain was still scalpel-sharp.

Maybe that's why it was such a shock to the system when I got a message from his wife, Eithne, that he had passed away. Even now, I still find it hard to believe. He had a say in so many big decisions I made in my life, even including the one to do this book. Yet he was so quiet and unassuming, wearing his success incredibly lightly all the time. We used call him a 'Tuam sham', and trust me, that was always a term of affection.

He had a different brain to most: a research brain. He always had his homework done. In that regard, he was a mentor to me in terms of me understanding brand awareness and the kind of questions that needed to be answered before committing to a commercial partnership. I always felt that John and I were singing off the same hymn sheet when it came to compatible sponsorship arrangements. He even had a role to play in me moving to Dublin to work with Liberty Insurance. I do think I had a big under-standing of brand awareness very early in life given how quickly I linked up with companies like Adidas and Bord Gáis Energy. But, for me, John was the ultimate sounding board. And one I miss terribly today.

Having the ear of someone of his calibre probably instilled a confidence in me within the realm of business. I have an involve-ment in four franchises of the Camile Thai restaurant chain today. I'm also involved in a pub in Athlone, named after my grandmother, Maisie.

Hurling gave me a lot of connections in life that have helped me evolve professionally. Hand on heart, I'd say I took up no more than 20 per cent of what was offered to me across the years. From the outside, it mightn't have looked that way. But I never wanted to be someone who just grabbed everything going.

I was once offered a five-figure sum to become an ambassador for one of the biggest supermarket chains in Ireland but turned it down. This would have been when I was just starting out as a senior inter-county hurler. It was a perfectly reputable company, but I just didn't feel that the fit was right at the time. A costly decision, but I went with my gut.

I was with Adidas from the age of seventeen and would remain with them for about five years until their GAA connections began to diminish. I got to meet Dan Carter when the All Blacks were in Dublin for a November international. I've a signed jersey from Richie McCaw.

I remember getting a truck-load of Adidas gear after winning an *Irish Examiner* Young Sports Star award in the same year as Rory McIlroy. I was in the Adidas 'stable' you see – same as some chap called David Beckham. Paul Moloney was 'Mr Adidas' at the time, and someone I found really decent to work with in terms of supplying anything I needed.

I knew this wasn't an environment too many other hurlers existed in, and in truth, my eyes were out on stalks half the time. There were maybe 13 or 14 hurlers and footballers in that 'stable'. Myself, Seán Óg, Ken McGrath, Tommy Walsh, Ben and Jerry O'Connor, Eoin Kelly and J.J. Delaney represented the hurling side.

For me, none of these felt like connections of short-term convenience. Even when Adidas drifted away from the GAA scene, I kept wearing their boots out of habit more than anything. Yes,

I got offers from other brands, but I turned them down on the simple basis that I didn't like their boots.

Then in 2017, I bought a pair of Nike boots online and they were the boots I wore as Galway, finally, got that monkey off our backs and won the All-Ireland. They're now in a glass case at home.

A random purchase that ended up carrying me to the mountaintop.

I never used an agent, though there were plenty of approaches over time from people offering 'help'. My brother, Frank, acquired the role without ever having any formal status in that regard. He was just someone I trusted implicitly; not simply in terms of the financial side of things but also in the matter of plain judgement. Frank was just very clued in to the concept of perception, and maybe more specifically, how things might look for Mam and Dad. Bottom line, he didn't want people bad-mouthing me.

If Frank thought something wasn't right for me, then it wasn't happening. His role in that side of my life was like a comfort blanket. He's 16 years older than me, and even in hurling terms, was always a voice of reason. Throughout my entire hurling career, his was the opinion I'd always seek out after a game, because he'd routinely challenge me and question my take on something.

The easiest thing when you acquire a certain degree of celebrity is to find yourself in an artificial bubble. In other words, surrounded by people who just want to humour you; say the things they think you want to hear.

Not quite sycophants, but something close, I suppose.

So I'd actively seek out Frank's opinion because I always knew it would carry a few sharp edges. I'd especially do so after a loss. Not because I enjoyed the process. I *categorically* didn't. And voices would be routinely raised as we'd go over and back about various incidents. More often than not, we'd agree to disagree.

I had more tough conversations with Frank across the years than with anybody else for the simple reason that I respected his view so much. He'd be one of the quieter, more understated members of the family. On the best of days, with him, it was never *you* did well; it was always more *ye* did well.

The danger with letting the wrong voices dominate your head is that you can always blame someone else for when things don't work out. It can always be somebody else's fault.

Even though I'd often end our conversations bulling, deep down I always knew Frank's voice was the one I needed to hear at key moments in my career. Sometimes, I'd hang up the phone thinking: *Don't know why I fucking bother!*

But I did know. I always knew. I wasn't stupid.

Funny, I had a small sponsorship for Marc Helmets that I chose to abort towards the end of 2014. It might sound a little OCD, but I felt I was chasing fractions at the time. Trying to make things better through a period in which my head sometimes felt like a jigsaw spilled on the floor.

It was just after we lost the delayed county final to Gort that I decided to change. I remember having an argument about it with Frank because he couldn't see the logic of forsaking that kind of sponsorship, however modest. After all, what difference could the brand of your helmet really make in a game? But I was always finicky about equipment. Before the sponsorship, I'd worn a red Cooper helmet and decided to change back now. And that's what I wore for the next couple of seasons until early 2017 when a part of it came away in my hand.

Then I noticed this white, old-style Cooper helmet sitting unclaimed in the house. I think Ollie had bought it at some stage and just never got around to wearing it. Anyway, that's the helmet I wore as Galway won the National League, and subsequently, the All-Ireland.

Just like the boots that finally got me over the line, the helmet was a random personal choice too.

And maybe there was a certain karma to it being one of Ollie's. After all, he wore my blue Mycro in the 1994 All-Ireland minor final and was still wearing it into the early 2000s. I vividly remember buying that helmet in Concannon's of Killimor and being very put out that he never gave it back.

Honestly, I always understood the status I was held in commercially, albeit it did strike me that people had a very inflated idea of what a top GAA player could make in sponsorships. The perception was actually a bit silly. I've heard it said, for example, that my deal with Red Bull was worth six figures. And I'm thinking: *if only* …

The truth was a million miles from that. In fact, I suspect people would be shocked to hear how modest the deals were. But truth and rumour always seemed hopelessly intertwined with these subjects.

There was this story that I myself only became privy to about two years after it was supposed to have happened. It ran that Cappataggle, James Skehill's club, had approached me to perform the official opening of their new pitch. Someone actually claimed at a club meeting that my reaction to the request was to ask for five grand. Now this conversation never took place. I was never approached by anybody to perform the opening, yet the story found enough traction in the end to be spoken of as gospel at a committee meeting in Cappataggle.

Just think about that.

'That bollix was looking for five grand …'

It was Frank who eventually heard about this from one of his own sons, but he decided not to tell me until years later, knowing I'd go absolutely ballistic. So the story around Cappataggle was that they got Brian Cody to do the job instead. In other words, the greatest manager in hurling history stepping in to do a job that Galway's own boy wonder couldn't be arsed doing.

It was complete bullshit, but then in a GAA life so many of the best stories are.

11.

A LONG WAY FROM CLARE TO HERE

When the circus comes to town, it's only natural to want a front-row seat, right?

That was how it felt for Galway hurling in September 2006 with confirmation of Ger Loughnane's return to the inter-county game after an absence of six years. You could sense a giddiness in our people, a belief that, finally, the county had access to some kind of evangelical presence for whom anything less than All-Ireland success would be tantamount to a personal slight. Loughnane as much as said so himself, making the bold declaration that he'd consider his tenure at the helm a failure if Galway were not in possession of the MacCarthy Cup within two years.

For many, this felt like our golden ticket. The man's optimism was irresistible. After an eternity in the wilderness, Clare had won the All-Irelands of 1995 and 1997, through what felt like sheer force of personality. Loughnane's personality. I was still just a child while that story was evolving, but there was no escaping the charisma of the man, the absolute conviction he carried with him into just about any environment.

Hurling might have changed in the decade since, but Ger remained one of the game's more compelling voices. He'd become a fixture in the TV studio as a pundit on *The Sunday Game* and was an often unapologetically withering newspaper column-ist with the *Irish Star*. In replacing Conor Hayes, he became Galway's first outside manager since Babs Keating in 1979. The appointment felt seismic.

I was neither deaf nor blind to any of that, given that Hayes had made tentative soundings about me joining the Galway seniors in 2006 (minors manager, Mattie Murphy, naturally batting away any enquiries about the availability of his captain). It was obvious that there'd be speculation around my intentions again now that the county had effectively gone to Broadway for their new man.

But my head was clear. I'd said as much the previous February at an AIB-sponsored event promoting the All-Ireland club semi-finals, myself, Ollie and Eugene McEntee pitching up to the Raheen Woods Hotel in Athenry as Portumna's representatives.

Heading into my third and final year with Galway minors, I was asked if it would be my intention to make myself available for the seniors in 2007. I pretty much said then that it wouldn't be, that there was still plenty I wanted to do outside of hurling, and that, in my opinion, life as a senior inter-county player could wait.

What people maybe didn't realise was that I missed out on playing minor again in 2007 by just two months. I was still, essentially, a kid. As I kept saying at the time, I wanted to live a teenager's life.

Maybe people assumed that Loughnane's appointment seven months later would flip that idea on its head, but if so, they didn't know me. I have always had an obstinacy that only deepens the moment I sense people making assumptions about me. Hand on heart, it never entered my head that I'd be missing out on some-thing monumental by not submitting instantly to the new regime.

Once I'd said something, I'd very seldom go back on it. But would I have been so stubborn had I genuinely believed they could win the All-Ireland in 2007? It's hard to see it. I mean, I wouldn't want to miss out on that, would I?

There were representations made, admittedly. Brendan Lynskey, one of Loughnane's selectors, met me one day at Kilmeen Cross near Loughrea. What do I remember of the meeting? Little beyond the fact that he drove a really big, eye-catching car and had the complexion of a man just back from a sunshine holiday.

Being honest, Brendan was trying to push open a firmly bolted door.

Louis Mulqueen, another selector, then met me in Limerick in early 2007 and bought me a pizza in Milano's. He even got me to agree to go to a team meeting in Athenry, and for the life of me, I still have no real idea why I did that. Probably just some kind of diplomatic reflex.

Louis's idea was that I might just 'get a feel' of what they were doing, but I knew I really had no place in that group.

I didn't go back.

There was no direct sales pitch from Loughnane himself, who I suspect might have been vaguely offended that I wasn't absolutely desperate to be a part of this new Galway story. My sense of it is that his ego could have been bruised.

In fact, when I won the Fitzgibbon as a first year in LIT just weeks into 2007, he delivered a fairly scathing verdict to the *Star* on where I might stand as a potential senior inter-county hurler. I didn't actually see the piece myself at the time, but my family did. They kept the cutting.

In it, Ger described the Fitzgibbon as 'a Mickey Mouse competition', suggesting that I'd be very foolish if I let the achievement of winning one go to my head. He warned that I was in real danger of never fulfilling my potential, arguing that I was being 'pumped up by people despite scoring very little from play'.

Loughnane's view was that I was 'way off the pace' of senior inter-county and that 'listening to ill-deserved praise is going to do him more harm than good'. His conclusion: 'I'd be very doubtful at this stage if he has what it takes to cut it as an inter-county hurler.'

It's kind of strange reading those words given that he'd already sent two of his selectors to try and get me to go in, but in hindsight, maybe he was having as much of a dig at Davy Fitzgerald in that interview as he was at me.

It was Fitzy's second Fitzgibbon win with a college that had never won previously, and he was clearly establishing a coaching and management reputation that, to this day, has kept him at the cutting edge of the game. I'm not entirely sure Ger ever warmed to the idea of his old goalkeeper making fresh history of his own.

To be fair, that thread of extremism in Loughnane's personality is almost certainly what got Clare to the mountaintop in the mid-'90s. Bearing in mind that their Munster title win in 1995 was the county's first since 1932, I imagine it would be hard to overstate the importance of a genuine revolutionary's voice in that dressing room.

But in Galway, that voice just never quite resonated with the same credibility.

In two championships, the county's only victories under Loughnane would be against Laois and Antrim (both twice). I always sensed in subsequent years that he never quite forgave the Galway players for this, specifically for not buying more unequivocally into the starkness of his gospel. To him, we just proved ourselves a soft bunch, and he was never subsequently slow to communicate that belief.

The day Galway went out of the 2007 championship with a

10 points All-Ireland quarter-final loss to Kilkenny, I watched the game from a pub in Brussels. It was a stag weekend for a first cousin of mine, Shane McClearn, and it's fair to say I was feeling absolutely no pain.

Ollie, now temporarily retired, was beside me, and apart from a few predictable comments along the lines of 'Fuck's sake! Ye boys should be in Croke Park,' I honestly don't think there was a genuine shred of longing from either of us to be in maroon that day.

No question the fall-out to our county final defeat by Loughrea the previous year still stung us both, but I was about to win an All-Ireland under-21 title with Galway in the coming months and had every intention of making myself available to the seniors once I felt the time was right.

And, hand on heart, I had absolutely no issue with the Portumna lads who did make themselves available to Galway seniors in 2007. Everyone had their own decisions to make, and I just wanted to move on now. I genuinely held no grudge against Loughrea players either.

At some point I suspect I mentioned in an interview that a lot of my friends were going on J1s around the world at the time, and that I didn't want to feel I had lost out in that regard. This was a comment Loughnane would subsequently revisit a little witheringly, saying something along the lines that I wanted to travel the world 'but only got as far as Limerick'.

He was right to a point.

The third-level life was proving everything I had hoped it would be – primarily an escape from Galway and the sense of always living in some kind of goldfish bowl.

My housemates, Gavin O'Mahony, Bernard Gaffney and James Skehill were all kindred spirits too – at least until James submitted himself to life as a Galway senior hurler under the incoming regime. From then on, we proved pretty pitiless, as our lifestyles began to diverge down profoundly different tracks.

Put it this way, if we had Apache Pizza and the local Chinese on speed dial, Skehill would arrive in from Galway training armed with barely the strength to eat a Jaffa Cake. Inevitably, we'd be mad for stories from the front, but James routinely seemed almost too drained to speak. He'd seldom last more than a few minutes before retiring to his room, the weight visibly falling off him from one night to the next.

Among their training venues, Galway were using the sand track in Tubber, a place notorious for burning off anyone remotely equivocal in commitment.

It was all, I don't doubt, a mental challenge that Loughnane was setting Galway's players now. A way of saying, 'Everybody says ye're soft, go prove them wrong!' You could recognise the logic to it too.

He introduced a baseball machine that spat out sliotars at lightning speed, the idea being to quicken up reaction times. Again, here, you could see what he was getting at. The most fundamental change to Clare's hurling in his time – fitness apart – was the sheer speed of their hurling. He'd transformed them in that regard.

But there had to be more to training than just hardship too.

Every night I'd see the ghost-like figure of Skehill coming in the drive, the only thought in my head would be: *Thank fuck I'm not in there!* The training sounded largely old school, little more than running lads into the ground to see who could survive the pain.

As poor James would arrive home, we'd barely lift our heads from *Pro Evolution* on the PlayStation. If I'm honest, there was an almost passive cruelty to how we'd greet him. 'Ah, James, ya poor cratur. Sit down here ...'

It would be March of 2008 before I was finally ready to experience the torture chamber for myself, specifically the week after Portumna's All-Ireland club final defeat of Birr.

We'd basically been on the beer since St Patrick's Day, when six or seven of us were called down to Athenry for a session. As the hurling field was flooded, we ended up doing a circuit of weights instead in the makeshift gym they'd made in the underground car park of Raheen Woods Hotel. It was a gym that never really made sense to me, the ceiling little more than six feet above your head, everything a little sooty and dusty, so much so that some of us found it nearly a struggle just to breathe.

The session proved little more scientific than challenging lads to bench-press the heaviest weights they could. After that, into our cars and out to what can only be described as a real cabbage-patch field with a tiny shed where we were sent off to run laps.

For the Portumna contingent, our guts still full of beer, this was pure hell on earth.

It was originally supposed to be just a ball-work session in Kenny Park, easing us back into it that evening. But that waterlogged pitch put paid to the idea, and we found ourselves instead doing the polar opposite of what had been flagged.

I'll always remember Andy Smith – categorically the toughest of our crew – hopping a wall at one point to get sick on the other side. Soon enough, he just abandoned. Actually, my most enduring memory of that night is of lads vomiting pretty much everywhere.

As a mental challenge, it failed abysmally for those of us still in celebration mode. Some of us even had a pint in the hotel before hitting the road home that evening where our drinking would continue. Not something to be proud of in hindsight, I agree. But after a marathon club season, we just weren't ready to bounce straight into that kind of back-breaking hardship, no matter the identity of the person cracking the whip. Barking and shouting alone was never going to win us over, but I suspect Loughnane had long concluded that that could be the very thing – maybe the only thing – that might put some much-needed steel into our hurling.

His first championship as Galway manager had left people generally unimpressed, specifically an Ennis All-Ireland qualifier loss to his native Clare now managed by his old sidekick, Tony Considine. In what struck the players as some act of kid-psychology, Loughnane had delayed naming his team for that game until just before throw-in. Galway's subsequent performance was predictably hesitant and disjointed en route to a two points loss that I suspect went a long way towards dissolving any sense among the players of having a managerial Messiah in their midst.

I've often thought it must have been much stranger for Ollie than for me, standing in that Brussels bar, pints of cider in our hands, watching the team then lose to Kilkenny for the limpest of championship evictions. Ollie, after all, had been a virtual fixture for Galway's seniors since 1996, winning three All-Stars up to that point (with a fourth to come in 2009, after his decision to step out of retirement in 2008). Loughnane would actually appoint him Galway captain for the 2008 campaign, triggering an outbreak of the most risible nonsense in some media quarters implying that Ollie had agreed to return only on certain conditions, which included demanding the removal of specific players from the Galway squad.

One newspaper in particular perpetuated this rubbish, something that was not merely ridiculous but also deeply offensive to Ollie, not to mention (I presume) to Loughnane himself, someone who I'd very much doubt was ever dictated to by a player in his dressing room.

As you will gather, it took time for us Portumna lads to adjust to Ger's revolutionary ways, specifically to the off-the-wall intensity of training.

Things that worked for him in 1995 seemed hopelessly out-dated now. One of the drills he had us doing was two lads standing maybe 10 yards in from either sideline driving the ball out over one another's heads, the idea being that you had to turn back, rise the ball and clear it away over your shoulder as far as you could. Striking it blindly, in other words. Ger reckoned we needed to be better at this.

When match day came, there were no identifiable tactics either; though, being honest, hurling at the time wasn't especially tactical anyway beyond Cork's short stick-passing and Kilkenny's withdrawal of their half-forwards to congest the middle third.

As might be expected, Loughnane's team talks generally compensated. He'd make the hair stand on the back of your neck with words full of fire and brimstone and rippling with questions targeting the very core of your being.

We trained a fair bit down in Daingean at the time, and my memory of it is of submitting myself to the equivalent of a torture camp. Weekends away were almost studiously unpretentious. I remember one during which we stayed at the Ardilaun Hotel where our night-time entertainment was this virtual racing game with one of the county board lads operating as bookie.

Broadly speaking, it being my first year in, I just kept my head down.

People might imagine that Ger would have been in my ear a lot, identifying the specifics of what he expected from me now. But he didn't say a whole pile to me – ever. In fact, I can't honestly remember us having a single one-to-one that year. He had his favourites in the group, a few lads that we came to call his 'lieutenants'.

They were the ones he spoke to, and I definitely never qualified.

To some degree, he might even have drawn some negative conclusion about me given my lack of interest in being a part of his first year. I don't honestly know.

Anyway, I made my debut in a National League semi-final against Cork, a game we just about won, having built up a wind-assisted 14 points lead in the first half. I did fine, scoring 0–4 and generally drawing positive reaction in the media, especially for a line cut I put over from about 50 yards.

Throughout my career, I loved playing Cork because it was always pure hurling against them, whatever the level. They were never overly physical. In fact, our subsequent All-Ireland qualifier loss to them would prove my only championship loss to Cork at any grade from childhood to retirement.

Ger was full of praise for me after that League semi-final, lauding my 'unselfishness' as a trait that people were inclined to underestimate.

But a Liam Sheedy-managed Tipperary was too strong for us then in the League final, where I was met with much steelier terms of engagement in the shape of my marker, Éamonn Buckley. I did score what some papers described as a 'wonder goal' when we were already seven points down, collecting a ball maybe 60 yards from goal and just racing the whole way in. It was a run I wouldn't have dreamed of attempting 10 years later, but in this instance, everything just opened up for me.

Given I had three years of senior club and two years of Fitzgibbon under my belt, it's fair to say I already felt comfortable in this environment and was hurling without any real physical fear.

But that defeat to Tipp meant that we went into the 2008 championship with few enough certainties around the Galway team-sheet.

That said, we still knew we were part of something profoundly different now.

It was decided we should fly to Belfast for our championship opener against Antrim in Casement Park, and on arrival back in Galway, some of us went in to town on an evening that gave root to what became known as the story of 'the Dew Drop 15'.

The Dew Drop Inn is a well-known city pub, and that evening we sat outside in glorious sunshine, never imagining for a second that there was anything to worry about, even though our next game – against Laois – was just a week away.

We'd beaten Antrim by 26 points after all, and would then have 20 to spare the following weekend in Pearse Stadium. My respective scoring tallies of 2–6 and 0–9 (1–4 and 0–5 from play) suggested that I was settling reasonably comfortably now into life as a senior inter-county hurler.

But that night in the Dew Drop turned a little sour when one of the lads in our company (not a Galway player) decided to save money by drinking cans he'd bought from the Spar across the road. Not unreasonably, this was something the bar owner took exception to. Word of the resulting argument got back to Loughnane, who decided to take us to task at the next training session.

We were just pucking around in Salthill when the word came out: 'Ger wants everybody back inside!'

He was demanding names.

'Who was drinking in Galway the other night?' he roared. To be honest, he needed to be more specific here because those of us in the Dew Drop hadn't been the only ones out that night for a few pints. Anyway, nobody put their hand up. Nobody was ratting anybody out here.

This infuriated Ger and his selectors, with Louis Mulqueen berating us for showing the management no respect. He talked of all the hours they were putting into us, so much so that his own kids barely recognised him anymore.

'Meanwhile, ye're out drinking!' he snapped.

Given the silence from the floor, they duly sent us out for our punishment. Wire-to-wire shuttle runs, one sideline to the other. Completely illogical in a week book-ended by two championship games, but that was always the tenor of it. The drinking shouldn't have happened, albeit that was pretty much how things worked at the time, but to then run the crap out of us afterwards was madness.

We'll show ye how it's done! We'll toughen ye!

Unfortunately, the runs then took their toll, Damien Joyce – a man who, incidentally, never touched a drink during championship – pulling a hamstring that would rule him out of the Laois game. Damien, probably the fittest hurler in Galway, thus became an unintended victim of our punishment.

That Laois game was played on a Saturday, and management had us in for an eight-kilometre run around Pearse Stadium the following morning. Rumour had it that one of the management team had been in conversation with Davy Fitzgerald that evening (Fitzy having taken over the Waterford team mid-championship after a player revolt against Justin McCarthy), and he'd indicated that they'd be running on Tramore strand that same morning, having hammered Antrim the day before.

Essentially, this would be a means of ensuring that the players didn't go drinking that Saturday night.

So that's what we did less than 24 hours after beating Laois. An eight-kilometre run around the stadium in Salthill, the vibe from management being: 'If Waterford's players are willing to absorb this hardship, it's high time Galway did something similar!'

Except, of course, Waterford never did have that run in

Tramore. I remember asking Fitzy when I got back to LIT. 'We did like fuck!' he replied, laughing.

As you will gather, intensity had become God in our world.

The week before we played Cork, we had a 15-on-15 game in Thurles during which Alan Kerins was momentarily knocked out cold in a heavy collision with Andy Keary. When Alan came around, he hadn't a clue where he was and would actually spend the evening under observation in Nenagh Hospital.

But the game just thundered on, Loughnane seemingly oblivious to what had just happened until he spotted Kerins sitting down on the sideline.

'What are you doing, Kerins?' he roared. 'Sunning yourself, is it?' I can still hear the disdain in his Clare voice, the tone of dismissal. We were soft boys in his eyes. He was right too, just maybe not in this instance.

Not realising that Kerins had been knocked out and might have had a concussion, Ger just talked up Andy as a warrior. 'Keary, the way you're motoring, you'd mark Ring if you had to!'

And Andy beaming: 'I would! I would!'

Both Kerins and John Lee subsequently had to do fitness tests before the game, but Ger clearly felt the only tests that truly mattered now were psychological. Anyway, Lee was a doctor, Kerins a physio. They knew their bodies.

So he sat them both down and told a story of how he'd once fallen off a trailer the evening before a big Munster championship game for Clare in the '70s, yet still played the following day. His message: 'Ye'll be fine too if ye want to be!'

There was a slapstick element to much of what he did.

The night he told us the team to play Cork was a case in point. We were all gathered in one of these huge Pearse Stadium dressing rooms, and he had his back to us, writing down the team on a flipboard. As he was filling in the names and numbers, he kept turning around, as if he'd forgotten his choice for a couple of positions. It was clear he didn't quite have his team off by heart.

Two of the positions were eventually left blank.

Anyway, Chunky Hayes would be wearing number 11, but lining out at full forward. Given I'd be starting in the corner, Chunky's instructions were unambiguous. 'You're in there to mind Joe!' he was told. I'll always remember Chunky's smile at the instruction. He was well used to minding me in Portumna colours at that stage, but he could play a bit himself too. And that smile said as much. 'Jaysus, Ger, there's a bit more to me now than just minding Joe!'

It's all too well documented what followed that day in Thurles, and I've said many times that scoring 2–12 of Galway's 2–15 total in what would prove Loughnane's last game as Galway boss didn't exactly do me any long-term favours.

On a rotten day for the team, that tally pretty much secured me a first All-Star, as well as the Young Hurler of the Year award. It also bred the wildest of expectations for my future. I'd been the youngest player on the field that day, and despite Cork winning, mine was the name in every headline.

Galway already trailed 0–6 to 0–0 when I scored a goal in the twentieth minute. In many ways, it was a goal that encapsulated our game plan. There were no identifiable tactics. Just a hit-and-hope ball launched in.

The fact that I caught it over the head of Diarmuid 'The Rock' O'Sullivan – one of the game's most fearsome competitors – shrugging him aside before finishing one-handed past Dónal Óg Cusack – came to put a specific, wildly unfair slant on the day.

The number of times I've heard it described as 'the day you took The Rock to the cleaners' almost beggars belief, given that Diarmuid was marking me for no more than five minutes of that entire game. It actually jars with me massively to this day that that's how people remember it.

Like, I got far more off John Gardiner and Seán Óg Ó hAilpín that day. They were my markers in the second half; Shane O'Neill in the first. That goal apart, The Rock had little or nothing to do with me. Yet it seems to have been written into history that that was the day he got destroyed by a kid.

I've no memory of anything said in the dressing room after-wards by either Galway management or players. But then I stayed out on the pitch, signing autographs for a good 45 minutes, some-thing that I subsequently sensed didn't sit well with everyone.

So speeches may have been made that I wasn't privy to. To this day, I've no idea.

The media certainly didn't spare Galway's inability to exploit an extra man after Cork lost their goalkeeper, Cusack, to a straight red on the stroke of half-time. If anything, our opponents seemed to thrive tactically from that moment on, reverting to the possession game that had won them All-Irelands in 2004 and 2005, a game almost perfected at the time by men like Ben and Jerry O'Connor and Joe Deane.

It was a shocking Galway defeat, no two ways about it. I, of course, was spared the vitriol, given I'd scored so much of the team's entire total, and in fact, the *Connacht Tribune* would even name me their Sports Star of the Week.

A perverse little consolation in the strangest week.

The morning after the game, Portumna had a League game to play in Liam Mellows, with a camera crew for company. They'd been following us for the year as defending All-Ireland club champions, offering a kind of fly-on-the-wall insight into the bonds that made a once-struggling club so special.

Pride of the Parish would accompany us all the way to Croke Park on St Patrick's Day of 2009, the day we retained that

All-Ireland with a final defeat of Waterford champions, De La Salle.

So it had footage of Ollie and me, both bleary-eyed and a little worse for wear after a very late night (maybe 5 a.m.?), pitching up with the rest of the Portumna contingent that Sunday morning for a low-watt League fixture.

We were all there: Hayesy, Chunky, Andy – everyone. Because it was never even up for debate that we might sidestep the game. I was dying, if I'm honest; absolutely hanging.

And my scoring tally against Liam Mellows less than 24 hours after shooting 2–12 against Cork? A single point and lucky to get it.

Loughnane had condemned Galway's defeat as 'a complete and utter collapse', describing the performance as 'inexplicable'. Reminded of that bold declaration on his appointment that he'd consider it failure if Galway hadn't won the All-Ireland within two years, he didn't shy away from the evidence now before him.

'We got nowhere in two years!' he declared bluntly.

Initial indications were that he wanted to continue, that he had no intention of walking away from a team that never came close to his expectations for us. I'd say, at best, the feelings in the dressing room were mixed about that. But if we were honest with ourselves, he'd been proved fundamentally right about a softness in our core too. A weakness in the white heat of championship, the same heat that invariably brought the best out of his Clare teams of the '90s.

Some of their Munster championship games with Tipperary especially had an almost feral quality: wild events, games played almost on the edge of reason. Games, in other words, that suited his conviction about how great hurling contests needed to be approached.

Loughnane judged that very mental and physical steel to be missing in Galway, and frankly, it was a view endorsed by subsequent Galway managers, John McIntyre, and especially, Anthony Cunningham. But they understood too that hurling was changing, and that that change maybe demanded better, more skill-specific coaching.

It would be October before the Hurling Board, under pressure from the clubs, decided that Galway's grand adventure with Ger Loughnane was over. Lorrha man McIntyre, the former Tipperary centre back, was eventually appointed his successor.

A long-time Galway resident and sports editor with the *Connacht Tribune*, he just seemed a safer pair of hands now. And Ger? He went down swinging!

Speaking in December of 2008, he lambasted the board as being responsible for a period of neglect in Galway hurling that meant we were now miles adrift of counties like Kilkenny and Tipperary. Wishing McIntyre well in the position, Ger even suggested that his successor would now find himself on safer ground 'because he knows where the bodies are buried!'

His colour, if not his coaching, would be missed.

12.
'FLAKY' TRIBE

Y ou'd probably need to live in our shoes to understand the scepticism Portumna minds might entertain for a Lorrha voice arriving into their hurling lives.

There would certainly have been very mixed feelings in the Canning household with John McIntyre's confirmation as the new Galway senior manager. The older lads especially would have been stung by some of his past newspaper articles, specifically any implying that Portumna had become the perennial *nearly men* of Galway hurling.

We'd accumulated so many heartbreaking quarter-final and semi-final county championship defeats prior to winning our first senior in 2003, I suppose it wasn't unreasonable to suggest that Portumna had built up a habit of never quite fulfilling our promise.

But border energies can take a perverse hold on people.

Because John was a Tipperary man, yet a next-door neighbour, I suspect we were always more sensitive to what he might say about us than was probably the case for any other club in Galway. Lorrha, after all, was just nine kilometres out the road. For most of Portumna's hurling story, the feeling would have been that they looked down their noses at us.

Put it this way: through the '80s and '90s, Portumna would have been laughed at had they sought a challenge game against Lorrha. They were just a higher caste. Maybe it was a Tipp thing.

Anyway, the *Tribune* was always read at home, and maybe there was a sense across some of those Portumna defeats that John mightn't have been slow to lower the blade a bit when addressing another tale of his neighbours' sorrow. I had little sense of this myself, but you are a product of your environment. So I wasn't exactly celebrating his appointment; not that I was overly judgemental either.

What I will say is that his arrival, along with a backroom team of 1980 captain Joe Connolly, John Hardiman and John Moylan, brought an immediate sense of everything stepping up significantly in the Galway camp. Feargal O'Callaghan, now Head of Sport in NUIG, was in charge of strength and conditioning (S&C). All in all, you got a feeling that no stone would be left unturned after the failed promise of the Loughnane years.

McIntyre had gone for the job twice before, losing out to Jarlath Cloonan in 1992 and Mattie Murphy two years later. By now, he'd been living in Galway for almost three decades, and through his journalism, was clearly well versed on our club championship. That said, there was an element of surprise in November 2008 when news came through from a board meeting in the Raheen Woods Hotel that he had beaten the likes of Noel Lane and Michael Bond to the job. It almost felt like a left-field decision.

Looking back, I don't think anyone could deny that McIntyre would prove an unlucky Galway manager over the three seasons that followed.

We exited the 2009 championship with a single point All-Ireland quarter-final defeat to Waterford in Thurles, and after winning the National League in 2010, we then lost another All-Ireland quarter-final by a single point, this time to eventual champions, Tipperary.

That Tipp defeat was especially galling from my point of view, Ollie having to go off late in the game after taking a bad bang on the knee from Eoin Kelly. Lar Corbett duly got the winning point from the corner Ollie had vacated.

In McIntyre's third and final year, we went down by a single point to Waterford in Walsh Park in our final League group game, when victory would have put us into another final. Tiny margins seemed to be killing this team.

By then, though, hindsight suggests that those margins were beginning to speak of a bigger problem. There had been a very negative reaction to a heavy defeat to Tipp in Salthill before that Waterford game in which corner forward Shane Bourke would help himself to 3–4 of the visitors' 4–23 total.

McIntyre presented himself to the media afterwards with a quip: 'I hope this isn't a lynch mob', before making the not unreasonable point: 'If they [the players] themselves don't realise and appreciate that what happened out there isn't acceptable, then Galway hurling is not in the place we want it to be.'

I had minimal enough involvement in that League, but did play in that final group game in Walsh Park.

And my abiding memory of John's time in charge is one of endless meetings. Every training session seemed to be followed by one speech after another, meaning we could regularly be anything up to 90 minutes in the dressing room before getting down to the Ardilaun (if in Pearse Stadium) or Raheen Woods (if in Athenry) for food. This, as any dietician would tell you, made zero sense. It meant that we were simply eating too late, and accordingly, far too long after emptying ourselves in training.

Management's eventual solution was a bizarre one – Papa John's pizzas delivered to the dressing room so that the speeches wouldn't have to be curtailed. Needless to say, this went down like a lead balloon with some of the more clean-eating players, pizza boxes now piled high around them. Some just chose simply not to eat at all.

It seemed everybody had to have their say in the week of a game. Like John Moylan's territory on a Friday night was to fill us in on what to expect from the referee: things he might be fussy about or the kind of stuff he had a name for letting go.

In fairness to McIntyre, he was clearly just trying to cover all the bases. But for me, this was leading to an information overload. We were simply hearing too many voices, and worse, hearing them far too often.

I felt that subsequent Galway managers understood this. If five or six people are always talking within a group, it just becomes noise. And I suppose that's how it came to feel after three years with John at the helm – that we ended up listening to noise.

That said, I have little doubt that his heart was in the right place. Actually, if John McIntyre had one overriding weakness as Galway manager, it was almost certainly that he tried too hard. I sensed he ended up overthinking things.

He's an innately confident type of figure, and it always seemed important to him that he was seen to communicate that confidence. So, in summer especially, he'd be a regular sight, togged out and running laps of the field while pucking a ball as we'd arrive for training. I don't doubt that this was John's way of telling us that he, too, was a decent player in his time, and that he wasn't asking us now to do anything he wouldn't have been willing to do himself.

He also had this habit of referring to himself in the third person, as in: 'John McIntyre will get a break one of these days, lads.' He clearly believed that in a previous spell as Offaly manager that break had been denied him.

To be fair, he was well liked by the players. He could take a joke, even if he himself was occasionally the butt of it. On his watch, there was a real sense of trying to engender a greater sense of place within the group, of understanding the culture of where we came from, the uniqueness of our county. To that end, Joe Connolly especially worked overtime.

I remember having a conversation with him once in which he was looking for my opinion on getting everyone in the Galway squad to wear maroon helmets. Joe thought this might communicate a sign of unity. Cork had already done this with everyone wearing red, but I remember thinking: *How in the name of God is the colour of our helmets going to help us win a hurling game?*

So I wasn't enthusiastic and told him so. But I could appreciate that management were constantly trying to think outside the box. Looking for any edge they could find.

Anyone who has ever heard Joe Connolly talk will know of his passion and eloquence, epitomised by that remarkable speech from the steps of the Hogan Stand in 1980 after Galway's first All-Ireland senior hurling win since 1923.

He particularly pushed the traditions of the West of the county, the Gaeltacht areas and all out around the Aran Islands.

We went out to Inis Mór once to accentuate that sense of identity. This would have been June 2011 before our Leinster Championship game against the recently crowned League champions, Dublin, and they brought us out to see Dún Aonghasa, a famous prehistoric stone fort perched on a cliff almost a hundred metres above the Atlantic.

The fort is said to be over 3,000 years old, and I'll always remember Joe leaning intently into the group as we were there and roaring, 'Where's Ryan O'Dwyer's Dún Aonghasa, lads?'

That was the mantra. A reminder that in our part of the world, we celebrated a culture that ran deeper than elsewhere. It was beautiful in many ways, genuinely moving. I'd say most of us didn't even know the place existed before we visited, and Joe's gift with words really gave us a sense of its emotional power.

We did a bit of training while on the island too and stayed overnight, the trip finishing up with an evening céilí at which everyone just let their hair down. At some point in the evening, a few lads thought it would be funny to dump the mattress off James Skehill's bed out an upstairs window, his hurleys tossed out with it. Naturally, this went down like a lead balloon with the hotel management, and soon, the local garda was up making a few enquiries. To him, hurleys stamped with 'J. Skehill' on the side offered compelling evidence.

We were called together, the garda demanding to know: 'Who is this J. Skehill?'

'That's me,' said James.

'You're coming with me so.'

'Why?'

'You threw that stuff out the window.'

'Yeah, that makes a lot of sense, all right, me throwing out my own hurleys!'

James's tone was a little sarcastic, I suppose, but his argument pretty reasonable. He clearly had been the victim here.

Anyway, the guard apparently insisted that James attend local Mass (as Gaeilge) the following morning, Joe Connolly by his side. He then escorted him down to the pier where we were catching the ferry, telling Skehill firmly, 'Don't ever set foot on this island again.'

Another time we had a training camp in Westport, after which there was an option to climb Croagh Patrick. Some of us took up that option; others stayed down on the beer. A priest said Mass at the top before we all went out that evening in Westport. The fun was terrific, albeit a few of us had League games with our clubs to play the following day. For Portumna, that meant a trip to Killimor to play Mullagh.

We had a job and a half trying to get Chunky Hayes out of

bed and onto the bus that morning, and eventually, McIntyre himself got on the phone. Chunky wasn't entertaining much of a conversation, presuming that it was one of us ringing the room again. 'Will you tell that fucker I'll be down in a minute!' he roared, not realising he was talking to the Galway manager.

This was where McIntyre was really good. He'd never get too uptight about stuff like that. He'd have a good laugh at it. And he was excellent at building up people's confidence, largely because I suppose he seemed to have so much of it himself.

It will go down in history that Galway never got beyond the All-Ireland quarter-finals in any of his three years, and I'd imagine that's a sore point given the tightness of those margins against Waterford in 2009 and Tipp in 2010. But there had probably been warning signs in that summer of 2010 when we really struggled to overcome Offaly in the Leinster Championship, beating them by a single point in a replay.

We followed that up then by being really flat in the provincial final against Kilkenny.

You might think we'd have been flying after winning the League, but it never really felt that way. Yes, on some level, you'd be telling yourself that Kilkenny often built All-Ireland runs on the back of League wins, so why not us? But I find it interesting that I've no vivid memory from that time of sensing that we were genuinely on to something big.

Much was made of us entering the Leinster Championship for the first time in 2009, and I've little doubt that over the years our presence elevated that championship to another level. Kilkenny had simply put too much distance between themselves and the likes of Wexford, Dublin and Offaly. They beat us by four points in what was broadly lauded afterwards as a terrific 2009 semi-final in Tullamore, Brian Cody among those now declaring Galway a 'serious' team. That game set in place a rivalry with

Kilkenny that would have a kind of defining presence in my life as a senior inter-county hurler. Even though we lost more than we won, I loved those battles – if only for the fact they were decent barometers of where you stood in the game.

And Leinster needed us, Kilkenny's 2009 final defeat of Dublin bringing them a tenth provincial crown in eleven years. Trouble was, we were a team inclined to take one step forward and two steps back. The consensus out there – and we all knew it – was that Galway teams were fundamentally soft; that if you got a run on us, we were pretty likely to fold.

Needless to say, we deeply resented that view. But our track record didn't exactly offer much of a contradiction.

The day in 2011 that we played Dublin in Tullamore – after our Inis Mór trip – a really withering piece on this very subject appeared in the *Irish Independent* in which three members of the 1987 and 1988 All-Ireland-winning team delivered a damningly unanimous verdict on where we stood in that regard. Conor Hayes, Noel Lane and Brendan Lynskey could see little in the way of character in the modern Galway. Given that Hayes and Lane had previously managed the county team, their voices carried a weight that was always going to hold traction.

But Lynskey's was the most strident view. He branded us 'a little cowardly', suggesting that too many fellas in Galway were afraid to put their hand up to catch a dropping ball.

You'd imagine that the article might have stirred something resentful within us and that Dublin would have paid the price. But after a bright start, we duly folded, scoring just nine times (2–7) over more than 70 minutes. In other words, everything the three lads had said proved utterly vindicated. When it came to type, it seemed that Galway just never let people down.

It was easy to feel sorry for McIntyre now as everything began to unravel. We may have offered the illusion of locating a pulse with easy qualifier victories over poor Clare and Cork teams before being drawn against Waterford in the All-Ireland quarter-finals. A Waterford team supposedly in crisis after the concession of seven goals during a cruel Munster final drilling from Tipperary. And what happened? Caricature kicked in again in the form of a 10-points capitulation, McIntyre offering a public apology, before, later, announcing that he was stepping down.

He'd been another victim of what was broadly termed a 'flakiness' in Galway hurling, the rap sheet against those of us wearing maroon proving more damning with every lost summer.

The new man in would have to tackle an old question.

13.

IN SEARCH OF STEEL

From the moment he stepped into our lives, Anthony Cunningham was on a war footing against the weak-minded. He didn't communicate it so much in what he said as what he did. There was an immediate cull of some senior figures in the Galway dressing room that echoed loudly with an old accusation. We were seen as the game's 'soft touches', men who could be relied upon to fold under pressure.

The charge sheet against us was, by now, too long for any of us to convincingly argue. Anthony had just won an All-Ireland under-21 crown and decided that that group, even those who couldn't get close to a starting place, now had more to offer Galway hurling than some of the county's most experienced men.

Think about it. When you're bringing even your under-21 subs into a senior inter-county environment, you're delivering a pretty withering assessment of those they are replacing.

And that assessment was brutally simple. Nobody had an entitlement to the jersey here, and anyone who thought they had wouldn't be slow in getting the door.

The sense of everyone having to earn their right to be there completely changed the dressing-room vibe; everything instantly ratcheted to another level.

There's a kind of scaffold humour that kicks in with players when a previously settled environment becomes edgy. In this case, the new intensity to training had us all planning imaginary escapes.

Through the winter months, those of us based in Limerick (myself, Paul Killeen and Johnny Glynn) trained under Tom Helebert's watch on the University of Limerick campus. After a few early sessions under Anthony in Galway, Iarla Tannian decided that maybe things might be gentler in our company. So Tan started driving to Limerick from Ardrahan for training, only to discover that this revolution offered no loopholes.

There's a graduated hill around the periphery of the rugby pitch in UL, this slow incline wrapping itself in an arc to the far corner. Tom would stand at the highest point and blow his whistle for the torture to begin.

From the bottom of that hill, the burning in your legs deepened with every stride.

We'd do that twice a week, or sometimes run laps of the hurling pitch in LIT, everything dialled to a new intensity. There were three separate training pods to begin with: ours in Limerick, Anthony's in Galway and a third under Mattie Kenny maybe somewhere in the east of the county.

The training was brutal, yet always referenced with input from nutritionists and S&C coaches.

I would have known Mattie from my time in with Galway under-21s and remembered him as someone with an edge who took no bullshit. But he was also a brilliant hurling coach, and in this, Cunningham now seemed to have struck a perfect balance.

While he himself was cracking the whip and setting new dressing-room standards, there was a sense of the hardship now being married to good, intelligent hurling practices. And Helebert, the third member of the triumvirate, was the facilitator. The 'good cop' you could go to whenever you had a problem.

Everything felt a little more scientific, but with some key, old-school principles.

Kevin Craddock was the S&C man, but it was Anthony

driving everything. On the nights we all trained together in Daingean, he'd have us doing 'suicides' where you basically ran out and back to every line on the field from one goal line to the other.

It was cruel, but it suited me because I finally sensed myself reaching a level of fitness that had felt impossible through 2010 and 2011 because of persistently niggling injuries.

Two issues especially dogged me. The first was plantar fasciitis in the right heel. The second, sciatica down my right leg. For the latter, cortisone was the solution. And intensive physio.

I got plasma injections for the plantar where a patient's own platelets can be injected into the heel to promote the body's natural healing process. I also got special insoles for my shoes, costing €500 each.

Nothing worked.

Eventually, an equine chiropractor in Cork was recommended by Mick Mangan, a family friend. We were at a training camp in Johnstown Castle, and Mick had been speaking to John Moylan, one of John McIntyre's selectors. It was decided that I had nothing to lose, having tried just about everything else. So I left the training camp, drove to Carrigaline and experienced probably the weirdest, yet one of the most beneficial weeks of my life under the eye of a Scotsman, Ian Law.

I was carrying a lot of weight at this stage, maybe 16 stone, with hips out of alignment and my whole posture out of kilter.

To begin with, Ian would position himself on a bench behind me, manipulating my body with lifts and twists. The strangeness of the experience was that each session might only last five minutes, but I would do it three times a day for seven days straight.

Pretty quickly, I felt something fundamental begin to change.

Whatever way he was working my body, I spent the whole week going to the toilet, all of this retained fluid beginning to free itself. And almost instantly, even the sciatica symptoms began to ease. It was extraordinary.

Ian would get me to do a few short runs and ask, 'Is the pain there now?'

It wasn't.

That week was transformative: a real turning point for my physique. My whole body had effectively been blocked up, and that week in Carrigaline changed everything. Over time, I would shed two stone, arriving into 2012 a completely different athlete to what I had been before.

In other words, the intensity of the Cunningham regime couldn't have been better timed as far as I was concerned.

I'll always remember a Walsh Cup game against UCD in Belfield, and Anthony getting us to do extra runs soon as the game ended. It was a clear psychological ploy designed to tell us and anyone watching that whatever else Galway might or might not be in 2012, nobody would be fitter.

You could sense people who'd attended the game hanging back to watch, intrigued by what they were witnessing here. I loved the sense of bodies and minds hardening now, of an entirely different mindset beginning to kick in.

And then, wouldn't you just know it – I got injured.

A Fitzgibbon game against GMIT; bending to flick a ball away, I left myself a little too open only to be met by a shoulder from fellow Galway man, Ger Mahon. The impact popped out my AC joint, meaning I had to have the shoulder strapped and sit out the group stages of the National League.

My first competitive game under the new regime was therefore a relegation play-off against Dublin. It went to extra time, and eventually, a replay, with some of the Dublin supporters giving me plenty of heat about my fashion sense over a new pair of blue and red F50 Adidas boots, which – against my better judgement – I'd decided to wear. Up to then, I'd always sided with boots that were predominantly black. Those F50s were never worn again.

We won the replay comfortably, before victories against Westmeath and Offaly pitched us into a Leinster final against Kilkenny that, it seemed, nobody in Galway truly believed we could win. This might have had something to do with the fact that our final group game in the League brought a 25-point April Fool's Day annihilation against Brian Cody's team in Nowlan Park.

I remember people calling up to buy hurleys in the family business and, without actually saying it out loud, communicating the view that we'd probably be wasting our time even going to Croke Park.

You'd know what was coming soon as you heard the words: 'How are ye fixed for Sunday?'

This was never an actual question, more a platform for someone to introduce their own opinion on the game. An opinion which was, inevitably, clouded in pessimism. So you'd be standing there, hearing their doubts about one Galway player or another. How so-and-so would be the wrong lad to be put on Henry or T.J. or Eoin Larkin.

And all you could do was be polite, waiting for the transaction to end.

To be fair, the pessimism was broadly understandable. We just didn't need to have it in our faces.

Were we bullish about our chances within the camp? Honestly, I can't say that we were. But about two weeks before that Leinster final, we played Waterford in a challenge game in Rathkeale and what happened immediately afterwards has always stuck with me.

I can't remember whether or not we won that challenge, but I'll never forget an address the Waterford manager, Michael Ryan, made to us in the dressing room afterwards.

They had a Munster final against Tipperary coming up, so you'd have thought any words he might have had for us would have been merely cursory.

But Ryan stood in the middle of us that evening and delivered a speech that, for me at least, carried the most incredible power. The basic premise of his words was: 'Why shouldn't ye beat Kilkenny?' And in the same vein, for his own team: 'Why shouldn't we believe we'll beat Tipp?'

His delivery was unequivocal. The so-called 'traditional' counties often won games because their opponents almost unwittingly went into them weighed down by an inferiority complex. You often hear the expression of something making the hairs stand on the back of your neck; that night Ryan's words had precisely that effect on me. Put it this way: standing in that dressing room in Rathkeale, I wasn't just ready to play Kilkenny, I *wanted* to play them.

I'd never encountered him before, but there was such sincerity in his words, such a desire to see us play that Leinster final free of any psychological hang-ups, I remember thinking: *Christ, I'd say the Waterford players would go to war for that man!*

I've gotten to know him a bit since and always enjoy his company. He strikes me as a very traditional kind of GAA man, someone with a really profound sense of loyalty. After managing Westmeath in subsequent years, he continued supporting them long after his term in charge had ended, even operating as their stats man for a while.

I love that in someone: the idea of the bonds you build in a dressing room running deeper than just the winning or losing of games.

I remember thinking that night: *He's dead fucking right, you know. Why shouldn't we beat Kilkenny?*

I'm not for a second playing that card of 'Oh, we knew that

night in Rathkeale ...'; I've always considered that stuff the height of bullshit. But what he said did register with me. It made me think: *Why shouldn't we?*

Who can honestly say if it impacted in any meaningful way when it came to the game? That Leinster final followed a path that absolutely nobody could have anticipated, one in which Kilkenny all but failed to come out of the blocks.

I scored a fourth-minute goal that itself had slightly improbable circumstances. Jackie Tyrrell was marking me at the time, and I remember going 'Oh fuck' as he got a step in front just as Tan was about to deliver the ball in.

Nine times out of ten, Tan's ball would have been delivered low towards the corner, where Tyrrell would have mopped it up, with me left chasing behind. But the delivery came in high this time, Jackie back-pedalling furiously. I always knew if I got the ball in behind a defender, there was a good chance of a goal. So I caught the ball, spun and kind of mishit the shot, Tyrrell almost getting in a hook, but the sliotar skidding into David Herity's net. One of Tan's normal deliveries would have made my marker a hero. But this one just sat beautifully for me.

I was always more comfortable with Tyrrell marking me than I was when J.J. Delaney was on my case. Jackie had a ferocity about him, but aggression never bothered me. The problem I had with J.J. was a problem I had generally with left-handers. Namely, I found it more difficult to protect the ball against them because their hurley would be coming in on my catching (left) side. That meant it was easier for them to flick the ball away.

The goal pretty much set the tenor for that first half, a half that had us at a scarcely credible 2–11 to 0–1 ahead after half an hour and 14 points clear by half-time.

Not in a month of Sundays had any of us seen that coming.

Maybe Kilkenny were guilty of a complacency given that awful trimming they'd given Galway in the League, who knows? If it hadn't been for losing the 2010 All-Ireland final to Tipp, they'd now – potentially – have been chasing a sixth Liam MacCarthy Cup win in a row.

They were a generational group, defined by the very character-istics we were so routinely accused of lacking in Galway. Why on earth would they have had any fear of us?

Our ploy of constantly rotating forwards definitely unsettled their defence that day, while Damien Hayes played a blinder for us operating as a third midfielder. If I'm honest, much of the day comes back as a blur now.

There was definitely a sense of shock in the dressing-room at half-time, Anthony trying to drill home the idea that we'd be starting at nil-nil on the resumption.

Kilkenny did win the second-half by four points, something management were only too happy to project afterwards as a flaw on an otherwise perfect day. But Galway's first ever Leinster crown had been delivered on the back of one of our greatest per-formances. Maybe, just maybe, we were finally toughening up.

'We've had great days in the past and not built on them!' Anthony declared to the media afterwards. And that was now our mantra. This Galway needed to be different to anything gone before. Winning Leinster had to be a stepping stone, not a destination.

The win pitched us into our first All-Ireland semi-final since 2005, my first in five years as a Galway senior hurler. A novelty, in other words. The usual thing in my first four years had been to be on the beer for Galway Race Week. This time, mercifully, that kind of blow-out would have to wait.

If we'd been true to type, we'd have fallen to Cork in the All-Ireland semi-final because favouritism was not – historically – a position that Galway handled well. For that reason alone, the fact that we outscored them 0–11 to 0–6 in the second half, having gone in level at half-time, felt like a real watershed.

Rightly or wrongly, I'd be ultra-conscious of how history plays out in these situations, and Galway's reputation suggested we'd have a dip now. I remember being at the golf Masters in Augusta in 2023 and having dinner on the Thursday night with Shane Lowry. We were talking about that weekend's upcoming GAA games. Mayo were due to play Roscommon in the Connacht Football Championship and looked to be in red-hot form, having just won the National League. I predicted that Roscommon would beat them. Why? Because that just seemed to be the rhythm of Mayo's world.

Shane was on the putting green before his final Masters round that Sunday when I caught his eye. 'Told you, didn't I!' Roscommon had won by four points.

Maybe Anthony had this kind of stuff in mind now too as he gathered us in a huddle afterwards by the corner of the Hogan and Davin stands, his animation leaving us in little doubt that there could be no backward steps this time. We were hurling's form team – the big story, the revolution boys.

Then one week later, Kilkenny beat Tipp by 18 points.

14.

THE €5-MILLION FREE

Would we have preferred a different opponent?

There's really no right answer to that. Being absolutely truthful, probably yes. But then beating Kilkenny – *that* Kilkenny especially – in an All-Ireland final ... not many people could claim they had that scalp. We now had the opportunity to back up what we'd done in Leinster.

In other words, everything we wanted to be seen to be as a team was on offer here. We just needed to be ready.

I made a beautiful hurley the week of the game and remember thinking it the nicest I'd ever held in my hands. It would break in the second-half of that final, a small, invisible detail to everyone but me. In my head, tiny things could always find inordinate weight.

So a perfect hurley had the status of a gift, not an achievement. The fact I'd made it myself couldn't alter that sense of uniqueness: the reality that it would be absolutely futile to ever try replicating it. This was nothing to do with measurable specifics, like shape, or weight or flexibility. It was all about balance.

I went into that 2012 final with a stick I felt just couldn't be bettered. The Galway routine in Dublin was to have a light lunch at the Regency Hotel in Drumcondra before swinging around the corner to the Na Fianna grounds on Mobhi Road for a puck around.

In this instance, we had left the hotel and were pulled up at traffic lights when someone got a call on their phone to say we'd managed to leave Conor Cooney behind.

And sure enough, there was Conor sprinting down the road behind us, having gone to the toilet just as the bus was pulling out.

A small, chaotic cameo like that is actually a welcome distraction in the countdown to a big game. Laughter eases the tension, drags people out of their shells. From a nervy quiet, the bus suddenly came alive with voices. Two hours before throw-in, that's exactly what you want. The illusion of normality, I suppose.

During the puck around, I knew my touch was in, every ball sticking. I was full of confidence. It felt as if we all were.

Nine minutes in, I got a goal – James Regan off-loading perfectly just as I arrived on his shoulder. I used the Kilkenny bodies coming to meet me almost as a catapult, bouncing left and a little further infield off each contact before drilling a shot into the right corner.

Just like in the Leinster final, all of the early momentum was ours. J.J. Delaney had been delegated to mark me, but having been given a roving role, I had the freedom to avoid being pinned down into any single position.

We were dominating again in most positions, and if anything, Kilkenny were probably flattered getting to half-time just five points adrift.

But the third quarter then turned ugly for us, Galway outscored 1–0 to 0–9 between the thirty-ninth and sixty-first minutes, Niall Burke sniping a vital fifty-sixth-minute goal after a mix-up in the Kilkenny defence.

Much would be made afterwards of Henry Shefflin's performance through that period and rightly so. Chasing his ninth All-Ireland medal, he'd been a man possessed at centre forward, battling, arguing, cajoling wildly, contesting almost every decision that Barry Kelly gave against Kilkenny. Having fought back from serious injury earlier in the season, Henry's performance was probably the definition of real leadership. Now in the autumn of a legendary career, he'd dragged his team back from the precipice.

James Skehill made a great save to deny Colin Fennelly, and then, with just two minutes remaining, Kilkenny were awarded a Canal End penalty that Henry chose to put over the bar. It seemed an act of mature wisdom as the clock ticked towards the seventy-third minute, Galway now a single point behind. But then Davy 'Darby' Glennon was tackled beneath the Hogan Stand by Jackie Tyrrell, and much to Brian Cody's fury, Kelly awarded the free.

A moment that brings me back to that pet hurley.

I've no clear memory of how it broke, though I suspect it was in the act of blocking someone down with maybe 15 minutes left on the clock. All I know for sure is that I was now hurling with second-choice equipment.

Was that in my head when I'd pulled a sixty-ninth minute free left and wide? Probably. I should have scored. Ninety-eight times out of a hundred, I'd have expected to put that free over. But the hurley in my hands wasn't the hurley I wanted in my hands. It wasn't the one I'd practised all my free-taking with.

Now Darby got to his feet, handed me the sliotar and said three simple words: 'Best of luck!'

I'll always remember seeing him out of the corner of my right eye, hunkering down then as if in prayer. I could just about hear Cody and Anthony jawing at one another directly behind me, and it made me laugh when I saw pictures of them afterwards, going at one another like rutting stags. In some respects, that moment captured what Anthony was trying so hard to put into us. Not many people squared up to Cody on the line and this was Cunningham's way of telling hurling's greatest manager that Galway would be nobody's soft touch anymore.

The Monday newspapers would christen what followed 'the €5-million free', a score to secure the first All-Ireland hurling final replay since 1959.

It was, absolutely, the most pressurised I've ever felt on a hurling field. I remember almost thinking out loud: *If I miss this, I'm fucked!* I know that's a selfish way to look at things, but just imagine losing the All-Ireland by a single point and you've missed your last two frees?

Human nature is that you can have a hundred good things said about you, but the thing that'll stay longest in your memory is a negative. Personally, I've always been more tuned into criticism than praise, taking energy from the bad stuff.

I knew if I missed that free, there'd be serious questions asked of Galway's mental strength. Mine specifically. Yes, most of those questions would probably come from faceless people on social media, but that wouldn't make it any easier to swallow. Ger Loughnane's view of Galway being soft and Joe Canning never fulfilling his potential would be recycled as gospel now. Stuff that we were all tired of hearing, weary of having pushed in our faces.

I knew that narrative still endured in some quarters, and there was only one way to genuinely challenge it.

We'd had all these minor and under-21 successes, but through the years 2008 to 2011 – my entire senior inter-county career so far – we'd never even made it to an All-Ireland semi-final. Now, in our first final, were we about to go under to a team we'd hammered in Leinster?

The free was actually trickier than the one I'd just missed, and yet, on some level, I absolutely loved that 30 seconds or so immersed in my own little psychological bubble, getting ready to strike. Just that sense of being in this incredibly intense personal moment, everything on the line.

And you know something? I actually mishit the free, topped

it a little, so much so that for one split second I feared it might fall short into David Herity's hands. So the relief on realising it had the legs was monumental. And then, almost instantly, Barry Kelly's whistle blew!

We'd gone toe-to-toe with Kilkenny here and lived to tell the tale. With three weeks to the replay, it genuinely felt like we had a certain emotional momentum too. In our heads, Kilkenny had to be slightly sickened by our survival.

And then I went and opened my big mouth.

15.

WHAT DID I JUST SAY?

I magine standing in Dublin Zoo and feeling like you were the one in a cage.

That was me as all hell broke loose over my comment about Henry being 'unsportsmanlike'. Frank had phoned early that morning, cutting instantly to the quick: 'What the fuck did you say yesterday?'

I was in a city hotel room with my then girlfriend and instantly switched on the TV. At that precise moment, my comments were being discussed on *Ireland AM*. They were also all over Twitter. I remember just collapsing backwards onto the bed and going 'FUCK!', my relationship with the media about to change forever. My own fault too, absolutely. My own naivety. Maybe I'd become complacent when microphones were put in front of me, because, until then, journalists always seemed broadly decent and supportive towards me. The coverage of my career had pretty much been universally positive, so maybe I mistook the GAA writers for some kind of circle of friends.

But now I had, supposedly, insulted one of the greatest hurlers of all time.

The truth is that I'd been trying to pay Henry a back-handed compliment, hinting at the absolute anger in his hurling that day in Croke Park. An anger that had him arguing against just about every decision that went against Kilkenny. An anger that made him spiky and contrary, and if I'm honest, more than a little annoying to be in close proximity to as an opponent.

But that single word now damned me in the eyes of the world. That, at least, was how it felt.

A routine Bord Gáis press conference in Thurles the week after our drawn All-Ireland final and BOOM! – I'd just taken the pin out of a hand grenade.

Ger Cunningham, probably Cork's greatest ever goalkeeper, was involved with Bord Gáis at the time and rang me almost as soon as the press conference ended. He'd been chatting to some of the journalists and was given the distinct impression that I'd just armed them with some kind of 'bombshell quote' about Henry. Ger, to be fair, could detect trouble for me on the horizon. He was asking if I'd like to reword what I'd said, and that maybe he could then email out the new version to those who had attended.

And there I found myself, reassuring Ger that there was nothing to worry about here. 'Ger, I said we needed to be more like Henry Shefflin in Galway. Why would I want to change that?'

He didn't sound entirely convinced. 'If you're sure Joe ...?'

I was. But I shouldn't have been.

As a Galway hurler, my profile always guaranteed a media focus that I can't say I was entirely comfortable with, because, often, that focus came without any active input from me.

People looking in from a distance maybe found it hard to make the distinction. When they saw something written about me, it would just be a case of 'Canning all over the papers again'.

In time, I restricted my media interviews to maybe two, maximum three a year, carefully choosing the platform. It was clear I had a higher commercial footprint than most of my teammates, and the last thing I wanted was any dressing-room resentment building towards it.

But in 2012, I gave them every reason to be resentful.

I've no doubt that some of my teammates would have been

thinking: 'Thanks a million, Joe! Would you ever shut the fuck up?' Nobody ever said it to my face, but I certainly felt, with some, that that sentiment was there. And I could absolutely understand why.

I had only myself to blame, and on reflection, I totally get that now. That single word, *unsportsmanlike*, negated just about every other sentence I delivered at that press conference. It was all anybody saw now. All anybody wanted to see.

We'd pre-planned a trip to Dublin Zoo that day, and I walked around the place as a silent ghost. To this day, I remember little or nothing of the visit, other than a constant sense of siege from my phone.

Every second message echoing Frank's tone: 'WHAT THE FUCK DID YOU SAY YESTERDAY?'

Maybe the benefit of hindsight allows me to see it from the journalists' viewpoint. It wasn't their responsibility to protect me. Their job was to sell papers, and in the context of the biggest hurling game of the year, I'd just delivered a line certain to help them do that.

But if I'm honest, a sense of resentment never quite left me after that. Given how the replay would pan out, it certainly settled like an ache in my bones through the winter months. I could be anywhere doing anything, and without warning, a voice in my head would whisper: *If only you hadn't said that about Shefflin ...*

Nobody within the Galway camp ever quite went there, but I did genuinely find myself wondering if some of them blamed me for the fact we didn't win the 2012 All-Ireland. It would only have been human nature if they did.

I was still living at home back then, but my family never really broached the issue. I'd say they understood what I'd been trying to say and recognised that losing an All-Ireland final under any circumstances hurts enough without someone exploring the specifics of your role in that defeat.

They also spared me the vitriol of a few letters that subsequently came dropping on the mat in Gortanumera from Kilkenny 'supporters', essentially taunting me over what they considered an attack on one of their greatest men.

The tone was always an unremitting: 'How dare you!'

My father has always had a wonderful intuition of what was inside an envelope just from the way an address might be written. It was almost a game he'd play as soon as the post would land.

'I'd say there's a cheque in that.'

'Is your car tax due?'

'Might be best if I open that ...'

In this instance, he never said anything. Just opened the letters, took a quick look and tossed them on the fire. It was years later before he told me about them. Apparently, one included a full match report of the replay, alongside a photograph of a smiling Henry, the Liam MacCarthy Cup in his hands.

I've often wondered about the kind of people who would be moved to send such a thing to a player. Imagine taking the time to basically try to ridicule you after you'd been beaten in an All-Ireland final. Is that the instinct of a grown man or woman? Of someone's parent?

It was Henry's ninth senior All-Ireland medal, the letters seemingly keen to remind me that I still had the grand total of none. I've no real idea what impact, if any, they had on my mother and father at the time. I'm sure they hurt, but if so, it was never something they articulated. To this day, my father likes to joke that they were as good as a sod of turf on the fire, and in this case, his humour has always been welcome.

After 2012, I would become a lot steelier in my attitude towards journalists generally. If I'm honest, I wasn't especially nice. I was angry towards them, and I suppose, absolutely determined that they would know it.

So I'd very intentionally glare at any posse of scribes waiting outside a Galway dressing room in the hope of speaking to one of the players. It meant they stopped asking me for a word, my expression instantly telling them that they'd be wasting their time.

I felt exploited. Yes, I'd carelessly used that word to describe Henry's performance in the drawn game, and I shouldn't have. But I felt aggrieved too that the focus was on a single word, not the context in which I'd used it.

One loose line and I'd been devoured.

At a press conference some months later, I remember challenging a GAA writer with the *Irish Examiner*, Diarmuid O'Flynn, about how they'd misrepresented that quote. And O'Flynn pretty much told me that I had only myself to blame; that the journalists had recorded my quotes accurately and any resulting fall-out wasn't their problem.

Technically, he was right of course. But I got a sense that he was almost laughing at my indignation here. Worse, it seemed to me that day that his colleagues were chuckling away with him.

Whether right or wrong, this was a red rag to a bull now: the idea that my discomfort was a source of entertainment to them. It left me absolutely seething.

If there were Galway teammates who reckoned I was in the media too much before that (and I don't doubt there were), you can only imagine their feelings towards me now. It was never articulated to my face, but I don't think I've ever felt less comfortable going in to training as I did for our first session back that week.

I was only twenty-three, but already deeply conscious that Galway's disappointments quite regularly ended up dissected in media through the narrow prism of my performance. There were three weeks to the replay, and for much of that time, I felt embarrassed.

Anthony Cunningham, to be fair, never broached the subject, but I knew full well that if someone in Kilkenny had tossed out a loose quote about one of our players, 100 per cent we'd have used it to create energy.

The biggest worry for me was that I'd given Kilkenny an edge now because these games can be won by tiny margins. I'd given them something they could use.

So losing that replay just compounded the sense of personal responsibility, and being honest, it sat with me for a long time. A huge part of me was thinking: *That was my fault!*

It left a real awkwardness there, and then some joker decided to put myself and Henry sitting side by side at the All-Stars presentation the following November.

We'd had a quick chat on the field immediately after that replay, me spluttering something along the lines of, 'Listen, I didn't mean ...'. Henry was sound. But then why wouldn't he be? He'd just won another All-Ireland.

The point I'd been trying to make was that Galway needed Kilkenny's brand of ruthlessness in their hurling, the willingness to challenge referees, that absolute tunnel vision for 70-odd minutes that could make you come across as manic and tunnelled in the heat of battle.

Did we honestly have that in Galway? Not routinely enough in my opinion.

My mam often used this expression: 'What's for you won't pass you by.' In life generally, I think she was right about that. But in hurling?

One of the first things I remember Davy Fitzgerald saying when I landed in LIT was: 'Nice guys win fuck all!' And over time, I feel I came to understand what Fitzy was getting at. The

Mascot for the 1995 county final in full Portumna kit.
Canning No.1 on the back!

With my best friend and
companion Ross.
Often it was just me hitting
sliotars and Ross retrieving
them for me.

All the family at Seamus's 21st birthday party.

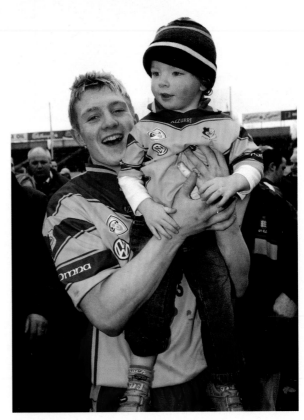

Celebrating with my nephew Seán after victory in the All-Ireland club semi-final, February 2006. (© Damien Eagers / Sportsfile)

Playing for Portumna in the 2006 All-Ireland Senior Club
Championship final against Newtownshandrum.
(© Damien Eagers / Sportsfile)

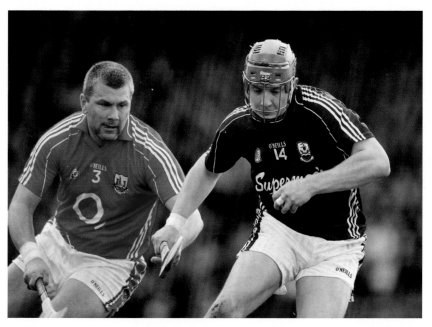

In my third championship game against Cork, The Rock keeping
close tabs on me. (© Brendan Moher / Sportsfile)

Myself, Damien Hayes and David Collins celebrating after
our win over Kilkenny in the 2012 Leinster Championship final.
(© INPHO / Cathal Noonan)

Just after missing a late free in the 2012 All-Ireland final
against Kilkenny. (© INPHO / Morgan Treacy)

From devastation to a €5-million free!
What a difference a couple of minutes can make.
This shot ended the game level, but Kilkenny went on to win the replay.
(© INPHO / Morgan Treacy)

Shaking hands with the great Henry Shefflin at the end of the 2012
All-Ireland final replay. (© David Maher / Sportsfile)

Bainisteoir Anthony Cunningham watches on as we play Dublin
in the 2013 Leinster final. (© David Maher / Sportsfile)

Holding up our captain (my brother Ollie)
after victory over Loughrea in the 2013 Galway club hurling final.
(© Diarmuid Greene / Sportsfile)

Pictured with my brothers holding the Tommy Moore Cup.
From right: Ollie, Ivan and Frank, who was also our manager.
(© Ray McManus / Sportsfile)

With Mam and Dad after a match against Offaly at
O'Moore Park in Portlaoise. (© Cody Glenn / Sportsfile)

Me and Meg at our friend's wedding in France.

With the younger Cannings, my nephews.
From left: Jody, Adam and Andrew, all representing Portumna
in Croke Park at the Go Games Provincial Days in 2017.
(© Eoin Noonan / Sportsfile)

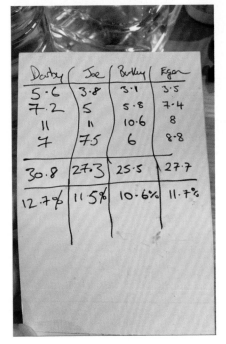

Darby	Joe	Burkey	Egan
5·6	3·8	3·1	3·5
7·2	5	5·8	7·4
11	11	10·6	8
7	7·5	6	8·8
30·8	27·3	25·5	27·7
12·7%	11·5%	10·6%	11·7%

Amazing the things you'll do to
pass the time! Myself, Burkey,
Darby and Brendan Egan doing our
body fat percentages the day before
the 2017 final.

Happy tears with my nephew Jack as we celebrate the 2017 All-Ireland final win. (© Ramsey Cardy / Sportsfile)

Waving to the Galway supporters who made it to Croke Park with Bainisteoir Micheál Donoghue after the 2017 All-Ireland final win. (© Ramsey Cardy / Sportsfile)

It's all in the eyes.
The look that tells me all
the sacrifices are worth it.
I hope Mam was proud.
(© Sam Barnes / Sportsfile)

Bringing the Irish
Press and Liam
MacCarthy Cups
back to Gortanumera
National School
where it all began for
me, my nephew Jack
and Martin Dolphin.

Dejected at the full-time whistle in the 2018 All-Ireland final
against Limerick. (© INPHO / Tommy Dickson)

Receiving a big hit under the headlights in the 2020 All-Ireland semi-final against Limerick. (© INPHO / Tommy Dickson)

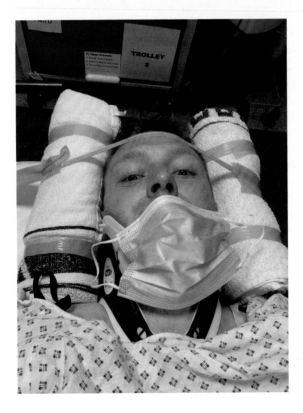

Precautions taken by the medical staff after that hit!

Before playing to an empty crowd at the height of Covid.
(© INPHO / James Crombie)

Walking down the tunnel after my final game in a Galway shirt.
(© Harry Murphy / Sportsfile)

In the largely destroyed city of Aleppo in 2017 as UNICEF ambassador.
(© Mark Condren / *Irish Independent*)

Working on *The Sunday Game* alongside Liam Sheedy
and Joanne Cantwell. (© INPHO / James Crombie)

best hurling teams are also the most ruthless. At times, maybe the most unscrupulous too.

They hurl as if there is nothing that matters more in their lives.

Ostensibly, the pursuit of a senior All-Ireland medal came to dominate the narrative around my inter-county career. But sometimes I felt it was more of an obsession for others than for me. I always argued that winning or not winning the All-Ireland wouldn't define me.

I meant it too. Hurling was never the only thing in my life. I always felt that I could park it and move on from disappointments.

I mean Ollie never won a senior All-Ireland, but I didn't look on him any differently because of that. To me, he was always right up there with the best we ever had in Galway. And often you'd meet players from another county who might have more than one Celtic Cross to their name but had won them essentially as part of extended squads. Men whose game time would have been minimal. Were they somehow superior hurlers to Ken McGrath? Or Tony Browne? Or John Mullane? Were they better than Ollie? Or Damien Hayes?

I'm talking about men who have left hurling legacies, not fellas who just made up the numbers. So winning an All-Ireland? God knows, I desperately wanted to do it, but it wasn't exactly keeping me awake at night. You only win an All-Ireland if your team is good enough. In 2012, I don't think we had quite reached that point yet – simple as that.

But maybe that's a thought that Henry Shefflin could never entertain.

16.

REPLAY BLUES

It's wasted energy to try figuring out where you sit in the opinions of others, but I spent a lot of time doing precisely that as the evenings darkened in 2012.

Some of the players believed me to be at least partly to blame for Galway not winning that All-Ireland. I sensed it then, and to some degree – even all these years later – I still sense it now. And that's fair enough. Nobody really said anything at the time, and I'm willing to accept it might just be a form of paranoia on my side.

But it was a vibe I got. Imagine being stupid enough to 'attack' Kilkenny's spiritual leader and one of their greatest players. For all of my attempts to explain afterwards, the story had already been written to fit the eventual conclusion.

I'd poked the Kilkenny bear, you see. What in the name of God had I been thinking?

Anecdotally, you get told that it didn't figure with any great prominence in their preparation for the replay, but I'm not sure I've ever fully believed that. If the boot was on the other foot, we'd have used it. I have absolutely no doubt about that.

Anyway, Henry became the first player in GAA history to win nine senior All-Irelands as a starting player. For those of us still chasing our first, that figure was almost impossible to process. In this instance, Kilkenny had come through the qualifiers to win their sixth crown in seven seasons. It now seemed that Leinster final defeat hadn't left them nursing a single psychological scrape or bruise.

They were better than us that second day, no question. Davy Burke's two early goals got us off to a flier, but we couldn't really sustain it. Kilkenny would eventually outscore us by double figures over the closing 20 minutes (2–8 to 1–4) to win by more than we'd beaten them in that provincial final.

Walter Walsh became the front-page story: an under-21 player making his senior debut in the biggest game of all, and eventually, leaving the field to a standing ovation, having scored 1–3.

We'd also had our moments before the walls caved in. Cyril Donnellan had the ball in the Kilkenny net after 44 minutes, only for referee, James McGrath, to call the play back for a Galway free. Four minutes later, I then rasped a shot against the butt of a Canal End upright, only for Kilkenny to break downfield from the rebound and score a Cillian Buckley point. A Galway goal would have levelled the game. Now Kilkenny were four ahead.

Seconds later, Donnellan got his marching orders for a challenge on J.J. Delaney and the game was well and truly up.

It would take us 70 minutes for a Galway starting forward to score a point from open play, by which time the black and amber bunting was already on the Cup. A damning statistic.

And yet, we felt we'd turned a corner. We were Leinster champions, after all. That 'soft' tag had surely been consigned to history.

Hadn't it?

17.
RUNNING
TO STAND STILL

I've been cheered by thousands, booed by thousands, but
nothing feels as bad as the booing inside your own head
during those ten minutes before you fall asleep.

Andre Agassi

The best book I've read is *Open*, the Andre Agassi autobiography, written with Pulitzer prize-winning author, J.R.
Moehringer.

On first reading it, there were just so many passages I found
myself doubling back on, momentarily spellbound by the clarity
of emotional intelligence. Ostensibly, Agassi's life had little if
anything in common with mine.

My childhood was certainly happier and much healthier, my
sport something I loved – as distinct from an obsession imposed
upon me by an overbearing parent. During his greatest days,
Agassi all but hated the game that brought him such wealth and
fame.

I never fell out of love with hurling, but I did fall out of love
with what it brought into my life.

It might surprise people to hear how vague my memories are
of hurling for Galway through 2013, 2014 and 2015. Much of

it comes back now as a blur, a great spilled jigsaw of games, all essentially leading to the same feelings and sounds.

Maybe, on some level, this endorses the idea of us still lacking that killer instinct in Galway, the notion of all those supposedly giant strides taken in Anthony Cunningham's first year being somehow bogus and illusory.

I mean, we lost the 2013 Leinster final to Dublin by 12 points, and I've no real defence to offer for that day. It was Dublin's first provincial crown since 1961 and, having won the National League two years earlier, they had real momentum under Anthony Daly.

But still … 12 points? In our first ever Leinster title defence?

Three weeks later, we got tangled up in a tactical web spun by my old friend Davy Fitz for Clare and our season was over. Only when I think about it in hindsight do I appreciate the starkness of that unravelling.

We were definitely complacent going into the Leinster final, with Dublin having needed replays to get over both Wexford and Kilkenny. I suspect few enough of us imagined they'd survive a second game against the latter.

But hand on heart, I didn't see our defeat at the time as a return of Galway softness. To me, we were simply caught off guard in pretty much the same way we'd caught Kilkenny the year before. In hurling, you just can't freewheel. You need to be psychologically ready for pain, because mid-game it's almost impossible to change gear if things start going against you.

I don't think we were arrogant, but we did probably make the mistake of believing that we were at another level to Dublin. Hindsight suggests that they could have gone on to win the 2013 All-Ireland, but Ryan O'Dwyer's red card early in their subsequent semi-final against Cork was a huge setback.

Nobody really saw Clare as MacCarthy Cup winners, but

Davy got them on a roll that summer with what, at the time, was the relatively novel deployment of a sweeper.

In our Thurles quarter-final, he put Pat Donnellan sitting in front of me for the whole game, and I just couldn't break free. With just about nothing coming in, there was this overriding sense of 'what the fuck do we do here?'

Tactically, we'd been outsmarted, meaning that so much stuff we thought we'd fixed in 2012 was open to question again.

Then, that October, we were hit by the shocking news of Niall Donohue's death by suicide. It was the week of the county final, and we were at training when word reached us.

There's really no way to process that kind of information, other than to slip into a state of absolute shock. Though I'd shared a dressing room with him for the previous two years, I wouldn't pretend that I knew Niall any way well. I suppose we were different generations essentially, and within a team, you naturally gravitate towards those closer to you in age.

He was a serious athlete who was a nightmare to be marked by in training. Niall just had this way of working his feet so that it was almost impossible to steal a yard on him.

As a person, I found him quiet enough, someone I'd always reckoned carried himself with a happy-go-lucky vibe. Just shows you how little we often know about people we pretty much end up going to war with.

I do remember a few of us, Niall included, spending a beery night in Ardrahan at one point but, broadly speaking, I found he was someone who kept largely to himself. Only those close to him were privy to his struggles – Anthony, I think, among them.

Sometimes I drop in to his grave in Kilbeacanty if I'm passing, just to pay my respects and say a quiet prayer. But even now, more than ten years later, it's hard to get your head around the fact that he's no longer with us.

You're hurling with this lad one day, visiting his grave the next. It feels terribly unnatural, and I suspect, always will.

Hurling-wise, I suppose I was in two parallel worlds in the autumn of 2013.

With Frank as Portumna manager, we'd found a fresh momentum that would take us to a first county title in four years and subsequent fourth All-Ireland.

This meant I pretty much missed the 2014 National League, my first outing being a four-points semi-final defeat to Kilkenny.

Anthony had surprised me by offering me the Galway captaincy, something I'd been a little torn over whether or not to accept. The offer came in a phone call to my office in Dublin, and I asked for a little time. On some level, I suspect I was worried how the other players would see this. Did some of them still hold me to blame for 2012? Given I wasn't even living in Galway, might they regard this now as some kind of populist appointment?

There was also the fact that I'd won precisely nothing as a captain in underage hurling.

The advice I got from home was conflicting. Frank was typically blunt, telling me not to take it on the simple basis that there was nothing to suggest the captaincy would suit me. Ollie's take was that it was an honour to be asked and that the opportunity mightn't present itself again.

Was I ever really going to turn it down? Probably not.

There's a selfish instinct that kicks in – a conceit, I suppose. Ollie had been Galway captain previously, so just imagine Mam and Dad's pride now if I followed suit.

I also suspect I thought it might be a good way of challenging myself. I was always comfortable speaking within a group because I generally believed that I could back up what I'd say. And I agreed with Ollie's view that if you were one of the best players in a team, you should always be a leader too, irrespective of whether or not you held the captaincy.

To me, Ollie had been pretty much a prototype of the perfect captain. Someone who always said the right thing at the right time, but more importantly, then backed it up on the field. I'd had other captains who were great orators but maybe not great players. Talking the talk was only one part of being a leader.

I also had to ask myself: if I didn't take it, who would?

The idea of having the Galway captain living outside the county probably suited Anthony too. It gave him the space to control things without having to interact almost daily with the players' main dressing-room representative. So there would be few enough conversations between us through the season other than at training.

This, I suspect, suited us both.

It was around this time that a huge image of me first appeared on one side of the Galway team bus, and I hated it.

I'm sure some people saw it as just another strand of the 'Joe Show': this idea that everything to do with Galway hurling had to be, first and foremost, about me and that this was something I actively encouraged.

The first time I saw it was when the bus pitched up in Loughgeorge as the backdrop for a team photo, and I remember a voice in my head going: *I don't need that!*

But who was I to object? Would I not have come across as a complete prima donna by requesting its removal?

We fell over the line in a Leinster quarter-final against Laois in Portlaoise, winning by two points. Laois were actually awarded a 21-yard free at the death that we just about managed to keep out, but I don't remember any of us being over-analytical in the aftermath.

There was a big wind blowing into the town-end goal, and with the benefit of it at their backs in the first half, Laois goalkeeper Eoin Reilly kept driving his puck-outs down into the corner where my old college buddy Willie Hyland made hay. Despite a second-minute Johnny Glynn goal, we trailed 1–7 to 0–16 at half-time and really only got to grips with the occasion (and the wind) as Laois tired in the final quarter.

When the game ended, I remember the Laois goalkeeper going to a spot out near the 21-yard line and rooting something out from under the turf. We subsequently heard that at training the week before their manager, Seamus 'Cheddar' Plunkett, had encouraged his players to bring in photographs of someone who meant a lot to them and bury them in the field.

I've never been able to get Willie to confirm this. He just smiles at me and shrugs. 'Oh, the day we nearly bet ye?'

And I tell him: 'Yep, *nearly* being the most important word!'

We then drew with Kilkenny in Tullamore, my late equaliser spoiling the script after Henry Shefflin had come off the bench to score what looked a likely seventy-second-minute winner from the left touchline. It was a game highlighting our two extremes as we rescued a reprieve, having trailed by 10 points with just eight minutes to play. Maybe netting three late goals in a five-minute surge obscured the fact that we'd let Kilkenny ease away from us at one point that day with an unanswered 1–8. The game was already in injury time when I netted my second penalty of the day, so we'd effectively come back from the dead.

Six days later, we ran out of road, Kilkenny winning the replay by eight points, my only score of the game a line cut. After my late return from Portumna duty, Anthony had chosen to keep Conor Cooney on the frees, a role, to be fair, he was thriving in.

The message was clear that he needed and expected more from me in general play, and it's also fair to say that that expectation wasn't met that second day in Tullamore.

One week later, our season was over with a defeat to Tipperary in Thurles that proved the very definition of a collapse.

Having looked in control of the game, with Glynn giving Pádraic Maher a torrid time, we were duly outscored 0–1 to 2–10 in the closing 20 minutes. From six ahead, we lost by nine.

Seamus Callanan was our tormentor-in-chief with a personal tally of 3–8 and maybe we consoled ourselves afterwards that three games in a fortnight had simply taken its toll on our legs.

Yet again the unevenness of Galway's hurling all but defied rational analysis. There's nothing much to be said in a dressing room when your season comes crashing down around your ears like that. I fulfilled the cursory obligation of thanking management for their efforts while Anthony tried to be as upbeat as he could.

And maybe a little delusion held its attractions now.

There's a voice in your head, saying: *Fuck. Beaten by Kilkenny and Tipp, probably the best two teams in the game.* That's the kind of nonsense you cling to because you have to cling to something. You ran Kilkenny to a replay. You hurled a great half against Tipp. All that went against you in the end was tiredness.

In the immediate aftermath, you become something of a cliché in how you deal with defeat. You go on the beer, revisiting mistakes made, identifying culprits. You go in search of (and invariably find) one scapegoat or another. You fool yourself that small things might have made a big difference. It's called taking solace in the consolation of bullshit. And in Galway, we'd become more than well-practised in the art.

18.

BREAKING POINT

When the tears came, they arrived in an unexpected torrent.

It was like a dam breaking: this huge weight crashing out through the stone. My first concern was probably that somebody might see me now, sobbing openly in the lobby of the Lucan Spa Hotel, a stranger for company.

It was 2015, and I'd just bared my soul to Fran O'Reilly, a man recommended to me by the Gaelic Players Association (GPA).

I'm not entirely sure how our meeting came about or even what Fran was supposed to be bringing into my world. Was he a sports psychologist? A life coach? A mentor? Maybe all of those things, maybe none. The one thing I quickly came to understand was that he was someone who knew how to listen.

I'd spoken to Dessie Farrell at some point about feeling a little beaten up by life in general, about having no real sense of being in control. It was as if I'd become a bystander to my own story – negatives just piling on top of one another. If I'm honest, I'd slipped into the trap of wallowing in self-pity.

No question, top of the list was Mam's diagnosis with breast cancer. There's a picture of me standing alongside her the previous December, immediately after our county final defeat to Gort, both of us looking suitably crestfallen. That defeat stung, particularly given we'd had to wait 10 weeks from our semi-final win over Craughwell because of a controversy on the other side of the draw. Not for the first time, Portumna were left feeling short-changed by those in authority within Galway GAA.

If you look at our expressions in that photo, that's probably what you see. But there was a lot more building now that was as yet invisible. For me, it was beginning to feel like a perfect storm.

A relationship break-up some months earlier had been hanging over me. Completely my own fault. I'd been a dickhead. I fucked up, and having only myself to blame, I found this very hard to deal with for a long time after. But I'd made the mistake and had to live with it. All part of growing up, I guess.

Working in Dublin was getting tiring too because of all the travelling. I loved the work, but it was just the journey up and down a couple of nights a week that wasn't suiting. Now the people in Liberty Insurance were brilliant to me in terms of time off and so on, but that can only last for so long. I didn't feel entirely comfortable leaving the office at 3 p.m. while others had to stay and work for another two hours.

That just never sat right with me.

There was an awful lot going on in my life at the time: my world an endless soundtrack of agitating questions.

At home, a recurring one was about the Galway captaincy. I'd had the role for 2014, and given the lateness of that county final, the Portumna contingent only really got back to Galway training around Christmas. We'd missed maybe eight weeks with the rest of the squad, and there were no big conversations on our return, certainly nothing beyond the physical specifics required.

But Dad, especially, was curious.

Almost on a daily basis, I'd hear: 'Well, what's the story? Are you captain again?'

My answer would exasperate him. 'I don't know,' I'd reply. I didn't.

Ordinarily, the captain would be announced at the beginning

of the season, but Anthony was choosing to keep his powder dry. Eventually, I ended up ringing to ask, but even then, he was non-committal.

It was more a case of: 'sure, we'll see in a while ...'.

Then David Collins was captain in the early stages of the League, and without any real declarations being made, that's essentially how it just stayed for the year. I'd lost the captaincy without any explanation of the reason why. Not ideal for a man nursing increasingly brittle confidence.

The commuting to training began to really drag now. Two and a half hours down every Tuesday and Thursday, sometimes three if traffic was bad. I found that incredibly wearing. Maybe Anthony could sense that too and possibly factored it into going elsewhere for his captain.

I've no idea. I was never told.

If he'd just said something along the lines of, 'Listen, we don't think this is working ...', I'd have been fine with that; I might even have agreed. But no reason was ever given, and selfish as it might sound, that knocked me psychologically. Normally, a captaincy lasts two or three years unless there's a change of management. After a single year, this felt like a demotion.

Then, that January, having broken a finger playing a Walsh Cup game against Offaly in Tullamore, I suppose a kind of black humour kicked in. I'd only been on for 10 minutes when I went in to hook someone and his hurley caught me. A clean break. Two pins inserted.

You might remember a scene from *Love/Hate*, the gangland drama that was a big TV hit at the time. It's where Fran whips out a human bone – taken from slain IRA man, Git – and pretends to wave it at his boss, Nidge.

'I've a bone to pick with you, Nidgy!' he cackles.

Well, I stole that line as the caption to a shot of my finger

X-ray that I put up on Instagram. Just trying to make light of a setback about to keep me sidelined for six weeks.

Then, in April, came the news about Mam. And it was around then that I had my sit-down with Fran O'Reilly.

One of the first things he said to me that day in the Lucan Spa was that for an athlete to perform at their best, every other aspect of their lives needed to be in sync. He listed four headings: 'Relationship. Work. Home. Hurling.'

Each one essentially impacted on the other, and in my case, the first three all felt problematic now. I was hurting on so many different levels, and basically, trying to internalise the pain. Bottling things up.

That's when the tears began to flow. I'm an emotional enough person at the best of times, so it wouldn't take that much to set me off. But generally it would only happen in the family environment. Otherwise, the guard was always up.

When I did a lengthy interview with the *Irish Independent* that appeared the day before our 2017 All-Ireland semi-final against Tipperary, Ollie said he was really taken aback to read how much the health issues of Mam and Dad (he was diagnosed with prostate cancer in 2016) had impacted on me. It just wasn't something I had articulated to anyone before that. It wasn't my style.

But as the tears began to flow that day in the Lucan Spa Hotel, I instantly felt a weight begin to lift. Why? Because I was being honest for a change. I was telling the truth rather than just acting out a role.

No question, it helped that I didn't really know Fran, because as soon as I'd got all that stuff off my chest, I was ready to move on. This might sound strange, but I just had this sense that I could leave a lot of baggage behind me in that hotel.

I probably cried for five minutes in total, then wiped my eyes and was ready to get on with things, feeling neither compromised nor judged.

Sometime later, I tried communicating some of this stuff at home to Dad, but he just couldn't see where I was coming from. At least, not in a hurling context. Funny, when I look at him in old Portumna team photographs, I see a man looking at absolute peace with the world. Someone who couldn't ever imagine being anywhere better or doing anything more natural.

His chest is always out, his smile forever confident.

Hurling to him, I sense, offered a kind of freedom when, at times, it seemed to me to be the polar opposite. So his attitude now was: 'What the hell's wrong with you?'

The very thing that could set him free was leaving me feeling trapped.

I like to think I handled the pressure of being an elite hurler pretty well across the years, but I do sometimes wonder if people understand how isolating huge public visibility can make you feel. It's actually where a lot of my crankiness would originate. From the sense of people making assumptions about what it was like to be Joe Canning.

Bottom line: the pressure of performing was always there. And with it a huge degree of presumption. People pretty much forget that you are human and that you experience worry and insecurity too. This can lead to contradictory feelings.

For me, it was almost a perverse conflict at times. The higher the stakes, the more I honestly felt alive.

Like taking that last-minute free in 2012 to rescue a replay in the All-Ireland final. On so many levels, the pressure of that moment was horrible. But if you'd asked me there and then would I abdicate the responsibility to somebody else? Not a hope in hell. Because that's precisely what I wanted to do, where I wanted to be at that moment.

When I was a young fella in the garden at home, imagining myself as Mikey Sheehy one minute, maybe Pat Fox or Joe Cooney the next, it was always in the last seconds of an All-Ireland final, the game hinging on what I did next.

So I came to love that pressure in real life. I mightn't have dealt with it successfully every time, but it was never something that unnerved me.

Even days when a game was clearly slipping out of reach, I still wanted to be there, still wanted to compete. I can honestly say I never found myself on a field wishing the game over. My mentality was always 'a couple of quick goals here and who knows?'

The issue I had in 2015 was that so much of my life outside the game now felt as if it was spiralling out of my control, and with it, so many things were just out of kilter.

Maybe one thing that people miss about me is that I'm fundamentally shy. I'm certainly one of the quieter Cannings whenever the family gets together. Even the nephews would confirm I'm an understated presence when we have a gathering at home.

As a child, you'd have struggled to get a word out of me through all those nights, pucking balls back out from behind the goals at hurling and camogie training. I was always fairly reserved, doing my level best to just stay out of the way.

In this, I inherited something far closer to Mam's personality than Dad's. I'd be inclined to generally hold my counsel. To let things settle.

Mam's was definitely the most powerful presence at home, the one whose voice carried furthest.

My siblings would say that Dad is almost more of another brother to us at times, an open book, someone who loves the craic. Mam was much more reserved. In a loud room, you'd never hear her speak.

And my inclination was always to follow Mam's way. To store stuff up inside. To never show weakness.

To some degree, I always sensed that the more you revealed, the more vulnerable you became. So I was always a little on edge, the poker face becoming a kind of defence mechanism. I felt that people had enough ownership of me on the day of a game, so I didn't want to give anything away beyond that if I didn't have to.

I'd watched the All-Ireland finals of 2013 and 2014 from corporate boxes in Croke Park, the former as a guest of Chill Insurance, the latter working for Liberty. There's a massive jealousy that kicks in watching players from other counties have that moment of marching behind the Artane Boys Band. The inevitable thoughts of what might have been …

And the corporate side of things can be a little surreal in that context, some guests choosing to stay in the box and socialise rather than go outside to watch the biggest game of the hurling year.

I found the 2014 final and replay a little easier to stomach, maybe because I was busier on both days, organising tickets for clients, doing a Q&A on the day. Was there a bit of resentment? Absolutely. But that's an impulse familiar to any serious inter-county player when they find themselves looking in from the outside on All-Ireland final day.

Having recovered from that broken finger, I played in four of our six League games in 2015. But it was another forgettable campaign for Galway, and Waterford comfortably evicted us from the competition at the quarter-final stage.

We then played Clare in Ennis in a behind-closed-doors challenge game, with Ollie invited along as an extra set of eyes for the Galway management.

As I bent to rise a ball, Pat O'Connor's hurley accidentally caught me, opening a deep gash between the index and middle fingers of my left hand. The Clare team doctor, Doc Quinn, took one look and volunteered to drive me straight down to Ennis Hospital for stitching. There was blood everywhere, and he had to open the windows of his car for fear I was going to faint.

From memory, we got to the Accident and Emergency department about twenty minutes before it was due to shut down for the night, and I was there maybe ten minutes when Johnny Glynn arrived in to the bed beside me, just a curtain between us. He'd been knocked out momentarily by a heavy hit and was now being checked for concussion.

We used to call Johnny 'Superman', and as they'd given me so much pain medication, I was almost hallucinating while this doctor began stitching me. I remember the nurses looking at me as if I had two heads because I was roaring at Johnny instead of talking.

'WHAT THE FUCK ARE YOU DOING IN HERE, SUPER?'

The wound in my hand required 15 stitches and every single one was a torture. I was begging the doc to give me more gas, but he was adamant I'd reached my limit.

'You'll just have to bear with me on this and the sooner you do, the quicker it's over.'

The whole thing probably took 15 minutes, but it felt like an eternity.

Our kit man, Tex Callaghan, came in to drive Johnny and I home to Oranmore, with Anthony driving my car.

The cut proved stubbornly slow to heal, and to this day, I have a tenderness in that part of the hand. I wore a pad on it on my first night back in training, but as soon as I went to catch a ball that familiar sting told me the wound had reopened. This happened twice, and I would need an injection before six of the seven championship games we'd play that summer.

Someone in Connemara, hearing of my predicament, sent me this little pot of lotion that you rubbed into the palm to harden the skin. I was trying everything just to get back to the point where I'd feel confident again putting my hand up for a ball.

The injections basically numbed the two fingers, making it just about possible for me to catch a sliotar so long as I had sufficient padding. It wasn't ideal, but at least those injections made me available for championship.

First up, was a Leinster quarter-final against Dublin. We drew the game, and I pretty much stunk the place out. Anthony took me off with about a minute to go, an act I interpreted as an expression of some disgust on his part.

The following Tuesday at training, he called Joseph Cooney and me into the referee's room in Athenry and duly tore into us both. I said to him that I'd have absolutely no issue with him if he dropped me. I meant it too.

Deep down, I knew I hadn't done enough to deserve a start in the replay, and I knew I wasn't the only one now holding that opinion. Sometimes, you can't help but look at certain journalists' player ratings, and one in particular had given me a five. On the one hand, I was instinctively offended. On the other, I recognised it was probably as much as I deserved.

Hand on heart, I didn't expect Anthony to keep faith with me for the replay, but he did. Cathal Mannion scored 3–3 and I got 2–3 as we blitzed the Dubs in Tullamore, winning by 13 points.

I had a good day against Laois in the next round too, a game delivering Galway's first back-to-back championship win since 2012. But then we faced Kilkenny in the Leinster final and a 26-minute spell without a score in the first half left us playing catch-up.

We got back to parity with a Jason Flynn goal just after half-time only to lose momentum again, Kilkenny eventually hitting five of the game's last six points to win comfortably by seven.

This had the echo of an old story just running on a loop.

From a personal point of view, it was the day of my so-called 'no-look goal' – Andy Smith driving a high delivery towards the Hill-end goal – which I fielded on the turn and fired, first time, past Eoin Murphy.

The finish was pure instinct, and nine times out of ten I'd probably have fallen on my backside trying to execute it. The ball from Andy was actually terrible: one that, ordinarily, would have left me glaring back down the field. In this instance, the goal possibly spun an illusion that we were all in perfect sync.

But this was, perhaps, what we had become now. A team of moments. Anthony accentuated the positives in his media interviews afterwards, insisting that we were 'very, very close' to Cody's men. Believing it was the challenge.

Three weeks later, we leaked 23 wides, yet still won our All-Ireland quarter-final comfortably against Cork in Thurles. Sweepers were becoming a thing in the game now, and the Cork management opted for Brian Murphy to play the role.

I decided to shadow him, meaning that my direct marker – Eoin Cadogan – was left in a bit of quandary. If Murphy looked like he was closest to me, did Cadogan then revert to sweeper?

We'd spoken about this beforehand and my attitude was: 'Lads, I know what to do here!'

Like a lot of sweepers at the time, Murphy was essentially still learning the position, and the last thing he'd have expected was me constantly coming out from behind him, left and right, endlessly in his line of vision. It meant I had pretty much two people marking me, something creating an ocean of space for those around us.

Sensing their discomfort, I was almost messing with Murphy and Cadogan. They'd imagined this was a game that would be played strictly on Cork's terms, but the opposite was now happening.

Johnny Glynn scored an early goal for us, soloing in unchallenged towards the Killinan-end goal before batting the ball past a static Anthony Nash. We'd noticed that Nash pretty much never left his goal line, so the instruction was to run straight at him if the opportunity arose.

And Johnny duly honoured that instruction within seconds of the throw-in.

It was the day of his infamous post-match interview, live on RTÉ television. 'What's this about Galway only having one forward?' asked Joanne Cantwell.

'Fucking bullshit between ourselves,' says Johnny, before realising that he was already live to the nation and interjecting, 'Sorry, sorry …'.

There was a very different feel to our semi-final against Tipperary, Shane Moloney getting an injury-time winner for us on his championship debut. But it was another day of a single individual inflicting big damage on the Galway back line, with Seamus Callanan scoring 3–9 for the beaten team. Colm Callanan made a couple of great saves for us too, so we got away with it and were back in an All-Ireland final. Back with an opportunity to right a small multiple of wrongs against Kilkenny.

This, after all, was a Kilkenny no longer graced with the presence of Henry Shefflin, J.J. Delaney, Tommy Walsh, Brian Hogan or Aidan Fogarty. A Kilkenny, in other words, that to all intents and purposes should have been struggling through a challenging period of transition.

All would be going to plan at half-time, Galway leading by three points. And then our performance just went tumbling off a cliff.

I have no explanation, no excuses. Kilkenny just seemed to work harder than we did, something unforgivable in the context of our respective circumstances. Loads of stories would emerge of rows in the dressing room at half-time, none of them remotely true.

Aidan Harte did go off in the first half, replaced by David Collins, but there was nothing to suggest any rancour in the camp at half-time. Why would there be? We were leading, hurling well.

But that seven-points, second-half turnaround had the knives out in force now. And though he didn't seem to know it at the time, they were being sharpened specifically for our manager.

19.

ANOTHER ONE BITES THE DUST

Exactly three weeks after that All-Ireland defeat, a delegation of four met Anthony in Ballinasloe to articulate feelings of unease among the players.

David Collins, our team captain; Andy Smith, vice-captain; Davy Burke, and myself – as members of the squad's 'leadership group' – spent maybe two hours basically alerting him to the fact that a majority of players had now begun expressing their desire for change.

A vote had been pretty overwhelming in that regard, the bulk of the squad saying they had lost confidence in his management team. The feeling was that the time had come for something and someone new.

This had been building.

It first kicked off after our fairly tepid National League quarter-final defeat to Waterford in Walsh Park at the end of March. Back then, two questions asked of the group had delivered unambiguous answers.

The first: did the players still have confidence in Anthony as our manager? Overwhelmingly, the reply to that had been 'No!'

The second: did the players believe that Galway's squad was good enough to win the All-Ireland? That was a convincing 'Yes!'

These findings were made known to him at the time, and he'd given the impression of a willingness to freshen up his backroom, but it never happened.

I was in a minority camp, answering in the affirmative to both questions. It wasn't that I completely disagreed with those now going after Anthony and his backroom. I, personally, felt that a lot of their complaints held merit. I just didn't think that everything should have been landed back at one man's door.

To me, as players, we needed to take responsibility here too. It was far too simple to blame management for everything when, in reality, you could trace far too much repetition running through the recent Galway hurling story.

We'd lost that Waterford game by eight points and been left with a sense of having been completely outsmarted tactically. Derek McGrath was being accused in some quarters of introducing football tactics into Waterford's style of play, an accusation he made clear he considered offensive.

You could see where it was coming from, though.

They were deploying big defensive numbers whenever out of possession, meaning that, routinely, they didn't have a single player inside our 45-yard line that day. It mightn't have been to everybody's taste, but it clearly had the support of their own people. As his team warmed down at the end of that game, a knot of local supporters gathered around the Waterford players in a clear gesture of approval.

Though we'd won the toss, Galway elected to play into the wind in a first half that would leave us trailing 0–5 to 0–14 by the midpoint.

We got that margin down to four points only for Waterford's web to then hold us scoreless for over 20 second-half minutes, by which time Pauric Mahony's frees had seen them safely home.

It was our fourth defeat in six League games, and arguably the most dispiriting.

Anthony's comments afterwards that the players 'didn't want it enough' didn't exactly sit well with the team. He'd fought vigorously to get a fourth year in the job, but there was little sense that that year was leading us anywhere positive.

When the feelings of the squad were made known to him, my sense of it was that he resented this. And so, six months later, unease among the players had begun climbing to a whole new altitude.

When we met Anthony that day in Ballinasloe, he proved naturally defensive.

There was a feeling that he just hadn't taken the players' reservations on board in March, and that, if anything, the idea of a players' mutiny would only encourage him to dig his heels in now. One of the stranger things he indicated was that he hadn't actually had the final say on some of the substitutions made against Kilkenny on All-Ireland final day. This only fed a sense of mixed messages coming from the line.

For the semi-final against Tipperary, the backs coach, Pat Malone, and forwards coach, Eugene Cloonan, had directly contradicted one another in their messaging to players. All of this stuff was on the table now.

Our meeting ended with Anthony declaring, 'I have two options: stay or fight it!'

He chose the latter, and so the next two months dragged by with plenty of rumour and innuendo doing the rounds, but little enough clarity on what might or might not happen next.

I'm a bit jumbled in my recall of the sequence of meetings. The squad certainly met a couple of times in Clarinbridge gym and another in the Shearwater Hotel in Ballinasloe. After that, another players' delegation went out to Anthony's house outside Athlone for one more 'clear the air'.

I've often thought since, could you imagine this happening in Kilkenny during Brian Cody's time? The idea of players demanding the manager change his way of working? Of insisting he alter his backroom team? It wouldn't happen, would it?

The players' view, broadly, was that a new backroom might be enough to revitalise things. But it was clear that Anthony's pride was stung by this. Essentially, he resented the idea of players telling him how he should do his job, and he knew too that he still had the county board's backing.

An intermediary, Kevin Foley, came down from Dublin to operate as a neutral in discussions and it all came to a head then in late November with both sides pitching up for talks in the Shamrock Lodge in Athlone.

This meant seriously awkward glances exchanged between players and management in the lobby, a sense of betrayal written all over their expressions. As someone who was still backing Anthony (if not his backroom), I found this deeply uncomfortable.

A secret ballot of the players produced pretty identical figures to those reached six months earlier. Specifically, 26 to 6 voted no confidence in Anthony continuing.

This, apparently, flew in the face of the message he himself had communicated to the county board the day after we'd met him in September, namely that he retained the players' support to continue. A board vote had accordingly been passed to reappoint him, but they hadn't reckoned on the depth of disquiet within the squad now.

For a group of people that had worked our way into a winning position halfway through the All-Ireland final just two months previously, this all felt a little depressing and even unseemly. We were washing our dirty linen in public, and none of it really sat well with me.

With the writing on the wall after a third players' vote, Anthony eventually stepped down. But he was never going to go quietly.

Branding the result the work of 'a kangaroo court', his resignation statement expressed a belief that the players' decision had been 'misguided'.

He observed: 'I consider it is unreasonable to express a lack of confidence in management – how else could we have reached a winning position in an All-Ireland final last September?'

Anthony's view was that some players had been 'motivated by a desire to unjustly extend their lifespan as inter-county players, placing personal agendas over the greater good of Galway hurling'.

In response to this, the players delivered a lengthy 'setting the record straight' letter to the county board that – inevitably, I suppose – then found its way into the public domain. It was all highly regrettable and a little undignified.

The letter made clear that disquiet with management stretched back a good deal further than merely the second half of the All-Ireland final. It referred to two months of 'unnecessary animosity' given the clear unambiguity of dressing-room numbers in favour of change.

On one level, I had a real yearning now to make public the fact that I was one of those who'd backed Anthony in the vote. I certainly didn't agree with everything he did, but neither did I feel that our consistent shortcomings in key moments on the field could rationally be the exclusive responsibility of someone who hadn't pucked a single ball. In my view, we all needed to ask ourselves: 'Can you stand by what you did?' I'd have said as much at meetings.

But when you're in a group, you have an obligation to respect the majority decision, to just suck it up and accept it as democracy.

I often wondered if the majority of the public imagined I'd been one of those agitating for Anthony's removal. I had, after all, attended most of the meetings. A part of me couldn't help thinking: *Jesus, I wish I could tell everybody my point of view here!*

A selfish impulse.

But you don't do it, because you can't.

Anthony himself knows the way I voted, and I'm still good with him today. But I'm not sure the same could be said for one or two of his backroom, given they were more than aware of broad unanimity within the dressing room that they – at a minimum – needed changing.

I'm not sure Eugene Cloonan, for example, would have much time for me today. The impression I got was that he thought senior players like me should have been able to assert greater influence on the group. That if we set our minds to it, we maybe could have saved them.

But would it not have been the ultimate conceit for someone like me to try overturning such a decisive group decision? My feeling might have been that all of us needed to look a little harder in the mirror here; that another lost year couldn't logically be deemed simply management's fault. I and a few others made our feelings on that known. But ultimately, you're just one player in a group, one voice in a commotion.

No question, there was a small split in the group now, a little unease between certain players. I decided not to go on the subsequent team holiday because it just wouldn't have felt comfortable.

And I found myself endlessly asking one simple question: 'Can I honestly say I'm not part of the reason we're not successful?' I knew I couldn't. When it came down to it, not one of us really could.

So, rightly or wrongly, Anthony was gone. And it was up to us to justify the execution.

20.

THE QUIET MAN

You wouldn't have to be a modern-day Einstein to understand the vibe coming our way now.

We'd shafted a decent man. For many, we'd lost the run of ourselves as a group given that Anthony had just guided us to an All-Ireland final. You could see what was building on social media now. A sense of people almost willing us to fail.

The majority of those within the group who'd wanted Anthony out already had their minds made up on who should be his replacement. I knew Micheál Donoghue as a selector to Vincent Mullins from my time with the county under-21s. He'd been manager of an All-Ireland-winning Clarinbridge team in 2011 and had just done a stint as a member of Eamon O'Shea's backroom team in Tipperary.

To me, Micheál always had a calm, understated presence. He was never one for ranting or breaking hurleys in a dressing room. He'd say little enough, but you always got the vibe of a watchful presence. Of someone paying attention.

That said, it was never a thing in my head: *Now that Anthony's gone, there's only one fella for this job!*

I didn't actually have any real sense of clarity about what should happen next. But a big positive was the presence of Franny Forde on his backroom ticket as a coach. Franny had an excellent reputation from his work with Galway minors, and he was coming in alongside Noel Larkin, who'd been an influential member of my brother Frank's backroom when we won the 2014 club All-Ireland.

To me, this was a pretty instant message delivered by Micheál Donoghue. He would surround himself with good people and delegate accordingly.

Our first team meeting was in the Loughrea Hotel, and he wasn't slow to lay things on the line. Micheál spoke of us working off 'a clean slate'. What we'd done had been presented to the hurling world as an exercise in player power, and whether we liked that or not, we'd have to live with the consequences.

In other words, if there was a perception that we had a target on our backs now, who cared? Micheál told us in no uncertain terms that everything would be player-driven from that moment on. That we needed to take ownership of our environment. Yes, people were waiting to pull the rug from under us. So what were we going to do about that?

Even though Davy Burke and I would have been in the minority that voted for Anthony to stay, Micheál also made a bit of a statement by naming us as captain and vice-captain respectively. I suspect this was his way of backing up that claim to a clean slate. This wouldn't, couldn't, be a dressing room with legacy issues from Anthony's departure.

It all felt and sounded hopeful. You're thinking: *Yep, there's a real positive vibe around this!*

And then we managed to get ourselves relegated to Division 1B in the National League!

Looking back, you could almost see this coming. There was still this sense of people refusing to take responsibility for what had gone before. The appetite to scapegoat hadn't diminished one iota. We were still a group attracted to the blame game.

True, it was a fine line in the end.

Bubbles O'Dwyer got a late equaliser for Tipp in Salthill after it seemed that my line cut had won us the game. We then drew our final group game against an experimental Waterford too, meaning we were pitched into a relegation play-off against Cork in Salthill.

Late goals from Seamus Harnedy and Patrick Horgan got Cork over the line, leaving us with an all-too-familiar feeling of flakiness in the group. We'd overcome an early deficit to be three points up with 10 minutes to go.

And then we'd done precisely what we always seemed to do. We'd let momentum slip.

That said, I can't remember any great sense of desolation within the squad over our relegation, as the League was never going to be the competition we'd be judged on in 2016. It was All-Ireland or bust for us now. And call it the innocence of the damned, the idea of some grand redemption possibly unspooling over the summer months still seemed entirely plausible within our dressing room.

But then, exactly three months later, we lost the Leinster final to Kilkenny by seven points and all the same old toxins seemed back in our bloodstream again.

This was the defeat that prompted Ger Loughnane's famous 'Fr Trendy' depiction of Donoghue, something – if I'm honest – we all found quite amusing at the time.

Players have a pretty juvenile default system when given that kind of material. I remember at one point a picture doing the rounds on WhatsApp of Micheál's head super-imposed onto an image of Fr Ted kicking Bishop Brennan up the arse. We thought it was hilarious.

Ger effectively eviscerated us in his *Star* column, which, on reflection, was something we all pretty much knew was coming our way now. For many, the most galling aspect to the defeat was how it absolutely mirrored our fade-out against the same opponents the previous September.

Loughnane wrote that it proved we had 'no guts whatsoever', suggesting it was *the* day we needed to stand up after what had been done to Anthony.

'This defeat showed they are made of absolutely nothing,' he wrote.

> You can forget about this Galway team. They are always looking for a crutch. There's always someone or something to blame. The manager, the trainer, the physio, the length of the grass on the training pitch, the weather …
>
> After pushing Cunningham out the door, the crutch was kicked away from the Galway players. They had to stand up for themselves. No one would listen if they played the blame game again.

All of this, I imagine, chimed with most people's view of us at this point. Could we honestly argue that we'd justified the push against Anthony in any shape or form? No, we couldn't.

But it was what he said about our manager that got the headlines with Ger suggesting that Galway would have been better served by a more aggressive sideline presence. Whereas Anthony had been 'prepared to take on Brian Cody', we now – apparently – had a manager who reminded Loughnane of 'the Dermot Morgan character "Fr Trendy" from RTÉ in the 1980s'.

He suggested that Micheál came across as:

> an amiable curate coming into a new parish … and they're expecting to win with him? Compare Donoghue's body language on the sideline with that of Cody. You don't need to be a genius to work out who's the king in the jungle.

Ger wasn't wrong on one level. As players, we now hadn't a leg to stand on in terms of defending the recidivist nature of our hurling story.

But he was wrong to personalise it against Micheál. In many ways, our manager was the one figure within the group who should have been deemed blameless that day. This was down to us as players again.

If you ask me to explain our fade-out in that Leinster final – and just as with the previous year's All-Ireland final, we were three points up at half-time – I find myself drawn to an idea that Kilkenny simply outworked us in the end. How that makes any sense, I can't honestly articulate. Kilkenny won the second-half 1–16 to 0–9, a fairly damning statistic by any measure. They were pulling up in the end.

When I look back on that day now, I see it as quite possibly the day the penny finally dropped for Galway hurlers. It was as if people – as a group – came to the same conclusion. 'Fuck, it can't always be the manager's fault! We've now done exactly the same thing under Micheál that we did under Anthony. So what's the real problem here?' Or maybe more pertinently: *who* is the real problem?

Loughnane wasn't the only one giving us a kicking now. Local media put the boot in; the Keith Finnegan show, *Galway Talks*, on Galway Bay FM was running hot with callers sick to the teeth of assessing what had become, essentially, the same story.

That said, Loughnane's words were the ones we used for energy, especially given our next opponents would be his native Clare.

Actually, by the time that game came around, our attitude was: 'Just let us out that fucking door!'

There would be a real edge to us for that All-Ireland quarter-final, and I have a specific memory of three of us hunting Cian Dillon down early in the game as a kind of collective statement of what we were about that day.

I scored a goal just 11 seconds after the restart, Clare left momentarily unsettled by my switch to full forward. Brendan Bugler had been marking me on the wing for the first half, and I always knew with Davy Fitz teams that the player he'd put man-marking me would make forward runs on the basis that I'd have to give chase.

As the second half got under way, I remember Pat O'Connor shouting, 'Who's on him?', after spotting me without a shadow. Johnny Coen won the throw-in; Burkey ran off him and passed it out to me. In the confusion, I had a clear path in on goal.

A few minutes later, I went back out to the wing. Normal service resumed. We won by two goals.

Knowing that Loughnane would be on *Sunday Game* duty that day, I turned to the TV gantry at the final whistle and shook a fist in his direction. Couldn't help myself. We'd taken so many kickings at that stage, I was only too happy to reciprocate now.

Just my way of saying, 'Fuck you!'

One of the first people to reach me on the field was given short shrift too. This lad had been giving us plenty of abuse on different forums – the kind of stuff that, ideally, I suppose, I shouldn't have been reading. But I knew who he was now, and I knew exactly what he'd been saying.

Just a few weeks earlier, he'd christened us 'a useless shower'. Now as he arrived to pat me on the back, I just looked him in the eye and told him to fuck off. He looked stunned.

Of course our season ended next day out with a single-point defeat to Tipperary in the All-Ireland semi-final. A Tipperary team that would then devour Kilkenny in the final.

My memories of that day are largely ones of hurry and impatience.

The county board didn't book a garda escort to Croke Park for us – early evidence, I suspect, for Micheál that he wasn't exactly engaging with like-minded people here. It meant that we were late arriving at the stadium and didn't have time to do a proper warm-up.

Basically, we pulled up in Croker at 2.52 p.m. and were due on the pitch at 3.02. It was ridiculous.

Did this have a role to play in what happened me? Who can say?

But running out to a ball, I took a nudge from James Barry in the back and instantly felt something go in my hamstring. It meant I had to sit out the second half and goals from Bubbles and John McGrath in the closing 10 minutes got Tipp just about home in the end.

At the time, I had no concept whatsoever of what was ahead of me.

It was probably a week later when I got up to Santry to see Dr Éanna Falvey, former doctor to the Irish rugby team, to get some scans done.

'I have good and bad news,' he smiled on seeing the results. 'The bad? You've done the tendon. The good? You've a centimetre and a half still on the bone. The other tendon has retracted about three centimetres.'

This was the first time I'd even heard of such a thing as a hamstring tendon, and now, I needed surgery on mine. Éanna said the normal rehab for such an injury was somewhere between seven and eight months.

I was absolutely speechless, having gone to the clinic believing I just had some form of a hamstring pull.

Frank dropped me down to the University Hospital in Cork that evening and I was operated on the following day by Professor James Harty. A man of dry wit, he came out to me afterwards to declare, 'All a success, you can go home now, and I don't ever want to see you here again!'

Ollie collected me and we were both back at Portumna training that evening, me on crutches with a knee in a brace to keep the leg at a 90-degree angle. The brace would have to stay on for six weeks, because if the leg was straightened, the stitches would tear.

And standing there that night, my mouth still soapy from the general anaesthetic, I got an overwhelming sense that the road back from this would be a long one.

21.

CHANGING MINDS

There's a heightened awareness that comes with being part of a team so accomplished in the art of making its own people angry.

You have to be careful not to allow yourself to be reduced to cliché. Because social media wants to do that. It wants to give you a kind of cartoon status, objectify you, diminish you. Every sports psychologist I've ever encountered has counselled against giving that kind of noise any space inside my head.

And I've continuously ignored them.

Anger has always worked for me, you see. From resentment, I take energy. I feed off negatives.

Maybe it's something to do with the isolation we've always felt while hurling for Portumna, but that's the mental setting I still actively seek out when there's a big game on the horizon. I'm sure it's not something the likes of Malcolm Gladwell or Bob Rotella would recommend. But you chase what works for you. You trust it.

I always felt I needed anger because it went without saying that I was going to meet it. People maybe wouldn't have seen this as much in Ollie, but trust me, he had the very same thing in him, this attitude of 'I won't be bettered today!'

It was never lost on me just how hard Ollie worked to become the player that he became. The way he trained. The life he led. The things he ate, or more specifically, those he didn't.

Whenever we'd have a family meal, sauces or stuff like mayon-naise were always off the menu for him. If the other lads were having a pint, he'd invariably be drinking water. Just this multiple of small, largely unseen sacrifices that made the game more a lifestyle choice than a hobby.

I savoured my time figuring all this out because he wasn't around home that often while hurling was getting really serious in my life. Ollie spent various spells at college in Dublin, Sligo and Limerick, and while at the Dublin Institute of Technology, I sometimes stayed with him in his flat in Phibsboro.

We'd go ice-skating in this rink near Mountjoy Prison, and though I might be tempted by the idea of a takeaway, he could always be trusted to win the argument against one. The hurler on the ditch doesn't see that kind of dedication, or in some cases, maybe they simply don't want to.

I always knew that it would kill Ollie if he ever thought an opponent had got the better of him. He had that ruthlessness. You could count on the one hand the number of substandard games he played during his entire career hurling for Galway.

For me, just being in close proximity to him fed an understand-ing that there was always a right and wrong way to do things. Ollie was captain when Galway got to the National League final in 2004, and I travelled on the bus with the team from Gort, assigned the job that day of 'doing' the hurleys. I relished that kind of intimate access to the Galway senior dressing room, almost using it to educate myself.

There's a lot of pain involved in being an inter-county hurler, both physical and psychological. And often a lot of solitude in trying to work your way through that pain.

When I think back on it now, I was trying to play through one injury or another for most of my adult hurling career. From a fairly young age, I became increasingly aware of a soreness in my abdomen, which turned out to be a condition called osteitis pubis.

This really kicked off around 2009, and I remember specifically struggling with it a little when we played Kilkenny in that year's Leinster Championship. It was probably just a case of doing too much at the time, playing for too many teams.

I'd be fine up to a point, once the game got underway and I was fully warmed up. But afterwards, I'd be in agony. How would I describe it? I've never been stabbed, thankfully, but I can only imagine that's how it feels to have a knife stuck in you. To cough or sneeze was torture.

Given this was a period in which I also had issues with plantar fasciitis and sciatica, it's fair to say that there were days I almost felt as if my body was being held together with masking tape.

As both the plantar and sciatica were down my right side, I suspect I ended up over-compensating to my left, a habit that then introduced even more problems.

With the osteitis pubis, I'd be in bits for two days after a game or training session. But you're young; you don't want to miss out on anything. The doctors and physios were aware I had an issue, and they'd be constantly asking me how it felt. And my trademark answer, almost always, was: 'I'm grand!'

I got a couple of cortisone injections into the pubic bone in 2009, after which I had to stay away from training for 10 days to allow the cortisone settle in the specified area. Dr Éanna Falvey would have done them in Santry, and he became a great support to me during that time.

It's not the most pleasant of sensations, having this big needle inserted into that part of your body, but I found it would then relieve me of the pain for two or three weeks before slowly wearing off.

My body was trying to tell me something, and the message

wasn't really complicated. I was nineteen and probably just playing too much hurling.

I had, after all, been playing with Portumna under-21s from the age of thirteen and the seniors from fifteen. I'd played under-14, under-16, minor, under-21 and senior for Galway. I loved it, and even now, in hindsight, I wouldn't change a thing in that respect. Hurling was all I wanted to do; it was that simple. But maybe my body didn't quite love it as much as I did.

That said, I was hugely lucky too. To the best of my knowledge, the first time I broke a bone was that baby finger in 2015. I would have dislocated the other one a good few times, but I just got over that through strapping.

I'm pretty sure I had multiple little fractures over the years too, but you'd just never bother getting them X-rayed. The attitude at home would be: 'Can you bend it? We've seen worse. It'll be grand in a few days.' There was always a manliness towards injuries in our house that, I suppose, I wanted to honour too.

But the hamstring issue I faced at the end of 2016 was arguably the most serious of all for me. Potentially career-threatening. In this, it wasn't dissimilar to Paul O'Connell's injury sustained during the 2015 Rugby World Cup, though in his case the tendon came completely off the bone. When that happens, it's as if you end up with a jigsaw in which the pieces never quite fit together. Chances are, had that happened to me, I'd never have been right again. It would have been the beginning of the end.

Personally, I never honestly entertained the thought of being finished for the simple reason that to do so would have been mentally ruinous. I'd be stubborn in that regard. Tell me there's something I won't be able to do and just watch me try to prove you wrong.

But the worst part of a long-term injury is how useless it makes you feel. From one week to the next, you routinely sense that you're treading water, getting nowhere. You're with the physio and the S&C people, doing everything they tell you to do. It's painful, boring and monotonous. Endlessly, you have to fight the negativity in your head.

I had regular arguments with physio Dave Hanley in particular. I was always impatient, pushing to get back on the field quicker than he'd allow. No doubt there were nights I'd be a bit of an Antichrist, feeling as if I was present in body but not in mind.

Sometimes I might ask Darby or Burkey afterwards how the session went, and they'd be looking at me as if I had two heads. 'Sure you were there,' they'd say. 'You saw how it was yourself.' But I hadn't. I could only read the quality of a training session by being fully immersed in it.

There's a huge sense of personal achievement when you come out the far side of that loneliness, and in my case, I was particularly chuffed to beat all the projections.

I was back hurling within six months, but I do remember, initially, being terrified that the tendon might go again. My first game for Galway in 2017 was a second-half substitute appearance against Wexford in Pearse Stadium. We lost it and the vibe in the ground afterwards was absolutely toxic.

The defeat meant we'd effectively surrendered control of Division 1B, leaving Wexford in the box seat.

I'd netted a penalty shortly after coming on, but Wexford pretty much took over after that, and we managed just a single point in the closing quarter. Micheál took dog's abuse on the field as we were doing our warm-down, and it's fair to say that some of the local media coverage the following week was reliably poisonous.

This is what I mean about the hurler on the ditch. A conclusion was drawn by many that day that Galway hurlers were going nowhere fast. Not just that, but that the man in charge deserved a good kicking.

I'll always remember one national newspaper headline declaring 'Galway flops blow a six-points lead'. The piece beneath the headline was written by a Galway man. I knew he didn't write the headlines, but I honestly didn't care. To me, all that mattered was that he wrote the piece. He was one of our own. He called us *flops*. In my head, everything was that simple.

Not long before this, another journalist had written an article with the title 'Nine players with a point to prove in this National League'. I was one of those he named – at a time when it was still a moot point whether or not I'd even be able to play in that League.

I accept that most people probably weren't aware of the seriousness of the injury, but for him to suggest that I was now someone with 'a point to prove'? Another person on his list was Patrick Horgan. I mean, seriously?

I still have those pieces on my phone, which maybe says more about me than the people who wrote them. I've no problem accepting that argument. My father has this expression when he hears me giving out: 'Christ, Joe, everybody can't be a prick!'

Like Burkey would often say to me, 'Ah, Joe, I don't think that's the angle …'. He'd see me as being too negative about something. But it *was* the angle for me. It was the thing that gave me an edge.

Anyway, we were just two games into the season now, and the script, for some, had already been written. But there was one person in Salthill that day who viewed things a little differently. We'd just arrived back in the dressing room, all manner of abuse still ringing in Micheál's ears, when he heard the words: 'You're needed outside!'

And this was the moment a truly remarkable man first came into our lives.

*

The morning before the 2017 National League final, Davy Burke and I spent maybe two hours in the company of John Walsh.

We'd gone to his home in Salthill at Micheál Donoghue's request, and it's fair to say that we came away afterwards with a sense of renewed ease about the game ahead. John was the man outside the dressing room looking for a word with Galway's manager the day of that Wexford defeat in Salthill.

Initially, Micheál's assumption had been that the journalists were just impatient for his post-game verdict. Either that or some irate Galway supporter was on the warpath.

But when he went outside, he was met by this man standing with his young daughter, an envelope in his hand. They chatted briefly, and Micheál remembers just tossing the envelope into his kit bag without opening it before heading away to meet the media. He was at home the following evening when he first thought of it again.

Inside was a letter in which John essentially described his passion for Galway hurling despite coming from Liskeevy, Tuam – resolute football country – and having gone to St Jarlath's with All-Ireland football winners, Michael Donnellan and Pádraic Joyce.

Also inside the envelope was a book he'd had published the previous November: an autobiography describing his extraordinary, near two-decade battle against a multiple of different cancers.

The book is called *Headcase: A True Story of Love, Life, Medical Miracles and Battling Against the Odds*. In it, John recalls the initial diagnosis in 2000, when he was just 23 and working in Germany, confirming a rare and aggressive brain tumour that became the starting point of what proved an almost ceaseless battle against inoperable cancers. John's condition was liponeurocytoma, something that, at the time, only 41 people in the world had ever been diagnosed with.

Once he began reading, Micheál was absolutely spellbound. Not just by the dreadful cruelty of a young person ending up with such a pitiless condition, but even more so by John's attitude. The optimism and complete absence of self-pity just sprang off the pages with a basic message that while you couldn't always change the cards you'd been dealt in life, you could choose how you responded to them.

John had left his phone number on the letter, and so Micheál now rang, apologising for not being able to give him more time that day in Salthill.

They agreed to meet, and a real friendship began to flower between the Galway hurling manager and this remarkable husband to Edel and father to Firínne, Ríain and Saorla.

For Micheál, the friendship came with one implicit message. Real pressure was trying to stay alive as long as possible for your wife and daughters, not trying to win hurling games.

By 2015, John was battling literally hundreds of microscopic tumours in his body, yet, between bouts of awful sickness, he was living every single day to the full.

Having met him, Micheál decided that it would be no harm if we got to meet him too.

So Burkey and I found ourselves sitting at his kitchen table the Saturday morning before that final against Tipperary. John's message was uncomplicated. Of the bad things that can happen to you in life, losing a hurling game should be pretty insignificant.

On some level, I think he'd come to recognise this instinct in Galway to almost catastrophise our bad days. To overplay the consequences of losing. We were in this bubble of reflex negativity, and we needed to understand just how out of kilter that overreaction was with the things that really mattered in life.

John probably knew that he was going to die soon, leaving his young wife and children behind. It was clear that he was desperate to live. Yet, his positivity was phenomenal.

'Lads, losing a game should never be a reason for devastation,' he told us. 'There's always a bigger picture.'

Throughout 2017, he became a regular sight at Galway training, Micheál often sending Tex Callaghan up to the house to bring him down. And I think it was before the All-Ireland semi-final against Tipperary that Micheál then got him to address the whole panel one Saturday morning in Pearse Stadium.

Basically, John just told his story and, honestly, you could have heard a pin drop. It was spine-tingling, and I'm not exaggerating when I say that every single player there that morning made a point of going to John afterwards individually to thank him for taking the time.

I'm not going to spin the line that what he said was a turning point in our season. If I'm honest, I think we'd already got there. The day we turned around a 10 points second-half deficit to beat Waterford in the National League quarter-final had gone some distance towards doing that. When we then beat Limerick by 10 points in the semi-final, it's fair to say that the Wexford defeat already felt a part of ancient history.

But I think meeting John that morning before the League final was just a well-timed reality check.

I suspect that it was completely against medical advice that he made it to the subsequent All-Ireland final and even our victory celebration that evening in Citywest. But on so many levels it was only fitting that he was with us on that famous day.

John passed away in June 2019, Micheál and I going to the funeral in Milltown. The eulogy was done at the beginning of the Mass, and then different gifts were brought to the altar representing the different passions in John's life. One of the gifts was a hurley, the priest explaining: 'This is to show that, even though he was a Jarlath's man, John's number one team was the Galway hurling team.' When he said that, the entire congregation got to their feet and delivered this sustained bout of applause while looking across at Micheál and me. It felt a hugely powerful and emotional moment.

Funny, you can have all manner of people come to speak to you, and we did. Other sports people like Paul O'Connell and Joe Schmidt. Comedians like Rory O'Connor of *Rory's Stories* fame, and Tommy Tiernan who spent an evening with us in the Galmont Hotel the following year, doing the equivalent of his Saturday night chat show with three players randomly selected by management. (He asked for subtitles when Skehill sat down for questioning!) But sometimes the voice that makes the biggest impact belongs to someone without a public profile.

If anything, thinking about John Walsh today leaves me feeling a certain guilt. Because I suspect it's only in hindsight that I could truly appreciate the mental resilience he summoned during that pitiless struggle with his own body.

Back then, I remember the selfishness of our quest for the All-Ireland overriding everything else around us. It's extraordinary how superficial your interaction with people can become in those circumstances. You're endlessly keyed to a kind of paranoid setting.

The easiest way to avoid hearing someone saying the wrong thing is, essentially, to always be in a hurry. To meet the world on the run. It wasn't that someone as worldly wise as John Walsh was ever going to deposit something stupid in our heads, but you're programmed to be defensive. To deliver sentences rinsed of any depth.

I sincerely hope that wasn't the impression any of us gave to John at the time, and hand on heart, my memory is of him always being a hugely welcome figure within the group. But I do wonder if I ever really took the time back then to truly process his predicament. Sport at that altitude can often leave you wearing blinkers, so that even an incredible story like John Walsh's can just gently lap against your consciousness without really making you stop and think.

There's plenty I'd love to say to John today if he were still around. Words of respect and admiration for how he dealt with the cruellest of circumstance. The truth is that every day he showed courage beyond measure, and in your life, you don't meet many people you can say that about. We were blessed to have him in ours.

Even with John Walsh as inspiration, beating Tipp by 16 points in the 2017 League final hadn't been predicted in anyone's crystal ball. They were flying as All-Ireland champions with the air of a team capable of winning another. But one of the things we did that day was to put Cathal Mannion on Pádraic Maher.

Pádraic had this style of sweeping in behind, which meant he'd always leave pockets of space on the wing.

And Cathal now duly exploited those pockets. I dropped deeper in the game too, and all in all, we just had a tactical clarity about us that Tipp found impossible to break. Everything felt insanely easy. And there was one specific detail which I could sense made this defeat especially unpalatable for some of their players now.

We'd managed to recruit the Polish S&C wizard, Lukasz Kirszenstein, with whom they'd won that 2016 All-Ireland. The stories we were hearing from Tipp suggested a level of disgust among some of their players that a greater effort hadn't been made to keep him as part of Michael Ryan's management team.

We could almost instantly see why.

Lukasz just had this aura about him. He's a very vocal, forceful presence, and there's an intensity to how he works that brooks no argument. Whatever he said in 2017, we did. If that meant doing handstands for the year, our response would have been: 'How many?' Training at six in the morning: 'Should we eat breakfast first?'

And Micheál's strength was a willingness to delegate responsibility to people who knew what they were about. So Lukasz drove us hard, and we followed without questioning.

It was Galway's tenth National League crown, and typically, some flak kicked off when the Cup was brought back that evening to St Thomas's. It wasn't a homecoming, but that was the convenient depiction now. Someone had simply asked Davy Burke (our captain, remember) if he could drop in to his home club on the way back from Limerick because the place was full of kids. So Davy and a few of the lads obliged.

Next thing they're reading a national newspaper column essentially accusing Galway of losing the plot again. A column pretty much asking: 'Who the fuck do these lads think they are having just won one miserable League?'

I loved this because it only added to our siege mentality. It was fuel for my fire.

The truth of how we celebrated that League win? We went in to Supermac's next door to the Gaelic Grounds to get a group photo taken for our sponsor. And then most of us just went our separate ways.

My night was actually spent working in Camile Thai in Castletroy. Some of the family were in. A few supporters too. Nobody was dancing on tables.

22.

DELIVERANCE

J ust to be clear, we weren't different people in 2017. Nobody managed to magically rewrite our DNA.

We just got momentum and we kept it. Yes, a seam of anger ran through our hurling, and we probably needed that. There was maybe a degree more honesty about us too. Micheál consistently challenged us on every conceivable level, cultivating a culture of players taking ownership.

I mean, five years had passed since 2012 and a campaign in which we thought we'd got the 'softness' out of our systems.

And five years is an eternity in the life of an inter-county hurler.

The 2016 Leinster final was a watershed of sorts in that, finally, we stopped using management as some kind of human shield. But it didn't happen overnight. I don't for one second believe that winning the All-Ireland would have been possible without the groundwork Anthony Cunningham had put into us as a group. But we were only too happy to let him take the flak too whenever things went wrong. Micheál just wouldn't let us away with that now.

He'd toss problems straight back on us, pretty much saying: 'Go solve this.' Leadership groups had to be more than talking shops. They needed to achieve rather than simply question.

And I suppose winning writes its own history in the end.

Eleven of those who would start the 2017 All-Ireland final against Waterford also started that Division 1B League game against Wexford that unleashed such vitriol towards the team and management. Fourteen players who got game time in Salthill that day would go on to play and win on the biggest day of the hurling year.

So maybe you'll get where I'm coming from with my indifference towards much of the noise that surrounds an inter-county life. So many people just have too much to say about an environment they palpably don't understand.

For me, social media is the worst. In a lot of cases, it is an echo chamber of fake machismo; of lads trying to better one another with their often unintentionally hilarious stories from 'inside' one camp or another.

Unidentified voices can casually denigrate players in a way you know they'd never dream of doing if they ever happened to encounter the same player in real life. And that's the kind of noise that pisses me off. The ease with which lads who've clearly never hurled in their lives can be so dismissive of people putting their bodies on the line.

That February defeat to Wexford in Salthill accommodated an abundance of this stuff. We were 'flops', 'bottlers', 'imposters'. Take your pick.

The decent supporters will express disappointment without ever letting it descend into abuse. They were the ones you could be happy for in 2017. But in Galway particularly we have become all too familiar with supporters who'd be hugging you one weekend, then cutting the back off you the next if you were playing against their club. It's almost as if they switch personalities without even noticing.

Anyway, we won our second Leinster Championship with more than a little to spare, beating Dublin by 14 points; Offaly by 19 points and Wexford by nine.

Maybe we benefited from the fact that Wexford had taken

Kilkenny's scalp in the Leinster semi-final, but this wasn't exactly a classic Brian Cody team, and they were subsequently removed from the championship altogether by an extra-time All-Ireland qualifier defeat to Waterford.

We would have been hugely confident facing Wexford, albeit I hurt my knee at training in Athenry that Friday night. We'd been down one corner of the pitch, just doing these short, snappy drills when, suddenly, I felt unmerciful pain. Subsequent tests on the ligaments all proved negative, but it was clear I had a problem.

There's a picture of me walking across the field with the Bob O'Keeffe Cup in my hands after that Leinster final victory with ice strapped to my right knee. I'd played most of the game in a certain amount of discomfort and would be soon headed to the Sports Surgery Clinic in Santry for a cortisone injection to allow me to continue playing through the problem.

In Santry, Professor Cathal Moran told me that had I been nineteen he would have recommended major surgery on the knee. Put specifically, it was a tear in the cartilage of the kneecap with inflammation of the underlying bone. My age dictated that a programme of management was the preferred option, and I'd end up getting the knee scoped through keyhole surgery that November.

That settled the issue, but not completely. To this day, that knee still gives me grief, so much so that I can't train for two days after a training session, given the swelling and the fact that there's basically very little cartilage left.

Our Leinster final tally of 0–29 meant that we'd won the title scoring an average of 0–32 per game. We were picking scores from every conceivable angle and distance. Even though Offaly deployed two sweepers against us in the semi-final, we still managed to score almost at will. Confidence was soaring.

I had committed to doing an interview with the *Irish Independent* the week after that Wexford win, but agreed to their request to hold off until the week before the All-Ireland semi-final against Tipperary. I didn't have to, but it didn't seem that big a deal to me either.

This meant the interview appeared the day before that game.

I will admit that seeing its prominence in the newspaper did trigger a certain anxiety that Saturday morning. There's a natural paranoia to being overly visible in the media coming up to a big game, for no more logical reason than if you end up playing badly, you know exactly where the noise will be coming from. Namely, the usual suspects attributing your performance to the fact that you've been too busy talking to journalists. It's garbage, of course, but that's the thought process: *If we lose, and I have a poor game, this is going to be an easy stick to beat me with.*

The interview was probably the most extensive I'd ever given a journalist, reaching into just about every single aspect of my life. Stuff I'd never really spoken about before, such as my parents' health issues, the loss of the captaincy in 2015 and my discomfort with having a giant image of me plastered across one side of the Galway team bus.

I remember reading the piece that Saturday morning, and I suppose the natural instinct was to wonder if maybe I'd said too much?

But then a one-line text from Micheál managed to settle my anxiety: 'Great interview today!'

I'm not sure many Galway supporters would have been inclined to agree with him halfway through that subsequent semi-final as I struggled badly to have any impact. My free-taking was off and I just couldn't seem to work my way into a really tight contest.

Was the interview now playing on my mind going in at half-time? No, hand on heart, it never even crossed my mind. For me, it was more a case of: *how the fuck do I get into this, because that was absolutely brutal!*

Apparently, it was at this point that someone put up a post on the BenchWarmers forum, along the lines of 'Things that disappear when you need them most', accompanied by pictures of keys, a wallet, a phone and me. How do I know? My nephews and nieces see everything and aren't exactly gentle with me in how they recycle it.

The post was, I am told, deleted after the game.

So it's four minutes into injury time, the teams are level and – for some mysterious reason that I will never fully understand – Johnny Coen turns back towards me. Johnny's pass gives me a split second to settle and shoot from the toes of the Cusack Stand. There would be some pretty spectacular pictures of me turning away and looking back over my shoulder with a smile as I realised the ball was clearing Darren Gleeson's crossbar.

My eleventh point of the game was about to become the most celebrated of my career.

It's been almost forgotten that Tipp still had a last-gasp chance to bring the game to a replay, but Bubbles O'Dwyer's shot tailed off wide. For three successive seasons, there'd been a single point between Galway and Tipp in the All-Ireland championship. This win put us two-one ahead in the split.

I sometimes wonder if fate always finds a way of balancing the books. When I scored that late line cut during our League game against Tipp in 2016, it looked as if we'd won an important two points. But it was Bubbles who got the late equaliser, pitching us into a relegation battle that we'd ultimately lose.

Similarly, what worked for Cathal Mannion in the League final also worked for me this time when I moved to wing forward in the second half. We had expected that there would be space in front of Pádraic Maher, and so it proved with me getting three points from play off that wing in the final quarter. Small margins but big success. Was this history rhyming?

There was a huge sense of satisfaction now that we'd shown the character to win a game of such intensity against the defending All-Ireland champions. But then, three days later, it was as if a bomb went off within Galway GAA with the shocking news that Tony Keady had passed away suddenly at the age of just fifty-three.

It's one of those moments that completely stops you in your tracks, similar to 2013 when hearing of Niall Donoghue's suicide.

Tony was a larger-than-life figure for anybody associated with Galway hurling, probably the best centre back in the country during the late '80s as Cyril Farrell's team went toe-to-toe with Babs Keating's Tipperary. But he was also this hugely human, easy-going character who never played the fame game. He would have been a regular presence at schools matches during my early hurling years, and over time, I'd gotten to know him – admittedly, on an superficial level.

His funeral would be one of the biggest ever seen in the GAA with people queuing for hours to pay their respects to Margaret and the children. If people were in shock generally, the impact on his teammates from the All-Ireland wins of 1987 and 1988 was vivid in their expressions.

To put it mildly, his death washed away any giddiness about Galway having reached the All-Ireland final. For those few days, as the county prepared to bury one of its greatest men, the final got little enough traction in conversations.

In any event, we had a month to prepare for that game, and the following Saturday, after training in Galway, Davy Burke, Johnny Glynn, Darby and myself headed to Dublin to take in the following day's semi-final between Waterford and Cork.

We stayed in Jury's Croke Park Hotel and the plan was a quiet dinner down in Temple Bar, then back to the hotel for an early night.

On our way across the Ha'penny Bridge, the inevitable words 'Sure, we'll go for one!' set in train a night on the beer that left the four of us in rag order for Croke Park the following day. In fairness, we still had three weeks to the final, and it was obvious that whoever won the Waterford–Cork game would themselves, most likely, be celebrating that Monday.

But it wasn't really in the script and anybody chatting to us at the game would, I suspect, have known instantly that we were hungover. Myself and Davy Burke were in one corporate box, Darby and Johnny in another.

Naturally, the whole management team was up for the game too, and having met them outside the stadium, we reckoned we'd delivered Oscar-level performances of group sobriety. But who were we fooling?

Micheál said it to us afterwards: 'Sure, I knew well looking at the cut of ye!'

This had been a big blow-out, but smaller ones were commonplace, harmless enough events that would, momentarily, help you escape from the almost robotic discipline of an inter-county life. I remember the same four of us stopping off in Killeen's of Shannonbridge on our way back from a League game in Wexford. Just a pint each, but you wouldn't believe the sense of freedom that simple act would give you.

Sometimes, there would be blow-outs with consequences, though, and a couple of times Micheál would have dropped lads from the starting 15 as a result. It was never a big deal within the panel. If anything, it just fed training-ground banter.

You need to come up for air in that environment, because if you don't, it can suffocate you. You also need to find levity in bad moments.

James Skehill lost sight of a ball in the sun during our final round-robin game in the 2018 Leinster Championship against

Dublin in Salthill, conceding a goal in the process. Luckily, we managed to win by a point, and that night, Johnny Glynn arrived into the bar wearing sunglasses, which he duly kept flicking up and down on his nose.

Harmless stuff really, but you'd be surprised by the craic we'd take from a little ribbing like that. Needless to say, Skehill was more than well able to take it.

When Waterford won through to the final, I have to say it strengthened our confidence that this, finally, was going to be our moment. True, Galway's championship record against them was atrocious. We'd never beaten Waterford in 10 previous championship meetings, but that kind of history felt immaterial now. After all, we'd backed up our National League win by claiming Leinster, and then overcoming Tipp in precisely the kind of game a so-called 'flaky' team could never win.

Yes, there was pressure bearing down on us, given Galway hadn't won since 1988. But Waterford were trying to bridge a gap all the way back to their heroes of 1959. If anything, the weight of history had to be heavier on them.

There would be a lot of talk of honouring Tony Keady's memory, which was only appropriate, but if I'm honest, that kind of thing finds a kind of abstract presence in the build-up to a big game.

This was something we had to fundamentally do for ourselves.

Time slows to a glacially slow dawdle when you are a player on All-Ireland final weekend. Killing it becomes the preoccupation. That and avoiding contact with anybody who might say something that deposits even the faintest negative in your head.

As I was sharing a house in Oranmore now with Burkey, Darby and Johnny, my family was, at least, spared the routine of dancing on eggshells around my reflex irritability. With all four housemates in the same headspace, we were comfortable around one another.

I'm pretty sure Johnny went home to Ardrahan that Saturday, but one of the Galway S&C team, Brendan Egan, was staying with us too, and we passed the time that afternoon in the kitchen with Brendan, who was roughly the same age as us, taking out his calipers and measuring our body fats. I still have the readings on my phone: Darby, 12.7 per cent; me, 11.5 per cent; Burkey, 10.6 per cent and Brendan 11.7 per cent.

We were in the shape of our lives.

At some stage in the afternoon, Burkey and I went up to what we reckoned would be the quietest pitch at Maree for a few pucks. Just as we were finishing up, he looked at me with a face full of anxiety, announcing, 'Jesus, I'm feeling awful weak. Think I need some sugar!' Not sure a nutritionist would have approved of our solution – a can of Coke and bags of sweets – to get the Galway captain back on an even keel. But given how he'd perform (Man of the Match) the following day, it clearly worked.

Nerves can play tricks on you in this way, essentially giving your metabolism mood swings.

That evening, Burkey and I walked down to evening Mass, hanging as inconspicuously as we could at the back of the church before the four of us from the house then went down the town for some pasta. After that, it was basically a countdown to bed. I'm not sure if we had *Up for the Match* on the TV, but if we had, it would only have been a kind of background music. By now, you are just impatient for the day itself. Hungry for the game.

Sleep came a little stubbornly, and as always, I was awake before the alarm, struggling to put away a bowl of creamy porridge before heading across to the nearby Maldron Hotel to catch the bus.

We had a stop in Ballinasloe, then on to the Carton House Hotel in Maynooth. As always, I sat down the back of the bus with the likes of Burkey and Skehill; others like Darby, Aidan

Harte and Joey Cooney never far away. That part of the journey was giddy, light-hearted. The more serious boys were up the front, management among them. Some reading newspapers. Some just sitting alone with their own thoughts. At this point, everything is about keeping the mind free of clutter.

I've always been a bit of a hard sell when it comes to sports psychology: not quite antagonistic, but routinely sceptical.

Throughout my career with Galway, I think we had eight different people with us in that capacity, and honestly, the only one I felt I had a connection with was probably the most unorthodox.

Ciaran Cosgrave – whose late dad, Liam, was the former taoiseach – was what I would describe as an extrovert in the field. He was a maverick, a storyteller, a character.

Micheál brought him into our bubble in 2017, and I suppose how that season ended identifies him instantly as a success. But I've never thought of it as being that simple.

Ciaran would tell us about his work with the highest level of clients, stories about involvement with people like Michael Jordan, with the LA Lakers and Manchester City FC. Hand on heart, we sometimes wondered if he was simply making stuff up to impress us.

He liked to wear this T-shirt with the message 'No off-switch' emblazoned across the front. Darby would take the piss out of him for that, routinely wandering over to Ciaran before the start of a session and pretending to flick an off-switch.

It's hard to put my finger on why I connected with Ciaran more than others. I mean, we also worked with Enda McNulty, Kieran Shannon, Gerry Hussey – all very well-respected people. But on a personal level, I just never really got what they were giving us. Dr Ciara Losty also came in for half a year in 2019, and I did find her quite good.

But of them all, Ciaran was the one I liked, the only one I

really connected with. I have this vivid memory of the day of the 2017 All-Ireland final against Waterford: Darby and myself sitting on the floor in this big function room in Carton House, and Ciaran talking to us about anything and everything. We were maybe little more than two hours out from the game, but Ciaran had Davy and me so relaxed it felt as if we had nothing unduly important ahead of us that day.

Was this intentional? Probably. The thing with Ciaran was that you never actually felt he was following any particular psychology manual. He just knew how to connect with people. How to rinse away pressure.

Others would have come in and done a lot of 'touch the white fence' kind of stuff. They'd have us wearing bands and going through power points. All the conventional stuff you'd become accustomed to with performance coaches. Stuff that never really clicked with me.

But Ciaran told stories. Just chatted.

Somehow, that approach always suited me better. We'd sometimes wonder among ourselves if there was ever actually a real line of psychological logic behind all the conversations or was he simply winging it? To this day, I couldn't honestly answer.

But the big thing for me was that I liked having him around the place. He knew how to relax people in an environment where that wasn't easily achieved.

And in some respects, I suppose the most important sports psychologist I had throughout my hurling career was probably my own brother, Frank.

But that day in Carton House, lads getting physio and doing stretches all around us, my memory is of Ciaran talking about his connections with Nike. They sponsored Chelsea at the time, and he was promising to get me a signed jersey for one of my nephews who was big into the club.

Not once was there mention of the game ahead. It felt perfect.

Because everything finds an almost militaristic precision for players at that point of an All-Ireland Sunday. You've been given the timetable on a group WhatsApp. There's little enough room for spontaneity.

I've always struggled with the pre-match meal, a culinary cliché of pasta and chicken and maybe some sweet potato that is strictly about fuelling up now. Maybe the alternative or supplementary option of a smoothie. I've often looked at some players horsing the pasta into them at that moment and wondered how the hell they do it.

Then a quick meeting before we left the hotel, Micheál reiterating the game plan. Everything still calm and measured. Five minutes of talking – no more – before getting back onto what feels like an entirely different bus.

People much quieter now. The vibe suddenly way more serious.

Down the back, Hartey had these giant headphones on, his music turned up so loud we could all hear it. Wild, throbbing anthems. God help those poor eardrums.

We came in along the Navan Road, a garda escort easing us through red lights. The sirens getting heads to turn. Grins from the crowded pavements. Gestures. Then the ribbed grey outline of the stadium. The bus slowing.

The height of the Galway bus meant negotiating the tight entrance under the Cusack Stand rather than swinging in directly under the Hogan, and I was always quietly mesmerised by the driver's precision. To me, the bus never quite looked like it would fit. But it always did.

Then the bags were loaded onto buggies, and we walked back across, under the Canal End part of the stadium towards the Hogan dressing rooms, the sounds of the crowd hissing above our heads, Galway and Cork already underway in the minor showpiece.

The dressing room is an oasis in one sense, a holding cell in another. Nerves and impatience feed anxiety.

And there's one truly bizarre aspect to the day that maybe only the GAA can explain. At half-time in the minor game, you are allowed onto the field just to get a feel of things. To read the wind. But you are barred from bringing your hurls out with you. Even if it's just to sit in the toes of the stand and soak up the atmosphere, your hurl is all but deemed an offensive weapon. Why? Not a clue.

It happened in Páirc Uí Chaoimh this year, the day Cork played Limerick in the Munster round-robin. There was a photograph taken of a steward blocking the path of Patrick Horgan as he tried to step onto the field with his hurl. Yes, the same Patrick who'd play out of his skin in a famous Cork win that day.

This is the kind of thing that exasperates me about the GAA.

I was genuinely delighted that Leinster got to play their Champions Cup semi-final against Northampton in Croke Park last May. As a GAA man, I'm proud of the stadium and only too happy to have it shown to the outside world. But it made my blood absolutely boil to see images of Courtney Lawes and other Northampton players messing around with hurls on the field the day before that game when that right is casually denied to hurlers on the biggest day of our year. Not because I thought the rugby players were doing anything out of the ordinary. They weren't. But because they were indulged something that the GAA denies its own stars literally an hour before they become the centrepiece of hurling's biggest day.

To me, this rule is stone-cold ridiculous. It speaks of nothing more than a lack of respect for its own people. Sometimes, the GAA really lets itself down with stupid stuff. And that's about as stupid as it gets.

Back inside the dressing room that day, I remember getting

this sick sense in my stomach. Not a nice feeling. Suddenly, I started to experience a kind of heavy fatigue, feeling incredibly tired. At one point, I was almost panicking. *Fuck, what's wrong with me? I've no energy!* The exact same thing that happened to Burkey in Maree the day before was happening to me now. Nerves had me in a vice grip.

You know you're in the best shape of your life, but your brain threatens to override that fact. There's a lethargy in your system. You have to just stay calm at that moment and wait for the feeling to lift. Sometimes that only happens when you're out there. When the sliotar is thrown in.

It's your mind setting traps. You need to just get out of there.

Funny, you often see lads yawning in a dressing room at that moment. But no matter how wrecked you find yourself feeling, you keep it to yourself now. No room for negatives here. You can't exactly turn to the lad beside you and say, 'I'm feeling terrible.'

It was almost a relief when Burkey and Micheál made their speeches. Short, high-octane stuff. All year, Micheál's message had been consistent and insistent: 'Enough is enough. No more excuses!'

It was decided that I'd start at wing forward, given the middle had been so congested against Tipp in the semi-final. Philip Mahony was my marker, but virtually my first touch inside 18 seconds brought a point, and for me, that was massive.

Pretty quickly I got into the flow of the game. We all did, really. It felt as if we were a team full of confidence.

People say to me now that we never looked like losing that final, but you never feel that comfort on the field. When a goal can change everything, you are forever wary, anxious, fearful.

We were 0–4 to 0–0 ahead when Kevin Moran got that fifth minute Hill-end goal, and suddenly, you're reminded that nothing's to be taken for granted here. We were three points up when a twenty-first minute Kieran Bennett delivery found its way to the net, and I remember wheeling away at that moment, thinking: *Fucking disaster!*

Both goals felt soft from our point of view. We were doing most of the hurling, but we just weren't getting clear.

I do remember a moment, though, in the second half, the momentum with Waterford and their crowd rising, when Kevin Moran hit a poor wide for them from just 30 yards out on the left wing. That gave us a bit of a lift. You could almost hear their groans as the umpire waved it wide.

It would be one of those games where the impact off our bench – people like Niall Burke and Jason Flynn – would prove vital. Maybe that was the story of our year. The fact that our starting 15 was constantly being pushed hard by those behind them.

This was something John Muldoon had articulated beautifully when Micheál brought him in earlier that year to speak to us. The idea that everybody had a crucial role to play, no matter the number on their jersey. Number two for any position needs to be pushing number one hard, while he himself is being pushed by number three. That really registered, and our in-house games pretty much reflected it all year. There was a constant edge to them. The match-day 26 was endlessly changing.

So when did I feel the wait was finally over?

Not until right at the death, not until Stephen O'Keeffe inexplicably hit Waterford's last free no more than 60 yards down the wing to Austin Gleeson when you're thinking they're surely going to fast-track the ball down on top of our 'square' here. To see that free go short was a huge relief, and when the ball eventually went out over the Cusack Stand sideline, I knew, as I went over to retrieve it, that we were surely safe now.

Then you hear the whistle, and it's this almost convulsive release of a pressure valve. You lose all sense of adult self-awareness for those few seconds, jumping around the place as if your body's overloaded with electricity.

But the best moment was tracking down Mam and Dad in the Hogan Stand lower tier and just losing myself in their tight embrace. The most private of acts between the three of us carried out in the full glare of public view. Photographers everywhere. Maybe it's a contradiction in terms because the image instantly becomes public property. But it's no less special for all that.

Mam and Dad had been with me through every single step of the journey and knew just how hard it had been to get to this day. They'd brushed aside my moods, the irritability with which I'd routinely meet their questions during game week. They just backed me in the unequivocal way that only parents can.

But there was the added dimension now of my nephew Jack winning a minor medal the same day. Both uncle and nephew in the winners' enclosure. This had to feel incredibly special for the family, given how long we'd hoped that Ollie and I might win an All-Ireland together. That of course never came to pass. As a family, we knew all too well how hard it was to get these big days to co-operate.

After that, I just stood on the pitch alongside Micheál, watching Burkey and the boys climb those steps up to the promised land. It just felt natural to stay down there. I've never really been drawn to the idea of climbing those steps. Even after trophy wins with minor, under-21 or club, my preference was not to go up. I made an exception after the 2006 All-Ireland Club final only because I got the Man of the Match award that day and had no option but to collect it.

In a strange way, the cup was almost irrelevant to me at that moment. I mean, I knew I'd get my hands on it eventually. Seeing Mam and Dad had been my one and only priority. Once that was done, just standing out there on the field was exactly where I wanted to be.

And out of nowhere, Margaret and Shannon Keady materialised beside us. It was lovely to have them there, the pain of Tony's passing still so incredibly raw for the whole family. If it brought them a few seconds of comfort – and I don't doubt it was nothing much more than that at such a difficult time – then I'm really glad I could be a part of that.

A lot was made afterwards of my decision to stay standing there – far too much in fact. But I just did what felt entirely natural.

After that, the day fell away into a noisy, congested blur.

There's a lovely privacy to the dressing room when you get back in: just management and players, soaking up the moment. Then it was up to the players' lounge where the bar stays open for what feels like less than an hour, when you'd quite like to stay there for the evening. The Waterford players couldn't have been sounder in that environment, and I like to think we were respectful of their emotions, having ourselves been on that side of things on final day in 2012 and 2015.

We'd actually meet again the following January when our respective team holidays brought us to Cancún at the same time. To a man, they were fundamentally decent. Likewise Derek McGrath, their manager. I have to say Waterford couldn't have been more dignified in defeat.

There must have been something close to 2,000 people back in Citywest when we got there, and it was chaos. Sitting for the meal was grand, but the moment you tried to leave the table, it was just a wall of people, all seeking a little of your time. Everybody pulling and dragging, chasing photos.

I can absolutely see why an All-Ireland winner's evening becomes a little unhinged. It's not just the team's victory, after all; it's your county's moment. People who had followed Galway through thick and thin since our last All-Ireland victory in 1988 were now fully entitled to seek out their heroes and look for a little time.

The trouble is, it ends up suffocating you. What you want more than anything at that moment is the company of your teammates and family. The opportunity to just quietly savour finally achieving the goal you've committed to for so much of your life. But you can't get to them. You can't even see them. The evening becomes this blur of people coming at you. I don't want to sound disrespectful. It was their day as much as ours. But I ended up that night feeling something entirely different to what I imagined I would feel.

I ended up agitated, irritated, desperate to escape. And around 1 a.m., that's precisely what I did. Up the stairs and into the calm privacy of my bedroom. An oasis of normality. The day we'd dreamed of had finally arrived. Yet I was almost in a hurry now to turn out the light.

Videos of the homecoming still give me goosebumps to this day, even if my proposal that we should cross the Shannon in Portumna was ignored. I was being mischievous to a point, knowing that the traditional route home was always through Athlone and Ballinasloe. But my contrary Portumna head would have liked nothing more than crossing the bridge in my hometown.

A bridge that, for me, will always symbolise our sense of independence.

God, how I'd have loved getting off the bus in North Tipp with the Liam MacCarthy Cup in my hands and marching into Galway. Deep down, I knew my proposal wouldn't get much traction, and honestly, it wasn't far removed from being tongue-in-cheek. Just a gentle Sunday evening comment to Micheál that drew a smile. But then if he'd shown even the slightest inclination of entertaining it …

We'd done the traditional visit to Our Lady's Children's Hospital, Crumlin, that morning, some of the lads still absolutely hanging from the night before. Maybe 10 of us in a minibus, players and management, fulfilling one of the better traditions of an All-Ireland Monday.

On the way back out to Citywest, we stopped for a few lovely, quiet pints in Eleanora's in Walkinstown, the few locals there clearly indifferent to the giddy blow-ins now temporarily in their midst. Then back to gather our things in a hotel still utterly swamped with a community of ruined, euphoric people.

The first bonfires would be seen in Athlone, and it was genuinely touching to encounter the support welcoming us back with the cup through counties Westmeath and Roscommon. The crowd around Duggan Park in Ballinasloe was absolutely wild, stretching all the way up the hill to the church as far as the eye could see. And for all of us, one of the most powerful images was of Micheál getting off the bus to meet his ailing dad, Miko.

Around the time Micheál was getting the Galway job, Miko had been diagnosed with dementia. A staunch GAA man who drove the victorious Galway teams of 1980, 1987 and 1988 home, he was now confined to a wheelchair. The disease was taking him further and further away from his family, but you could absolutely see the recognition in his eyes when his son now came to him with the cup. I know that Micheál said afterwards he'd have preferred that moment to have played out in a more private setting, but God, it was hugely powerful for us all to see.

There's a famous Morgan Treacy photo of the moment they embrace, and I'm not sure any other single snapshot captures the emotional power of what Galway's win meant to our own people than that image. In a sense, it spoke to us too of just how driven Micheál had been to make this happen.

For me, Ballinasloe was full of familiar East Galway faces,

certainly much more so than Pearse Stadium. But I look at photos of Salthill from that evening, and the sheer size of the crowd is breathtaking. Galway city isn't strictly a hurling city, but the stand and pitch were absolutely swamped with people.

The great Paulie Fla – Paul Flaherty – would do his Luke Kelly thing on stage, but there is one image from that evening that really jarred with me.

The teams, minor and senior, were brought in through the Knocknacarra end to a stage set up just in front of the goals. Traditionally, it's the winning captain that then brings the cup on stage, but the minor manager, Jeff Lynskey, decided that he would do it instead.

I was not impressed when I saw it.

For me, Darren Morrissey, the minor captain, should have had that moment. I mean, there was never any question about who would bring the Liam MacCarthy Cup out that evening. That was the job of our captain, Burkey. Nobody else's. Micheál would never have countenanced taking that moment from him. Not for a second.

I just thought it was bad form for Lynskey to deny a young fella this once-in-a-lifetime opportunity. It shouldn't have happened. That just stuck with me.

Paulie Fla's rendition of 'The West's Awake' inevitably rekindled memories of Joe McDonagh singing it from the Hogan Stand steps in 1980, an image we'd all grown up with. Honestly, it was gorgeous.

After that, the week is a blur. Tony Keady was remembered that Thursday with an exhibition game between us and the team of 1988, on which he'd been such a charismatic presence. Again, the crowd was massive – borderline suffocating.

And after that, we drank and we sang and we hugged for what felt like an eternity.

The cup would go on a county-wide safari, and being honest, I maybe have a slight regret today that I didn't immerse myself more deeply in that. I'm not the most comfortable in those situations, and so I broadly did what I had to do, and – in the case of Gortanumera – what I really wanted to do.

But hearing the stories after of the fun that was had bringing the cup to Connemara, I had a certain regret that I didn't experience it. Burkey and our kit man, Tex, took it to Ashford Castle. People might not know that the castle itself is in Galway, but the lodge you drive past into the castle grounds is in Mayo. Burkey and Tex were given a bagpipe procession across the bridge over the Corrib into Galway, where it seemed the entire hotel staff came out to applaud them home.

I was sorry I missed that. Sorry I missed a few others too.

Micheál emphasised strongly the need for us to carry ourselves properly as winners. Even when we weren't physically wearing the jersey, we were still Galway hurlers. We were still representing our communities.

And I like to think we did that. I like to think that we were good All-Ireland champions.

23.

ONE THAT GOT AWAY

I n my head, 2018 will always be an All-Ireland that slipped through our fingers.

If anything, we hurled better than we had when winning the crown, but we found a capacity for self-sabotage that just kept mining the road beneath our feet. We were certainly good enough to become back-to-back champions, and our failure to do so had a two-pronged consequence.

Firstly, it armed our doubters with fresh impetus to be abusive. Secondly, it gave Limerick a final push to freedom from the ghosts of their past. Their first All-Ireland win since 1973 lifted a huge weight off Limerick chests – as the rest of us have seen since. Maybe it even created a monster. If so, in Galway we will always feel partly culpable for that creation.

All year we seemed to be giving our opponents a leg-up in games just when we should have been going in for the kill. We acquired the habit of squandering big leads and conceding soft goals. It was as if we weren't sufficiently street-wise, or maybe more accurately, cynical.

I missed most of a National League campaign in which defeat by two points to Limerick in Salthill meant we lost out on the opportunity to bounce out of Division 1B. Maybe that game meant more to them than it did to us, as they'd been trying for promotion since 2010.

Some of their players would talk later of the belief it gave them, coming away with victory from the home of the All-Ireland champions. If I'm honest, I didn't see them at the time as a team we'd be hearing too much of that summer. I don't think any of us did.

We lost a subsequent quarter-final to Wexford, but then duly won all four of our round-robin Leinster Championship games to make the provincial final against Kilkenny. It would take us a replay in Thurles to win that, and it's fair to say that we did our damnedest to make a mess of it.

Eleven points up after just 19 minutes, we ended up conceding three goals that were all of a soft variety. The third of them, scored by Richie Hogan in the fifty-fifth minute, brought the margin down to a single point. All the momentum with our opponents now, we dug really deep then to outscore them 0–8 to 0–2 through the remainder.

In fact, those two Kilkenny points were both from T.J. Reid frees, meaning we'd held them scoreless from play through the closing 15 minutes. On one level, that spoke of the character and confidence building within the group. But, on another, it left us questioning how on earth we could keep losing our footing in games.

We needed two contests to see off Clare in the All-Ireland semi-final too, building up nine point leads both days, but ultimately, ending up in absolute dog fights.

Again, the concession of sloppy goals threatened to be our undoing.

In the Thurles replay, Shane O'Donnell waltzed through our defence for a Killinan-end goal when there had been at least three opportunities to stop him with the concession of a free. It was the kind of goal that Cody's Kilkenny never conceded.

Peter Duggan got a soft enough one too, and we might well have been evicted from the championship but for Aron Shanagher's sixty-eighth minute effort rebounding off a post after his initial effort had been parried by James Skehill.

Seconds later, I managed to convert a line cut from under the Ryan Stand, but even then, Duggan had a virtual shank from a Clare free that could have tied up the scores. Then, with almost the final act of the game, Tony Kelly overhit a delivery aimed for Shanagher on the edge of the square, and so – courtesy of 19 Clare wides – we were back in the All-Ireland final.

It was our thirteenth championship game without defeat, a statistic that would have been unimaginable in our recent history. One that spoke of a team that, character-wise, could be depended upon.

But we needed to stop leaking goals … and that's where Limerick got their kick-start.

Because we didn't stop that leakage, conceding another three in the final to leave us trailing by eight points with two minutes of normal time remaining. The third of those goals, scored by substitute Shane Dowling in the sixty-eighth minute, was a perfect example of our defensive vulnerability.

Peter Casey got a block in, cut inside, and though his attempted pass was mishit, a virtually unmarked Dowling still had the time to lift and pick his spot into the far corner of the Hill-end goal.

The game was effectively over at that moment, but then, during eight minutes of added time, Conor Whelan got a goal, and I managed to bury a 20-metre free to leave us just a single point adrift as I stood over that last free about 100 yards out from the Canal End goal.

I speak elsewhere of my regrets over how I struck that free, the ball dropping into the hand of Tom Condon, who came charging out to arguably the loudest roar ever heard in Croke Park.

Basically, I swung too hard. And swinging too hard meant I lost distance rather than gained it.

I often think how Limerick were still a fundamentally brittle team back then, displaying absolutely zero indication of the dominant force they were about to become.

In my head, we gave them a vital leg-up, and it's fair to say that they've hardly taken a backward glance since. Our capacity for self-sabotage got in the way of what might very easily have been a successful All-Ireland defence.

And it left us facing into a long winter of regrets.

24.

BOARD GAMES

For Micheál, the end came in 2019 with a sucker-punch that none of us saw coming.

Out of a blizzard of contradictory rumours of how things had finished in Wexford Park, we finally got confirmation of a draw between Wexford and Kilkenny. To begin with, the implications of that news didn't even entirely register.

In a Parnell Park dressing room, we were still wrestling with the immediacy of defeat to Dublin. Then someone asked, 'What does that mean? Are we out?'

The question, suddenly, caught collective attention, almost as an after-thought. One week earlier, we'd beaten Kilkenny in Nowlan Park, the idea gathering steam that we could be serious players in this championship. I had wanted to play in that game, but the physios continued to frustrate me with their advice to be patient.

I'd trained fully the week before and was hungry to get going now. But why risk it?

We were playing a long-term game here. Almost three months after damaging my groin in a National League semi-final defeat to Waterford, my return to action would be held back for probably my least-favourite venue in hurling.

To me, Parnell Park was a place to be endured. It always had a claustrophobic feel to me, a sloping pitch that felt deceptively tight, and a surface routinely speckled with the shit of seagulls.

On top of all that, a crowd you knew would be mouthy and reliably hostile.

I hated the place just as, I don't doubt, plenty of players from other counties hate the wind and salty showers of Salthill. But hating it never equated to a sense of fear, and I couldn't wait to get on the field that June day. There were roughly 20 minutes remaining when I was sent on for Adrian Tuohy, the game tight and still clearly in the melting pot.

I felt good. I scored two points from play and began savouring the feeling of simply running freely again. But as each minute passed without us pushing clear, Dublin became increasingly emboldened. Then, three minutes from the end of normal time, Chris Crummey's goal sent the place into orbit. The score sickened us, and we just couldn't recover. They beat us by four points.

The realisation that four counties had finished on five points, and that survival in the championship would now come down to scoring difference came swinging at us like a wrecking-ball. What that meant was that our failure to beat Carlow by more than six points in our opening game was about to cost us dear, Colm Bonnar's team subsequently going down by 14 points to Kilkenny, 12 to Dublin and 15 to Wexford.

But we'd spurned a seven points lead to end up drawing with Wexford in Salthill too. Self-harm had left us in this predicament.

I have a vivid memory of the dressing room suddenly going quiet, everyone now in shock as somebody mumbled, 'Fuck, I think we're gone!'

We'd had an unconvincing League, drawing with Carlow in Carlow, losing a 10-point lead to go down against Waterford in Walsh Park, then coming up short against the same opponents a fortnight later in a semi-final that I left on a stretcher.

We'd gone almost half an hour that day without raising a solitary flag to lose control, and I was basically on a retrieval mission, running in on goal a minute from the end of normal time when Kevin Moran's jostle caught me off balance, and I landed shoulder-first onto the Nowlan Park grass.

I could feel the tear in my groin immediately.

It looked like an unremarkable collision, but I knew instinctively that I was in trouble now. People said afterwards that they were surprised I didn't get up straight away, but for me, my season was now over. That's how bad this felt.

After a delay, I was stretchered to the dressing room, and I remember Ivan coming in after asking, 'What's the story?' He got his answer from the tears streaming down my face.

It was quickly established that I needed surgery, a full recovery from which would take between 14 and 16 weeks. My old friend Professor James Harty duly met me in Cork University Hospital with the tongue-in-cheek welcome, 'I thought I told you I didn't want to see you here again.'

But beyond the levity, there was an understanding that this wouldn't be simple now. A urologist had to sit in on the surgery, because the tendon being operated on was so close to a tube carrying sperm. He had to make sure nothing was inadvertently clipped that might impact my ability to be a father.

But my only focus was hurling – the thought of having children still feeling a million miles away.

Post-surgery, I had to sleep for a time with my legs tied together as a sudden movement risked tearing the stitches open.

I injured my groin on the other side in a club match in 2021, the first game I played after bowing out as an inter-county player. Picked up a ball, went to turn to my left, and my right foot got caught in the ground. I felt the tear and knew straight away what I'd done.

There's obviously some kind of weakness there, possibly related to the fact that I've always had tight hips. Anyway, in this instance, I chose not to have surgery as the injury meant I was already gone for the entire club championship.

Looking back now, I honestly believe that if we'd survived the Leinster cull, Galway could have had a right crack at the 2019 All-Ireland. But Parnell Park proved our endgame, and soon enough, Micheál announced that he was stepping down.

I didn't see that coming. None of us really did.

We all knew that he'd had a pretty fraught relationship with the county board, but it wasn't something he ever brought to bear in the dressing room. His attitude – rightly – was that we didn't need to know about it.

But we did know. Too much had gone on around us for us not to be aware. Stupid stuff.

Like us turning up for training in Ballinasloe one night only to have to climb in over locked gates. We were aware too that management were having to access their own business contacts to fund various training camps. There was a sense, at times, of the board almost actively putting obstacles in the way of success for the team.

During his time at the helm, Micheál certainly found himself at odds with people seemingly blind to the tools required for creating a high-performance environment. Generally, he kept that frustration to himself, but there was little doubt in most of our minds that that decision to go now had as much to do with levels of exasperation in that regard as it had to do with our disappointments on the field.

Just four months after his departure, a loss of over €250,000 would be revealed in the county board accounts, compared to a surplus of almost €400,000 the previous year.

Incoming Treasurer, Mike Burke, was horrified to discover what was termed 'serious abuse' of the Galway GAA credit card for personal expenses and the accrual of almost €500,000 in ticket debt. In 2018, an independent audit of Galway GAA, conducted by the international auditing and corporate finance company Mazars, had identified major governance deficiencies. One of the most glaring facts to emerge was that in November of that year, Galway GAA paid €390,000 to Croke Park for ticket money still owed from the 2015 All-Ireland final.

All of this now was on top of the abandoned Mountain South project for a once-planned Centre of Excellence near Athenry. This was described by Burke as 'a financial disaster' that would come in with an eventual cost in the region of €3,000,000.

That, then, was the environment we were trying to build success from. One in which it was exasperating even trying to deal with these people. I had my own experience of it in July 2020 when I got a straight red card in a televised county championship group game against Sarsfields for allegedly pulling off the helmet of their captain, and former Galway player, Kevin Hynes. It was a shocking decision that video evidence showed clearly had been wrong.

Basically, the two us fell wrestling to the ground, and on impact, his helmet came loose. Needless to say, Kevin got up, roaring for the referee to take action. And that's when everything got a little blurred. The ref claimed afterwards that it was a linesman's call. The linesman in question insisted it had been the ref's.

Anyway, video evidence showed it to have been wrong, and we subsequently got an email from the referee admitting as much with an apology. That email was copied to a prominent member of the Galway County Board.

The game had been televised live on TG4, and accordingly, the clip of me getting the line ran on that evening's RTÉ *Six One News*. I was absolutely disgusted. The following week, I had to go to a hearing to plead my case, and on my way to Loughgeorge, stopped off for diesel in Oranmore. At the petrol station, I met the board member copied in the referee's email.

He seemed to think my predicament hilarious. 'You're coming down to the hearing, are ya?' he said, with what I interpreted as a dismissive smirk. 'See ya down there so.'

It was clear as day to me that this fella didn't give a flying fuck for my sense of injustice. This was all just a game to him. Ivan, as club chairman, came to the meeting with me, and naturally, we instantly brought up the referee's email.

'What email are you on about? I didn't get any email!' this fella replied.

We could clearly see that he had been copied on the email.

'Is this your correct email address?' we asked. Confirming that it was, we suggested he check his inbox again. Then the return of that grin.

'Oh yeah, I have it here.'

To me, he was just laughing at us. We simply didn't matter.

By now, the board's financial scandal had been laid bare, and all of us were now familiar with the kind of stuff that ultimately pushed Micheál over the edge. Everything achieved in 2017 seemed to count for nothing with some of these people.

I'd gone to Micheál's home in Clarinbridge within 24 hours of his announcement, pretty much begging him to reconsider. As far as I was concerned, there wasn't a single member of the Galway panel that wanted him to go. At the time, his public stance was that family and work commitments were getting in the way.

But we knew he'd just grown sick of dealing with a dys-functional board.

We had loads of meetings trying to get him to change his mind, but he wasn't for turning. I remember then meeting Franny and Noel in St Raphael's school (where Franny teaches) one night, and it was clear that they both had the appetite to continue if Micheál could only be persuaded. It was also clear that they felt we, as players, now needed to take some kind of stand on the issue.

But how could we do that?

We'd made it clear we wanted the same management team to stay and said as much in meetings with the board. But the response we always got was: 'Sure we've no problem with Micheál either. We gave him everything he wanted.'

On some level, what had happened in 2015 left us in an invidious position now. Could we really justify another show of militancy given we weren't in a position to contradict anything the board was telling us?

In the absence of Micheál going public with his grievances, we couldn't really challenge them or contradict anything they were telling us. Sure, you can be militant if you feel in possession of all the facts. But we knew we didn't have that licence.

Micheál chose to keep his powder dry, and so over time, we realised that he simply wasn't coming back. Before long, Galway was awash with rumour of who the board might have approached to come in as his successor.

So to some degree, I decided to take the bull by the horns myself.

I pitched up in Sixmilebridge, arriving at Davy Fitzgerald's door with a pack of Jaffa Cakes and a bottle of MiWadi in a kind of light-hearted nod to the meeting that supposedly had turned Clare from beaten Munster championship dockets to All-Ireland champions in 2013.

Davy laughed when he saw me. We hadn't spoken in a while, because you don't when there's the possibility of coming up against one another in battle.

But he'd just had a cracking year as Wexford manager, leading them to a first Leinster title since 2004 and giving eventual champions, Tipperary, an awful fright in the All-Ireland semi-final.

I sensed Davy was interested in being Galway manager, but the Wexford lads were desperate to keep him too. We had over and back conversations on the phone for a few weeks with genuine enthusiasm among the Galway players for him to become our new manager.

Honestly, if he was up for it, I don't think county officials could, logically, have rejected the idea. But Davy eventually rang to confirm that he'd decided to stay put with Wexford. I was gutted. The search for our next manager was back in the hands of an, admittedly, now fast-changing board.

25.

PANDEMIC

The silent season didn't suit me. Just too much time alone.

When the need is there to endure pain, I struggle with my own company. Training alone disorients me. Always has done. Covid sold everybody a pup in the end, I suppose; not least Shane O'Neill – the Limerick man finally appointed Galway's new hurling manager three months after Micheál Donoghue's announcement that he was going.

Imagine trying to get to know the players in your care when suddenly denied the regular access of physically meeting them?

I think back on the strangeness of 2020 now with two conflicting emotions.

Firstly, I think of it in personal terms and a palpable sense of losing status within the Galway dressing room. There was a distinct shift of energy within the group now generally under Shane and his right-hand man, John Fitzgerald.

Determined to put their own stamp on things, they made clear a desire to identify a new leadership core within the squad. Put simply, players like Pádraic Mannion and Conor Whelan now had the kind of interaction with management that David Burke and I previously had with Micheál.

That took a little time to get used to.

It would have been routine for us to meet Micheál in the Claregalway Hotel before training in Loughgeorge so that he could identify the specific focus he wanted for that evening's session. Simple 'you need to point this out tonight' kind of stuff. He'd have used the likes of Johnny Glynn and Joseph Cooney in the same way. Just his means of getting the players to drive things on.

When Shane and John took over, I quickly got a sense that they were more interested in talking to other people now. And I'll admit that that required a certain psychological reset on my part.

You're used to feeling central to everything and having management's ear. Of feeling one of the group's leaders, in other words. Now you're just another player.

But the other emotion I have is a certain sympathy for the new men. I can only imagine just how difficult that season must have been for them, trying to keep the energy right with players they barely knew through Zoom sessions, monitoring individual videos and basically judging people on the sterile evidence of GPS readings.

For much of 2020, we weren't even entirely sure that there would be a championship at all.

I got injured less than an hour into our second League game against Limerick in the Gaelic Grounds. That was on 2 February, and my next competitive involvement with the team would be a 31 October Leinster semi-final against Wexford.

In between lay probably the weirdest nine months of my hurling career. Actually – make that of my life.

As the pandemic hit, everything shut down around mid-March, leaving players to maintain some level of personal fitness by training on their own. I absolutely hated it.

I've always taken energy from training within a group. Denied that now, I struggled badly, especially in trying to cope with the early, more penal restrictions.

As those eased a little through summer, I could at least go down to this big park beside Castletroy College with a playground and a soccer field and run personalised time-trials on a path around the perimeter. Some days, there'd be this little pod of Munster rugby players doing pretty much the same, guys I'd exchange a knowing nod with like Keith Earls, Jack O'Donoghue, Mike Haley and – on occasion – Conor Murray.

I remember one day seeing this lady videoing them as if she considered them guilty of some terrible crime, and next thing, the gardaí materialised. It's only looking back that you realise just how crazy everything became. These lads just doing runs out in an open field, and a woman feeling compelled to report them in the way of a modern-day Stasi official.

It was around this time too that the story broke of some Dublin footballers facing condemnation for doing a few runs on a field in Malahide. True, by the letter of the law, they shouldn't have been doing that. But I find myself wondering now do some people feel embarrassed on reflection by their militant reflex towards something as harmless as lads running around an open field. It strikes me now that we lived through a time of abject madness.

Another place I'd go to was one of Monaleen's pitches in Castletroy, a place called Peafield next to the ring road around the city. I managed to get the code for the gate, so I could drive the car in, park it as discreetly as I could and just do a bit of individual training on the field. As our S&C man, Lukasz, was living in Limerick too, he'd sometimes come and train with me.

Once restrictions allowed, we'd also use the FIT 100 gym on the Ballysimon Road, which is a training base for the Limerick hurlers too. Occasionally, we'd entertain ourselves by looking through the sign-in manual, identifying who and when specific members of John Kiely's panel had trained that day.

A few times, we even met them as we were leaving.

Apart from a diminished interaction with management, I suppose another change I took as a discouraging sign was their decision over time to move me out of centre forward, the position in which I always felt I could operate as the fulcrum of an attack.

As an 11, I saw my job as organising people, and generally, being vocal on the field. A lot of lads probably didn't like that side of me too much; and I'm sure plenty of opponents – not to mention referees – had days when they were thinking: *Jesus Christ, he never shuts up!*

I couldn't blame them, but that was the competitor in me. I was always comfortable organising those around me and felt I could do all of that from centre forward, where generally, I had the freedom to drift into pockets of space.

But Shane and John, I suspect, felt I didn't have it in me anymore. That first year with them, I was generally used on the wing, while in their second year, I would start at midfield and end up eventually planted inside at full forward.

Maybe, on some level, they were right. Given the unique circumstances of the year, I can't say I was feeling at my sharpest.

At the request of then Hurling Committee chairman (and soon to be new county board chairman), Paul Bellew, Burkey and I had met the new manager before his appointment was formalised, spending a couple of hours chatting to him in the Clare Inn, beside Dromoland Castle. He was basically picking our brains to get a sense of the players' perspective on where we felt we now stood as a group. One thing that struck me instantly was how similar a personality he was to the man he was replacing. Just like Micheál, he's a quiet, understated character. We were impressed.

There was a rumour at the time that approaches had been made to Henry Shefflin too, but that he considered it too soon to take on a county job with so many of his Ballyhale clubmates still central figures with Kilkenny.

Anyway, as we saw it: Shefflin as Galway manager? Pigs might fly!

When O'Neill was eventually confirmed, he named a strong backroom team of Fitzgerald and former Galway players, Fergal Healy and David Forde. He also kept on a lot of key dressing-room figures from Micheál's time, not least Lukasz.

In that Covid season, our championship would extend to four games played out in eerily empty grounds over the course of a single month. The weather was cold, the atmosphere surreal.

Having beaten Wexford comfortably, we lost yet another Leinster final to Kilkenny, having seemed in control until a moment of wizardry from Richie Hogan brought a Canal End goal followed instantly by another from T.J. Reid. In roughly 60 seconds, we'd gone from five up to one down and never recovered.

Then we looked to be labouring in an All-Ireland quarter-final against Tipperary in Limerick until their defender, Cathal Barrett, got the line for a second yellow. From six points down, we rallied to win by two.

We remained a team inclined to hurl only in moments.

Looking back now, even at this remove, I'm still not entirely sure how to frame our subsequent All-Ireland semi-final against O'Neill's native Limerick. The 2018 champions had been sucker-punched by Kilkenny one year later, but had come through Munster now, putting up big scoring totals of 0–36, 3–23 and 0–25 in their three games.

But this championship was being played out now in a virtually silent vacuum. On so many levels, it struggled to feel real.

A score would be greeted by training-ground acoustics, maybe 30 voices at a time instead of what might in normal circumstances have been 60,000. And that absence of sound seemed to transfer into an absence of palpable momentum for either team. It felt as if we were just treading water at times. Working but not moving.

The game? We played with a sweeper (Pádraic Mannion), and it was a kind of stalemate in many ways, both teams just picking scores from distance, like prize fighters feeling one another out.

I find it incredible to think that the sides were still level at the end of normal time, because if I'm honest, while we were always in it on the scoreboard, I'm not sure I ever felt that we were going to win.

By then, of course, I was already in the dressing room, having been stretchered off just moments earlier after an accidental collision with my teammate, Joseph Cooney.

I've no actual memory of the collision, but watching it back, I'm trying to flick the ball back over Kyle Hayes when Joey gets a nudge from someone and ends up barrelling into me. I do remember coming round in the doctor's room and asking to know the score, but nobody seemed quite sure. I was actually hoping it might end in a draw, and I'd get another chance, but then the news arrived as I was being put into the ambulance.

Another championship gone.

I had played wing forward, and without pulling up any trees, my contribution of four sideline cuts and eight frees had been pretty decent. But Limerick were better than us. Deep down, I suspect we all knew it too.

One statistic that maybe tells a tale is that Limerick created 39 scoring chances from play that day and Galway just 19. On another day, it's quite possible they'd have hammered us.

In the Mater Hospital, my neck in a brace, I underwent a series of scans (CAT, MRI, etc.). At one point, the Galway team doctor, Ian O'Connor, arrived in with my phone, and one thing I remember is seeing a story go up on the RTÉ website suggesting I'd been given the 'all clear' before they'd even brought me up for a single scan.

I remember too the Limerick chairman, John Cregan, sticking his head in the door just to say, 'Hope you'll be okay, Joe.' Apparently, he'd come in with Aaron Gillane, who was being supervised somewhere else in the hospital after he too had taken a heavy knock.

It would be close to midnight when I was told I was free to go, and Ollie, who'd been working on the game for Sky that day, came in and drove me home to Gortanumera.

I felt as if I'd been hit by a train and remember being in a chair in the kitchen the following morning, Mam sitting opposite me.

She asked me how I felt, and fully programmed for self-pity, I began to itemise my issues.

'Awful pain in my shoulder and down along my arm, fair sore now ...'

I was in mid-sentence when a little adult perspective made me stop. Mam's cancer had returned that summer. She'd had a few fainting episodes and was struggling to eat. We knew she was feeling dreadful, but her way was always to play down her own troubles.

She'd never, ever complain about her own predicament.

'How are you?' I asked a little sheepishly.

'I'm grand,' she declared.

And I'm not sure I've ever felt guiltier in my life.

26.

THE LAST DANCE

My final season in a Galway jersey made retirement feel like the only sensible course of action.

Our championship lasted just two games, both pock-marked with periods of pretty shocking ineptness from us as a team that rendered any possibility of a prolonged run a fairytale.

Maybe it's a human instinct to downplay failures of the past once the great wheel prepares to spin again and I suspect that was our collective mindset at the start of 2021.

We'd hammered Wexford; been cruising against Kilkenny until that two-goal hit within 60 seconds; beaten Tipperary, and been level with Limerick after 70 minutes in the previous year's championship.

Why shouldn't we dare to believe?

On some level, I fear we bought into that crooked logic a little too willingly. Especially after a summer National League campaign that finished with Galway top of Division 1A, and accordingly, sharing the title with Kilkenny who'd topped 1B.

The idea was that, if we happened to meet in the looming championship, the fixture could double up as a League final. This never came to pass, though.

Our fault, not theirs.

In the modern history of Galway hurling, I'd imagine our defeat by Dublin on 3 July 2021 ranks right up there with our very worst days. Hand on heart, I had an inkling it might have been coming too.

We had a training camp in Johnstown House before that Leinster semi-final, and in their closing address to the players, management kept alluding to looming battles against the likes of Limerick, Tipperary and Kilkenny.

Dublin all but carried the silent status of a ghost in the room.

As the meeting ended, I made a point of approaching John Fitzgerald and articulating that view. 'John, we need to focus on Dublin before we even start thinking about other teams,' I told him. The message from the top that evening was essentially that we had bigger fish to fry. Dublin would be just a stepping stone.

It was a narrative doing the media rounds too: the idea that Galway might be the biggest threat to Limerick's All-Ireland defence now. We'd beaten them by six points at Pearse Stadium in the League, and there was definitely a belief within the group that we could match them on any given day. To be fair, at the time, they still hadn't yet quite developed into the powerhouse they would ultimately become.

Anyway, it seemed to me that Dublin were in nobody's conversation as championship contenders – certainly not ours. And they duly caught us cold.

I didn't train at that camp as I was nursing a slight hamstring tear picked up during our June National League win over Waterford. I'd just felt it go towards the end of the game when chasing Conor Prunty (dismissing it initially as cramp) and it certainly wouldn't be a game I remember with much fondness given that I also broke a thumb and suffered a rib injury on the day.

While the other issues healed with time, the hamstring never came fully right for me. I could train for a short while, but the leg would be getting weaker by the minute, and eventually, it would leave me virtually without any spring.

This wasn't ideal given that management had begun the

season trying me out in positions demanding real mobility like midfield and wing forward. I had the latter role in that League game against Waterford, and Calum Lyons continually stretched away from me, running into the distance like a gazelle.

To spare my blushes, I was eventually moved to full forward, which worked out reasonably well as I scored 1–3 from play.

That was where I started that Leinster semi-final against Dublin too, but it turned into one of those days when virtually nothing we did seemed to generate an ounce of momentum. Anthony Daly accused me on TV of disrespecting Dublin in the early stages when I went for goal from two 20-metre frees, both saved by Alan Nolan. But the truth was that Shane O'Neill had noticed the Dublin backs were slow to get themselves organised on the line when defending those frees and he told me before the game, 'Go for goal if we get an early 21.'

Had those frees gone in, who knows? But my shooting radar was off in that first half, especially with me alone guilty of six wides. Why were we so flat? It's hard to put a finger on it, but I do suspect that – above all – we were guilty of already looking beyond Dublin.

For me, personally, I knew that management didn't really trust me anymore. The accumulation of injuries meant I was barely able to train at all, and though I'd managed to overcome that handicap in 2018 (between knee and foot injuries), this was proving much more difficult three years later.

On some level, the very fact that they were putting me in at full forward left me asking myself if I even deserved to start in 2021. I do remember at one point thinking: *Jesus, I'm slipping here!*

But it wasn't really my ability that I was doubting. It was my body.

The changed dynamic of the dressing room was working even more brutally against Burkey now. Having been taken off at half-time in both championship games against Tipp and Limerick the year before, he came on as a sub just approaching half-time against Dublin, and then did not feature three weeks later when we made our championship exit against Waterford in Thurles.

On the evidence of training, I personally thought he was still good enough to be starting, but management clearly saw things differently.

O'Neill's management style was very stats- and numbers-driven. In fact, I've no hesitation in saying that some lads who started that All-Ireland qualifier against Waterford were picked entirely for their speed. There was a preoccupation with being able to match the runs of fliers like Jamie Barron, at the cost – I would say – of picking a team to hurl.

On the day, it was a real car-crash of a Galway performance, with Waterford a ridiculous 16 points clear coming out of the second water-break despite being reduced to 14 men with Conor Gleeson's red card on the stroke of half-time.

I'd been centrally involved in that incident, stepping across him to check his run, only to receive an awful dunt from the butt of Gleeson's hurl into my right forearm. I actually thought at that moment that he'd broken my arm the pain was so sickening. In the dressing room, the doctor thought so too, and I could see the startled look on his face as he was strapping it up and giving me painkillers when I said, 'This is probably my last game.'

We were 12 points down and needing a miracle.

I wouldn't say I'd categorically decided to retire, but it was definitely something hanging around in the back of my mind all year. Between the injuries and just not feeling really needed by management, I'd begun to sense that I was on borrowed time.

And if I'd lost a lot of things from my game, I still had my pride.

It was hugely important to me that, when I went, I would do so on my own terms. As a friend said to me once, 'You can never go too early, but you can always stay too late!'

I knew for sure that I could never accept being selected as a token gesture, someone getting a run only because of things done in the past. But that's how it had started to feel for me with Galway now. I'd got to the stage of genuinely wondering if I was getting selected because of who I was, rather than for what I could still do for the team.

The move back in to full forward certainly compounded that feeling given it's a very different place today to what it was when I was starting off. A different place that presents a different battle. There's much less space now for starters, and you need to be very fast in there to survive.

It was beginning to feel as if an accumulation of different factors was now pushing me towards the one door. An exit door.

That day against Waterford was the day I overtook Henry Shefflin as top scorer in the history of championship hurling, but I can genuinely say that it was the last thing on my mind going to Thurles that day. After all, it's not as if you get something for achieving that record.

And given the GAA itself isn't exactly great at keeping tabs on this kind of stuff, there's always a certain element of a guessing game to figuring out who might hold the record for what at any given time. I think I needed eight points that day to overtake Henry, but I genuinely didn't know the figure. As it happened, I got nine.

At the final whistle, I met Dad and Ivan on the field with two of the nephews, Jody and Andrew. There were a few people from Portumna there too, everyone a little shell-shocked by the tameness of our championship exit.

I do remember Dad was wearing a mask as I said to him, 'That's it. That's me finished!'

I'm not sure what he said in reply, or even if he said anything. I have a vague memory of Ivan protesting gently, 'What are you on about? Will you *stop*!'

Someone put me on the phone to Mam, and she was saying something similar. Hold your horses. Don't do anything rash. Deep down, I don't think any of them thought that this would be my last day. There'd been bits of speculation in some quarters that it might have been my final season at inter-county level, but I hadn't really said anything at home.

It was just a thought I'd been entertaining in silence.

I don't doubt there would have been a degree of consolation for them all that I was getting out on my own terms. It certainly made it easier for Dad going down for his pint and being asked 'Why did he retire?' rather than the alternative 'Why *didn't* he retire?'

There's a lot that goes charging through your brain when you're making that decision, though. What if Galway won the All-Ireland in 2022? Would I ever forgive myself if that happened, all the time thinking that I could still be in there with something to offer.

The truth was, though, I couldn't see it. If I could, no question, I'd have hung in there.

But there was another factor too, making the exit option the appealing one. Leaving Thurles that evening, I presumed that the same management team would be in place the following year. And it was clear that that management team didn't have much trust in me.

Covid hadn't helped given how much it impeded on collective training in 2020, and then in 2021 I just couldn't seem to get my body injury-free. So for two successive seasons, I lacked a certain physical sharpness, and I knew it.

I mean, you get three separate injuries in a single game, and you can't but help begin to feel that you're banging your head off a wall.

In the Semple Stadium dressing room, I told the Galway players that that was it for me, but that I didn't especially want my decision to be made public. I've always hated this thing players do these days of getting the GPA to issue a press release on their behalf. For me, it always has the air of an incredibly self-important act, and I've slagged plenty of good friends to that effect for doing it.

It's become something we specifically pick up on in the old college WhatsApp group. We gave Willie Hyland an awful going over when he announced his retirement from hurling with Laois, and I'm convinced the only reason Seanie Collins didn't go down the press release route in Clare was because we'd have given him such a hounding if he did.

So my approach was genuinely to slip away quietly. Say nothing. Do nothing. Allow the penny to drop with people over time. I told the county board that too, asked them to desist from saying anything.

And in true, clichéd fashion, we then took to the beer now that our championship was over. Probably a dozen of the Galway players ended up staying in my house in Limerick the night of that Waterford defeat after a session in the Kilmurry Lodge.

I have a blurry memory of Brian Colcannon volunteering to mow the lawn, then quickly abandoning the job with just a single stripe visible in the grass.

It was home to Galway then on the Sunday and more drink, more clutching at straws for a season that had turned so sour so quickly.

Back in Limerick the following Wednesday morning, I had a pre-arranged interview to do with the *Off the Ball* guys at Newstalk. Inevitably, the question came up in conversation.

'Any thoughts about your future?'

'Ah, that's for another day,' I lied.

I had a Bord Gáis Energy photo shoot to attend in Portumna that evening, which would involve more Zoom interviews and – I began to realise – inevitably more questions about retirement. Was I just going to keep dancing around the subject?

As I usually did in times of self-doubt, I rang Frank. 'Am I better off just saying it now and getting this over with?'

Pointedly, he'd been maybe the one person who hadn't baulked the previous weekend when hearing me speak of retirement. He'd have questioned a lot of decisions I made in my career, but not that one.

I'd say Frank could recognise a certain writing on the wall in management's decision to stick me in at full forward. In other words, he could see the same things I could see.

So we agreed that, yes, it was probably best just to come clean now, and so, when the question duly arose that evening, I confirmed my intention to retire. After 14 years of hurling senior with Galway, I was calling it a day.

The journalists had their story, and soon as the Zoom call ended, I knew I owed the *Off the Ball* lads a big apology.

27.

OLD DOGS, HARD ROAD

In Portumna, our story has no end.

We won an under-20 B championship two years ago, and a lot of those players were teammates of mine in 2024. After a brutal 2023, during which we basically had no real management set-up, some life sparked in the jersey again.

With Seán Treacy as manager we did at least reclaim the semblance of a plan. I think I was one of only four survivors from the 2014 All-Ireland-winning team, among them Ivan, still going strong in goals at forty-three.

We were Senior B this year, and honestly, it reminded me of why I fell in love with hurling in the first place.

Routinely, we had an entire Canning half-forward line: me on the 'forty' and nephews Andrew (Ivan's son) and Adam (Davy's son) on the wings. Maybe I was a little harder on them than I was on other teammates because I suspect that's something instinctive that happens within family. When I was a young hurler, my brothers never spared me criticism, and hindsight suggests it didn't do me any harm.

Of course, you look out for family in battle, but not to the extent of mollycoddling. Ultimately, young lads have to find their own way in adult hurling, figuring out stuff for themselves. And there's a balance to be struck in that respect. Occasionally, they end up trying too hard to show they can stand up for themselves and fall into the trap of needlessly playing the hard man. When that happens, you have to calm them down. To remind them that the best way to hurt a mouthy or overly physical opponent is by putting scores on the board.

I've made a kind of pact with another nephew, Jody, that I'll do my best to hang around until he's ready to play senior. He was in with the Galway under-16s in the 2024 season, so that commitment needs to survive another couple of years. Jody pretty much lives for the game and given all the rest of the Canning boys have hurled alongside me at this stage, I'd say he just doesn't want to feel left out.

Will I make it? I hope so. But even warming-up brings pain these days, and I am routinely in a lot of discomfort the morning after training. The knee is still the problem. But surgery is hardly an option at this late stage of my hurling story.

Routinely you came up against lads looking to make a name for themselves by softening up the old county man. It's just something you get used to. Anyway, nobody should be laying down a red carpet for Joe Canning, albeit sometimes it can get a little stupid.

You can tell with some of them that they just want something they can brag about to friends in the pub later. So they try to rattle you by pushing and shouldering you before the ball is even thrown in.

It comes with the territory of the profile, I suppose. Honestly, that stuff has never bothered me. My reaction is generally: if you want to go down that route, we'll go down that route.

I'd be much more troubled if a young fella was out-hurling me, because if he's just concentrating on hitting me a dig, then I'm pretty confident I can get the better of him. For an ageing hurler, the scariest thing is being marked by someone who has better legs than you. Someone who keeps getting to the ball first. That's when you know you're in deep trouble.

I'm still comfortable enough going toe-to-toe with someone. I mean, I was never the fastest, and I'm hardly going to be covering 12 kilometres in a game now in my mid-thirties, am I?

But the hurling is still there.

One thing I was reminded of this year is that it is so hard to beat the feeling of winning a really tight game. To me, that's still the ultimate buzz. The comradeship in the dressing room immediately afterwards. The tightness of those bonds. The sense of having one another's backs. Of having been taken to the edge and survived. God, that's still an epic thing.

One of the best I can remember was in the 2021 county championship, and I wasn't even playing. I'd torn a groin tendon off the pubic bone against Ballindereen in my first club game after retiring from inter-county. This meant my championship was over.

But we ended up playing Beagh in a relegation play-off in Tynagh and beat them narrowly. Standing on the line that day, I'd say I was as thrilled as I've ever been after a game. It was an unbelievable win by the boys to keep us up, and you just can't put a price on the feelings that kind of victory gives you.

Your club, after all, is who you are.

The following year, Mam's death had left me in a deep hole psychologically, and without knowing it at the time, I think the run we had in the club championship helped pull me out of that hole.

Ollie, Chunky and McEntee were over the team, and there was this overriding feeling for all of us of not wanting to let them down. We ended up genuinely confident that we'd beat Sarsfields in the county quarter-final, a hurling altitude few imagined we'd be at just a few short months earlier.

Sarsfields were still a top Senior A team and, man-for-man, clearly better than us now. But we gave them an almighty scare before losing narrowly. Everything about us in 2022 was stamped with a flaring defiance that kept kicking in all year. Nobody gave us much of a chance in our preliminary quarter-final against Craughwell either, but we beat them.

Embedded deep within us every step of the way was that absolute belief that we were outsiders here. That nobody outside of Portumna wanted to see us be successful again. It drove us. It's always driven us. It still does. The idea that the rest of Galway considered us – as we were often told in club games – Tipperary c—s!

You know a lot of clubs around us have amalgamated in recent years, but we are still Portumna, undiluted. That's something I really like. The idea that we remain strong as a club. That we're growing again.

We've just won two under-11 Community Games All-Irelands in a row, and to me, that's unbelievable. Yes, I know not every club in the country enters. But those young Portumna lads have now won something. The game already has their hearts.

I'll be long gone by the time they get to adult hurling, but my nephews won't. I believe a decade from now, Portumna could be really strong again. Maybe not quite winning All-Irelands or even county championships, but still vibrant and very much alive on the hurling landscape.

I love that thought.

I brought the Galway under-20s to train in Portumna this year, and it was so good to see the number of kids that came to watch. Galway teams across the years never trained in our town or anywhere close. We've always been on the outside in that respect. And even though I'm based in Limerick now, I'm determined that my children find a strong sense of Portumna identity in their lives. A selfish part of me would love them to play for the club, but that's not really realistic. I joke at home that, if my kids are any good, I'll personally be driving them to Portumna for training.

You see, it's never really been overly about Galway for me when it comes to who I am. It's first and foremost about Portumna.

Initially, I had big plans for inter-county retirement, among them the idea of doing a few triathlons. But then I started running on the road and realised pretty quickly that the pain in the knee made that idea completely impractical.

For a while after Mam's death, I had no great appetite to do anything. I didn't stay in shape and put on about a stone. The gym held no appeal for me. In fact, taking any kind of exercise on my own just didn't interest me. Still doesn't, if I'm honest. That's why the training nights in Portumna were a godsend this year. It's about a 55-minute drive from Limerick, and I always timed it so that I could sweep out to Gortanumera beforehand to see Dad for maybe half an hour. Not once did that ever feel remotely like a chore.

I did have to balance my time this year between training with the club and making sure I wasn't an absentee selector for Fergal Healy with the county under-20s. Given training nights often clashed, I togged out regularly in Loughgeorge for under-20 practice matches, something I genuinely felt was beneficial to both sides. While it helped me maintain a decent level of fitness, it also offered an on-field insight into the character of young men we all hope can play a big part in Galway's hurling future.

On the field, you see things – or maybe, more accurately, sense things – in players that you'd never be able to detect sitting in a dugout.

It also allowed me to have the craic with fellas little more than half my age and, trust me, you never lose the determination to win a training match, no matter the circumstance.

I'd certainly never describe myself as a coach, and being honest, I'd find it hard to come up with a full training session if challenged to do so. That's something you never really think about as a player. The amount of planning that must go into every single session if an environment is to remain fresh. It sounds simple, but it isn't.

Players expect something different every night and won't be slow to grumble if anything begins to feel remotely stale. Personally, I always favoured simple drills that involved plenty of touches. For me, you can adopt all the science and various avenues towards aerobic fitness, but ultimately, it's what you do with the sliotar that will always matter most.

I was surprised when Fergal rang last year, inviting me on board with the Galway minors. It wasn't something I had planned or expected to do so soon after retiring from the inter-county scene. Yes, I saw myself maybe doing something with the under-15s and under-16s in Portumna, and I had started a few bits and pieces with Johnny Kelly and Seán Treacy. But my suspicion is that I wouldn't make a good manager because I just don't have the personality to have a handle on everything at one time. That's a skill in itself. The ability to communicate authority while delegating smartly, and above all, remaining even-tempered.

The latter part especially is where I'd struggle.

In some respects, being involved with the under-20s has been even more fulfilling than my role with the minors last year, for the simple reason that you're in closer contact with the senior set-up.

The lifestyle required to hurl at senior inter-county level today isn't far short of actual professionalism. And for some, that just isn't compatible with their personalities or life circumstance.

Like my nephew Jack was in for a while with Henry and the boys but decided eventually that it wasn't really for him. When that happens, you have to park your own ambitions and expectations for a family member on the basis that everyone must choose what's best for them.

After his heroics in the 2017 All-Ireland minor final, Jack

hurled with the Galway under-21s in 2018. But he'd shown a lot of promise on the rugby field too as a flanker with Cistercian College, Roscrea, and moved to Australia to play professionally with Northern Suburbs in Sydney, returning home in 2020.

Having the Canning surname probably presents its own pressures in Galway too because people almost want to write a story for you rather than give you the space to write your own.

Jack was Portumna captain in 2023, and it's fair to say it was a challenging experience. We'd had that great year in 2022, playing seven championship games and winning six. The only game we lost was that county quarter-final against Sarsfields. Topping our group propelled us up to Senior A, but in 2023, everything just seemed to fall apart. The management team stepped down; we had a bunch of retirements that arrived together, and some lads simply decided to take the year out. It all felt like a perfect storm that left us completely ill-prepared for Senior A hurling, meaning we took some heavy beatings and ended up relegated.

But some who took a year out were back in 2024, and generally, the vibe around the group was just a good deal healthier. It's a long shot to think the club will ever get back to the heights we reached between 2006 and 2014, but then I don't suppose anybody in the town really saw that stretch of glory coming either.

When I think of the four All-Irelands we won, that last one in 2014 strikes me as the most improbable. Put it this way, I will always still seek Frank's counsel before making key decisions in my life, but the idea of him becoming Portumna manager in 2013 didn't exactly feel like anything seismic.

He lives in Roscommon and had been managing Pádraig Pearses hurlers there for three years without winning a county final (played in three, lost three) when he got the gig with us. We'd struggled for the previous two years under separate management teams and hadn't won a county title since 2009.

So what was his secret? I think he managed to remind us of who we were and what we had been. He tailored training to the needs of players he himself had soldiered with for years. He saw it as a one-off deal that would either work or it wouldn't. Looking at his CV, you'd have been inclined to predict the latter. But I think people, generally, underestimated us that year. They saw us as an old team chasing a distant past. It allowed us to catch a lot of people off guard.

I scored 0–5 from play from midfield in our drawn county semi-final against St Thomas's, and to this day, Davy Burke says to me, 'I honestly don't know what the fuck you were doing in midfield that day!'

Thomas's probably thought we were pulling some kind of stunt by putting me out there. We weren't. We were just approaching things differently.

Under Frank, there was no flogging of people on the training pitch either and no effort to intellectualise something we all knew to be inherently simple. You either hurled for one another or you didn't. You either lived on the field or you died. Our dressing room became incredibly tight again, and it's fair to say we pounced on any imagined slight we could detect coming our way from an opponent.

Before we played Limerick and Munster champions, Na Piarsaigh, in the All-Ireland semi-final, their manager, Seán Stack, depicted us in some interviews as yesterday's men. That, at least, was our – enthusiastic – interpretation of what he said. Eugene McEntee had come out of retirement, and Shane Dowling was quoted afterwards as saying that he'd never actually heard of him. You can just imagine how that sat with people in Portumna.

Na Piarsaigh had a cracking team with serious fire-power in the likes of Dowling, Kevin Downes and David Breen. And playing midfield that wet evening in Thurles: a certain Will O'Donoghue.

But we were old dogs for the hard road, and they couldn't live with us. You could say there was an element about Portumna that day of the band getting back together. We knew this was our last shot, and it felt as if nothing was going to stand in our way.

I sense people underestimated that depth of defiance in us.

There was an AIB TV advertisement for the club finals at the time, built around a dressing-room scene with Mount Leinster Rangers before their semi-final defeat of Loughgiel Shamrocks. It featured one of their players, James Hickey, delivering this rousing speech in which he declared: 'If we genuinely, genuinely believe that we're going to win today, we will win. I am 100 per cent convinced we will win. I am 100 per cent convinced! Do not let yourselves down today, lads. I want to go out in Croke Park on Paddy's Day. I want it more than anything in the world!'

To be fair, it was a great speech that got a lot of traction at the time, especially after they'd beaten Loughgiel. Sadly for Hickey, he subsequently sustained cruciate ligament damage in a challenge game against Offaly, meaning he then missed the final against us. But he was still absolutely determined to make his presence felt that day in Croke Park, and he did.

As we were coming out for the second half from under the Cusack Stand, he happened to come running behind me and decided a heavy shoulder from behind might be in order. So he hit me hard, roaring something along the lines of: 'We fucking have ye now!'

But as he ran away, still mouthing, my midfield partner, Leo Smith, absolutely buried him with a dunt. You could see Hickey was sickened, trooping off to the dugout without another word.

He'd made the mistake a lot of people made about Portumna that year. He mistook us for a group that could be bullied.

28.

SUFFER LITTLE CHILDREN

I look at the pictures now and can't help but wonder about the children.

Are they safe? Have their lives been reconciled with even the faintest idea of fairness? Can they see a future now? Are they dead?

Sometimes I want to stay as far away from the memories as I can because faces can be haunting. There was this little maybe four-year-old girl, Nour, I met when visiting Aleppo in 2017. A year before I went there, she'd been found traumatised in rubble by a soldier, barely able to say her name.

This tiny, innocent child already hopelessly brutalised by war.

Nobody really could be sure of her age because none of her family had survived to verify it. In other words, she could have no birthdays in her life. At least, none that were anything more than notional.

How she is today, I can't honestly say. The earthquakes in 2023 brought such chaos to the border region between central Turkey and north-west Syria, it was as if God's back was turned towards the people living there.

I mean, Aleppo was no longer even a viable city when I visited: it was a landscape of ruin, hardly a single building left intact from the bombs of their own president. Then, just as some spirit of recovery began to express itself, two earthquakes came.

What kind of God allows this to happen? What kind of world can be indifferent to these people?

In November of 2011, I travelled to Eswatini (then known as Swaziland) with Kildare footballer Dermot Earley, as GPA ambassadors with UNICEF. It was the first step in a relationship with UNICEF that continues to this day, and I am now on the board of directors of UNICEF Ireland. It's a role I take extremely seriously, and in case anybody's wondering, it doesn't come with any financial reward. Over the years, other charities have approached me to get involved with them, and I've often felt bad resisting their approaches. But I don't want to run the risk of my commitment to UNICEF being diluted in any way.

That first trip to Eswatini took Dermot and I into the heart of one of Africa's poorest countries, a place with the highest HIV prevalence in the world and one in which a staggering 40 per cent of the children suffered from stunted growth because of malnutrition. UNICEF runs clinics and hospitals there to monitor these children and try to ensure they get, as a minimum, some kind of therapeutic feeding. One of the things that always stuck with me was how a teacher in one of the schools said that many of the children dreaded the summer holidays because, out of school, they no longer were guaranteed that single daily meal.

As a father myself now, just thinking of that makes me sick to my stomach.

In 2016, I visited Gazientep on the Turkish–Syrian border, the destination for so many refugees from Aleppo. The thing that strikes you in such places is that these people are left essentially with zero possessions beyond the clothes on their back. Their lives have been destroyed.

In Aleppo a year later, I saw the children collecting spent bullet shells in the way our children might collect Pokémon or soccer cards. They knew the weapons that different shells came from and could identify them just from the sound. It was heartbreaking to see the lethally dangerous environment they were growing up in. An environment they end up accepting as normal.

On both my trips to Gazientep and Aleppo, I was accompanied by the *Irish Independent* photographer, Mark Condren. It's on those field trips that I can be of most value to UNICEF because of the attention I can bring to their work in these areas. That work focuses hugely on psychological support, not just for the children, but the staff working with them. It's about trying to give them some element of escape from the trauma, be it through sport, art, drama, music – anything to take their minds off the chaos around them.

In May 2024, I visited the Zaatari refugee camp, about 15 kilometres from Jordan's border with Syria. The camp is home today to roughly 80,000 people, about half of them children. War has driven these people into this ad hoc model of community: a bewilderingly dense landscape of tents, huts and galvanised sheeting – shelter for those thrown together by conflict and who now have nowhere else to go.

It is an old cliché, I suppose, that you routinely encounter the most beautiful spirit in the most desolate of circumstance, but that is the truth in Zaatari. One street in the camp they call their Champs-Élysées – a few hundred yards of stalls selling just about anything they can get their hands on. It is their market, the beating heart of their community.

To put it mildly, conditions are hard in this place. Only one person per household is allowed to work so that everybody gets access to some kind of income. Identity cards are mandatory. Electricity is restricted to maybe seven or eight hours a day and water is strictly rationed.

UNICEF's work in Zaatari ranges from sinking wells, putting in sewage systems, building schools and organising vaccinations. The organisation's hope is that people can access a future here through education, although you have to be respectful of culture in how you do that. We make no distinction between boys and girls in class, but some families still believe that women should stay at home. That attitude may seem backward from our perspective, but it's maybe worth remembering that not too long ago women in Ireland had to give up their profession once married.

Almost everybody in the camp has a story in their lives that would horrify you. We met one young man who had tried to end his own life. His whole family moved to Zaatari to try to escape the memories, but you can tell there is no escape from that kind of horror. While the boy himself and his mother were talkative, the father was broken. He barely spoke, and I was struck especially by the defeated look in his eyes.

We spent two days there, and if I'm being honest, I find it embarrassingly easy to do the required mental reset of arriving back home. Certainly easier than it should be. It's remarkable how quickly you can lose perspective again. Even on the way out to Jordan, a four-hour stop in Istanbul allowed me tune into that afternoon's GAA games on my laptop. I was, essentially, a tourist dipping in and out of a completely messed-up world.

A couple of days after arriving home, I bumped into another car at a traffic lights, and for the next few hours, that harmless little tip had me completely preoccupied. I was mortified. I had to remind myself of where I'd been and what I'd seen just a few days earlier. I'm not saying that what I see on these trips doesn't affect me. It absolutely does. I don't see any way I'd still be involved with UNICEF after all this time if it didn't. But I wouldn't be doing anybody any good coming home depressed by the experience.

My job is to use my profile to highlight the work UNICEF do, the reasons for it and the endless need for funding. The last bit of that has been getting harder because of the wars in Ukraine and Gaza. In some respects, displaced Syrians can feel like the world's forgotten people these days.

The people in the field are extraordinary. Honestly, I don't believe I could have more admiration for anybody than I do for those who live in those conditions, striving to save the children. After all, I'm not there to build a shelter, I'm just there to tell a story and be back home within a few days.

Some people consider it reckless on my part to go to these areas. Like Zaatari is basically 90 minutes from the West Bank. But it certainly helps that Meg isn't the type of person to fret in these circumstances. She's a strong, independent person who believes – as I do – that just because you're in a relationship shouldn't mean you can't still do your own thing.

I got plenty of advice prior to that trip to Aleppo that it mightn't be entirely safe for us to go there. But my view was that UNICEF and the people they work with on the ground would do their utmost to ensure our safety. That they wouldn't exactly be cavalier about the circumstances of our visit.

To get to Aleppo, we flew to Beirut and then a 10-hour journey in an armoured vehicle, taking us through places like Homs. There were massive posters on either side of each checkpoint we encountered: Bashar al-Assad on one side, Vladimir Putin on the other. You could cut the tension with a knife every time as our papers were scrutinised.

I particularly remember being in this small village one day, listening to stories from the children about what they'd been through. Next thing, this jet thundered by directly overhead. I instinctively ducked, but the children and staff around them never even flinched. This was their normality. Driving back into the city about half an hour later, I could see this huge cloud of black smoke rising in the distance, maybe a kilometre away. The jet had hit its target. Assad and the Russians were dropping barrel bombs on hospitals. Not unlike Gaza, Aleppo also has this huge network of caves, and often they'd just blow up the buildings from underneath.

In Syria alone, it is estimated that there could be as many as five million children in desperate need of help, be that in terms of food, water, warm clothes, education or even the simplest access to sport.

In the compound we stayed in, the window frames vibrated to the sound of gunshots at night. Just imagine living with that as your daily reality. The psychological damage it inflicts has to be momentous. I personally found that sound hugely unsettling, and for children to become immune to it is utterly depressing. To be there for a few days, immersed in that landscape of ruin, I had to keep reminding myself that this wasn't a movie set. It was our world.

And on so many levels, we ought to be utterly ashamed of it.

29.

TOOLS OF OUR TRADE

In my head, a favourite hurl all but has a personality.

When you find one, it is far more than just timber. It becomes something almost animate in the rhythm of a hurler's life, something settling and sure. I grew up in a world where hurls were never taken lightly.

With three carpenters in the family, I suppose they couldn't be. We were always fixing them, banding them, honing them into some vague concept of perfection. Long before hurls became a family business, they were in our blood.

The first hurl I made was the one with which I won my first ever senior county title. It was 2005, I was still in school, and God alone knows how many hours were spent spoke-shaving it down to something that felt almost weightless in my hands.

You never really know what you're chasing until it's right there in front of you – an accident of time. They almost become scrapbooks in their own way, spinning out memories both good and bad.

For almost a year after the 2018 All-Ireland final, I had this love-hate thing going on with one in the boot of my car. It was the hurl with which I hit that last second free that could have earned us a replay against Limerick.

If I could get one moment back from my inter-county career, that would be it. I'd give anything to be standing over that free again. Why? Because I'd trust my swing a bit more and not try to hit the ball so hard. The free was so far out I was easily forgiven for not quite having the range, but the memory actually sickens me.

Living in Limerick, I get almost daily expressions of gratitude now for not spoiling a day that became the launch pad for their team's recent dominance. It's always said in jest, of course, and naturally, I just smile. But Christ, it sticks in my craw.

I loved that hurl, but every time I opened the boot, there it was reminding me of a moment I could – and in my own head maybe *should* – have seen to it that history was written differently. I was still using it in club matches, but all I ever saw when I looked at it now was that Canal End free beginning to drop short.

So I was playing golf in Adare one day, spotted J.P. McManus and handed it over, telling him, 'Listen, you might appreciate this more than I will.'

It was, after all, Limerick's first All-Ireland win since 1973, and for someone as passionate about their county as he is, I reckoned it might be a souvenir he'd appreciate. To some degree, it offered a little closure too. At least, no longer looking at that stick, I wasn't having to revisit one of my biggest regrets on a daily basis.

It was during the downturn, when the construction industry all but ground to a halt, that the idea of setting up a hurley-making business gathered steam at home.

Eventually, in 2010, five of us got involved: Frank, Ollie, Ivan, Deirdre and me all putting in a few bob to set up the business in a converted garage behind Ivan's house. And from there it just took off in a way that none of us could ever really have anticipated.

Strangely, Seamus, who was the first real hurley-maker in the family, stayed out of it, choosing to focus instead on his farming.

Bonanza time became the Ploughing Championships, a mysterious world to most people but – to the farming and, accordingly, the GAA communities – a great September institution.

We sold out of hurls in our first year taking a stand there, and that taught us a costly lesson. Demand would almost always outstrip supply at the Ploughing, so you needed months of preparation to be ready.

Maybe over 200,000 people would attend across the three days, and though you could have up to 13 or 14 separate hurley-makers taking spots, the queues seemed never-ending.

We were invariably positioned beside the O'Neills stand, and in time, crowd control actually became our biggest issue. Together we learned on the job, creating this one-way system that eased congestion through barriers and security personnel. Over time, it was decided to remove me from the selling process altogether as my presence began slowing everything down.

Things went bananas in 2017 especially when I brought the Liam MacCarthy Cup with me, so much so that I ended up just putting it away under a table. Eventually, it was agreed that I'd just stand in for photographs and sign autographs, with the others doing all the selling.

We shifted huge numbers in that environment and were always proud of the fact that we were selling a hand-made product.

After running out one year, a rival hurley-maker offered to deliver 300 machine-made sticks to our stand the following morning, inviting us to put the Canning stamp on them and sell them as our own. We turned him down. It was never just about making money for us. That business had our name, and therefore, our reputations to uphold.

My high profile was a selling point for children especially, and there were plenty of days when family tensions would boil over about my availability to meet customers in the week of a big game. Ivan, who basically ran the business, always reckoned I should have been far more available.

It might be the Friday before a Leinster Championship

semi-final or final and I'd get a call: 'There's a family driving all the way down from the Glens today, you'll have to be here!'

And I'd be instantly indignant.

'Not a fucking chance!' I'd bark, my head already locked in game mode.

This would have been a routine source of tension, Ivan probably thinking I needed a kick up the backside; me thinking he had no real concept of the pressure I'd feel under coming up to a championship Sunday.

Over the years, I actually became less and less visible around the family home from the Wednesday of such a week – the idea being that I could avoid questions about the coming weekend.

I would have been there right through all the summers from 2010 to 2013 while still in college, but once I moved to Dublin in 2014, my presence became far more sporadic.

Ivan was often exasperated by that. As he saw it, I had an obligation to be on site to meet customers. To be fair, I could understand his position. My frustration was just that he could never seem to understand mine.

Galway getting to the All-Ireland finals in 2012, 2015, 2017 and 2018 was massive for the business, but curiously, our hurls tended to sell far better outside the county, specifically in Cork, Tipperary, Clare, Limerick and even Dublin.

It was great while it lasted.

But you work off certain margins, and over time, the costs began to spiral. As with every hurley-maker, the ash dieback disease – first detected here in 2012 – became a major issue in the most basic terms of supply. When we were starting off, you could buy an ash plank for maybe €7.50. By 2022, it would have been about twice that.

We decided it was just no longer viable to keep the business open, and eventually closed it on 1 April 2022. People probably thought it was an April Fool's joke when they saw the announcement, but Canning Hurleys had simply run its course.

A sad decision for us all. But a sensible one.

30.

SHORT FUSE

I'm a contrary sort, that's something I can't deny.

There have been times I'm sure I've been a nightmare to be around, be it at home or on a training field. The joke in Galway was always that Davy Burke was Good Cop, I was Bad Cop. Davy was accomplished at putting out fires, and he needed to be. Because I was often on a mission to set them.

Actually, Burkey's on the record in describing me as 'an unbelievably contrary trainer', and I don't doubt he'd have plenty of support for that opinion.

I could certainly be a bit of an Antichrist if ever I suspected standards slipping, specifically someone just shrugging their shoulders at a mistake. Like a ball overhit into the corner that just runs out harmlessly for a puck-out. Oh, sweet Jesus, that kind of thing could really trigger me. I'd go ballistic.

'What the fuck are you at?'

Being an inside forward, stuff like that would infuriate. Or a high ball put in on top of a small corner forward. It's not complicated. The ball delivered in has to give the forward some kind of advantage, however marginal, on the fella marking him.

Another thing to really grind my gears would be someone taking a tap-over point when it was clear that there was a goal on offer. This was always a thing with me. If the goal is on, go for it!

So over the years it's fair to say I'd have rubbed a lot of lads up the wrong way. Just ask James Skehill. The grief I'd routinely give James over puck-outs, there must have been nights he was fit to come charging out of goal and break a hurl off me.

So plenty of arguments, plenty of crap. A lot of lads looking at one another as if to say, 'Ah fuck, Joe's gone off on one again!'

I just always wanted to be in an environment with a hatred of losing. You look at that Michael Jordan series on Netflix, *The Last Dance*, and it's fair to say you don't come away from it under any mistaken impression that he was pleasant to be around during battle. His ruthlessness didn't leave any room to be either sensitive or considerate. He was a killer on court. And to be a killer on court, you were left in little doubt that he was a killer in the locker room too.

Now I'm not for a second comparing myself to Jordan, but watching that documentary, I felt I could understand the less pleasant side of his personality. Being a nice person doesn't always feel compatible with having an edge in competition. If anything, it sometimes even gets in the way.

I wasn't contrary every night, far from it. But I was a stickler for standards. On some level, maybe it was even a selfish thing. For my own standard to be up, I felt I needed everyone else's to be up also. I was always a little uncomfortable if it felt that everything was running too smoothly. If there wasn't a physical, even cantankerous, edge to training, it worried me.

The normal thing would be a 15-to-15 training match the week before a championship game, and for me, that had to be played in a contrary environment.

You'd hear these stories of Kilkenny especially, and the insinuation that it was sometimes only the grace of God that people weren't transported away from Nowlan Park training games in body bags. Exaggeration, of course. Maybe even an element of propaganda. But you just knew that Brian Cody loved people having that perception of Kilkenny training.

A word I often saw media use in relation to Cody's preparatory games was *lawless*. That became the acid test of teams then. Can you cope with Kilkenny's intensity? Can you too convey that appetite for hurling in a *lawless* environment?

In my senior inter-county career, Galway played nobody more often than we played Cody's Kilkenny. And I loved those games. I loved them because I always felt they told you a certain truth about your hurling. If you could stand up and be counted against a Cody team, you were alright as a hurler.

So sometimes a sloppy training session would leave me driving home like a demon. Occasionally, I'd nearly try to start a row just to change the energy. Maybe by just saying something. Arguments and even little physical flare-ups were commonplace, and as I saw it, broadly healthy.

But there was one night during John McIntyre's time as manager when I genuinely thought my physical safety might be in jeopardy. We were in Pearse Stadium and Eugene McEntee, a Portumna clubmate of mine, was pulling and dragging out of me. Now I was well used to Mac's close attention, and to be fair, it was attention that always stood me in good stead for some of the more unscrupulous markers you'd encounter in the club game. If you could cope with Mac, you'd cope with most.

But this particular night in Salthill, the Galway management seemed to have decided that a practice game without the awarding of any frees might be the best preparation for what lay ahead. In other words, Eugene was given free rein, and I was slowly becoming more and more resentful.

Anyway, I got past him this time and, sure enough, instantly felt myself being dragged back again. I flicked back my hurl as if trying to shrug him off only to hear the sickening sound of timber smashing against his helmet. And down Mac went.

Being honest, I'd been trying to make some kind of physical

contact with the flick-back, just not across the head. So this was trouble.

I kept going, scored a goal but could sense every single person on the field take a deep breath now. It was almost as if there was a collective 'Oh fuck!' from the group.

Now did I say that Mac is mad? Hard as nails and perfectly happy to play hurling on a war footing. But this was an awful belt, and as he slowly got back up on his feet, I actually thought it might be a good idea to get the hell out of there.

For the next five or ten minutes, I nearly feared for my life, knowing I'd gone too far.

But Mac showed no reaction, sauntering back over to my patch again and mumbling, 'Right, let's go!'

Funny, McIntyre used often say to him, 'McEntee if you had a fraction more confidence in yourself, you'd be some player!' But the truth was Mac lacked nothing in confidence.

I'd say if it had been someone else who hit him this night, things might have been different. But Mac and I were good. I'd have got harsher treatment off him in Portumna training than I got off anyone, but it was perfect preparation.

No doubt, my crankiness got on a lot of people's nerves over time. I hated losing A versus B games. Winning one? I'd sow it into the lads we'd beaten. 'Ah hard luck, lads!' My accompanying grin dripping with sarcasm.

Lose and I was a pure bull leaving the field. Not the most likeable characteristic in a teammate, I can't deny that. But we all survive on personal energy. Mine was always, I suppose, keyed to some kind of adversarial wavelength. I'd shake hands, take my medicine. But there was always a side of me wanting to better the person I was up against.

It was something that I could park reasonably quickly once a game was over, though. As my national profile grew, signing autographs became a thing that I did. It wasn't to everybody's taste, especially after a Galway defeat. I understood that.

Sometimes our kit man, Tex, would come out to say, 'Joe, you're needed inside.'

If he didn't come, there'd be no limit on the time I might end up outside, the rest of the lads togged out and gone by the time I'd get back to the dressing room.

Why did I do it?

Because I always knew Mam and Dad would have hated the idea of me ignoring young kids looking for a simple signature on a hurl. Their attitude would always be: 'You were a kid yourself once. How hard can it be?' I knew they'd be disgusted if they ever heard I'd been ignorant with someone in that regard.

It wasn't something I especially enjoyed doing, though that, clearly, was the impression some took from it. If we'd been beaten the same day, I don't doubt that some of the lads would be asking, 'What the fuck is he doing out there?'

That often played on my mind: the idea that some teammates saw it as me just chasing the limelight. Maybe it looked as if I was loving the attention, yet there were days I genuinely hated it. Trouble was I just couldn't bear the idea of someone saying, 'Canning's got too big for his boots!' So I'd be standing there, thoroughly fed up, but still signing.

Adults were often trickier than kids, and there were times I'd have to ask them to stop pushing. They'd want to get something signed quickly and just get out of there, maybe on the basis they had a car-load of children to get home. I understood that. But the idea of pushing kids out of the way so that you can get something signed quicker isn't the most adult of behaviours, is it?

Over the years, an element of superstition kicked in with me too. Total strangers could come up to me in the street handing me Miraculous Medals, and Mam would then have to stitch them into my togs because it would play on my mind that if I didn't use them it might come against me.

This probably started around the time of the 2012 All-Ireland final, with people calling up to buy hurls and saying, 'Look, this might just bring you luck on the day.'

I remember once getting this piece of green material from a St Brigid's Cross around 2017 or 2018 that had been blessed and being told to tape it onto my hurley. When something like that happened, I felt I just couldn't ignore it.

Stuff like that would actually freak me out because I always felt if I didn't use it and we lost, I'd forever be blaming myself. Conversely, if I used it and we won, then the compulsion was there to use it every day.

Believe it or not, this plays on your mind, niggles at you endlessly. It might sound absurd putting such store on symbols like that, and I genuinely never wanted to be given any of it. If anything, I found it annoying.

But if someone was adamant that it would bring me good luck …

That's how vulnerable you can feel emotionally coming up to a big game. You don't want to leave anything to chance.

And it became another reason for me to try avoiding meeting people. I was desperate to sidestep any sideshow in my head.

Because sideshows were the enemy.

The older I got, the more on edge I started to feel. The smallest thing could leave me irritable. Like something as simple as a family member saying, 'Oh, I heard you were in such-and-such a place yesterday …'

I'd instinctively bristle when I'd hear that, seeing it almost as an invasion of my privacy. It wasn't that I was trying to conceal anything. I wasn't. I just felt I had the right to be somewhere without everybody knowing. So a single sentence might leave me uncomfortable, resentful even. I might have just gone for a coffee somewhere, but to have the detail of my day recycled like that just pissed me off hugely.

And that edginess seemed to grow and grow. I became increasingly self-aware when I was out somewhere.

This is hard to explain without sounding a little precious and I get that. But meeting someone for a pint, I'd easily get it into my head, rightly or wrongly, that it was now common knowledge within a mile radius of the venue that I was there. Joe Canning drinking, in other words.

During a meal out with Meg, well-meaning people would come over to say hello and effectively talk right over her. They wouldn't be remotely aware of how ignorant they were being.

On some level, I probably started to overread stuff in this kind of scenario.

Just someone looking across a bar or restaurant in my direction would irritate me. Ridiculous, really. But with the advent of smart phones came this paranoia. You might have fellas pushing their phones in your face without even attempting an introduction, and my only thought would be: *Would you ever just fuck off and leave me alone!*

You'd never say that, of course. You couldn't. But often the only thing you wanted to do was blend into the background.

Funny, Meg and I spent a week in Tenerife last January, and my father was asking me if we'd met anybody over there. My response was something along the lines of 'No, thank God!' The last thing I'd want on a week away with my wife would be bumping into people looking to talk about hurling. In some respects, for me, going on holiday is a means of escaping that.

And Dad's a little incredulous when I say that. He's looking at me as if to say: sure isn't that part and parcel of going on holidays? That you meet someone else from home that you can chat to about the GAA or whatever? People from different counties?

And I'm trying to explain that what works for him doesn't work for me.

Because for me, the simple transaction of dropping into a petrol station for a coffee or bottle of water routinely involves stopping to let someone have a selfie. Even now, this happens four or five times a week. People are lovely, and I'm more than happy to oblige. I also like to think I'm broadly decent and respectful when they ask. I understand the privilege of being who I am, the stuff that comes my way because of hurling. But if this side of my life could disappear tomorrow, honestly, I'd be perfectly happy to be done with it.

To Dad, the idea of being recognised is great. Something to be welcomed. To me, it's been a part of my life for so long, I just love the idea of going somewhere I know I won't meet anybody.

So going for a few pints, my preoccupation is that they will be quiet pints.

The pressure of having to be sociable, of always being nice to people; in other words, the pressure of constantly having to perform, really grates sometimes.

I don't think even my own family has ever fully understood that. They'd just see me as being unreasonably irritable some days. Whenever I felt they were asking too many questions, I'd be inclined to snap back. With the hurley business, one all-too-familiar sentence would exasperate me: 'We need you here today!'

Did meeting people have a negative effect on my performance? Probably not. But at the time, you're just trying to insulate yourself from someone saying the wrong thing. The last thing you wanted to hear was 'Ye'll beat them handy!' or 'I hear they're going to be missing so-and-so …'. These tiny mental deposits that might soften your focus. It felt like a constant mental battle, and that's why I wasn't especially nice to be around coming up to big games. Mostly, I'd be barky and snappy. A ticking time-bomb that eventually even the family stopped trying to dismantle.

When I retired from inter-county hurling, I started writing stuff down, almost as a subconscious mechanism against forgetting. There were things I felt that were important to me: emotions that I didn't want lost through the passage of time.

My relationship with journalists was one. Generally, it wasn't good. Post-2012, I pretty much came to the conclusion that 90 per cent of them were to be avoided. This, I don't doubt, was unduly harsh. But it was an attitude that came to serve a purpose in my career. It fed a certain anger. And, from anger, I drew energy.

Now that I'm working within the media myself, I see things from a different perspective. It's been a surprise to me how much negativity a simple observation can trigger. The hostility. The paranoia.

I was golfing in Adare one day last year during the week after one of Limerick's championship games. I'd made some comment on *The Sunday Game* about Gearóid Hegarty getting into a little scrap. Something along the lines of 'There's no need for him to get involved in that'. I'd also made a point during Limerick's game against Cork of suggesting that they'd actually thrown the ball rather than hand-passed it for a couple of goals. Basically, I just offered an opinion.

But this day in Adare, two fairly elderly Limerick supporters arrived into the halfway house as I was just getting a bottle of water out of the fridge. They were coming off the ninth hole; I was only about to start. Almost instantly they started jabbing fingers in my direction, accusing me of being a 'disgrace' because of my bias against Limerick. They were going on about how outrageous it was that their tax was paying for me to be on RTÉ when I hadn't a good word to say about the All-Ireland champions.

To begin with, I thought it might actually be a wind-up, that someone had put them up to it. But then I began to realise they were deadly serious, and I started trying to reason with them, asking what exactly it was I'd said that they considered to be factually wrong. They were having none of it, though, and kept coming at me until the staff in Adare had to intervene, telling them to back off. These two men in their late seventies, early eighties, could not be persuaded that I didn't have some anti-Limerick agenda. There was a third chap with them, and my impression was that he was totally embarrassed by their behaviour towards me.

My own playing colleagues felt a need to intervene too, arguing: 'Lads, will ye leave it go, for Christ's sake! This isn't the place or the time!' Eventually, they just pulled me away.

Having started out laughing at first, I was now angry. I was also racking my brain, wondering if maybe I had said something unfair on air. Had I actually had a go at Limerick? Or did I just give an opinion that they were throwing the ball?

That was probably the first time I got a sense of how people can so casually interpret an opinion expressed in the media as some kind of mean-spirited agenda. Maybe two hours later, as we reached the ninth, the two Limerick supporters were finishing up.

We were back in the halfway house, and the third fella in their company was clearly dragging them sheepishly in to apologise. So they came over to me, pretty much staring at their shoes as they murmured, 'Sorry about that earlier on ...'

I'd been stewing about it for the nine holes, getting angrier the more I thought about it. So my response now was: 'That's grand, lads. Just don't ever talk to me again!'

Maybe I could have been more forgiving, but I was absolutely fuming. As they walked back out, the Adare staff were apologising too. 'That shouldn't have happened ...'

I've been down to Adare since and seen the two old Limerick boys out on the course, but they haven't come near me since. To be honest, that's how I'd prefer it.

I'd never encountered anything like that as a player, and it really brought home to me this tendency of people to see an agenda where none actually exists. You point out something negative about how Limerick are playing, and suddenly it becomes an anti-Limerick agenda.

Passion overtakes reason.

It's taken a little time for me to understand that side of punditry: the appetite in some places to interpret what you say through a prejudiced lens.

I can accept now that I myself was guilty of that on some level while playing with Galway. I was too quick to take exception to what could, on occasion, have been a reasonable criticism of something I'd done in a game or failed to do. My reflex instinct was 'Fuck them!'

In other words, I was wired to look for something personal in the commentary, something I could use. And once you do that, it's almost impossible to have a pleasant relationship with those commenting.

It's only when you step out of that bubble that you realise you were probably over-analysing stuff, overreacting. I know now, and I can openly admit, that some of the stuff I took greatest exception to was in reality probably factually correct. But it's only from outside the bubble that I can acknowledge that.

One thing I found consistently infuriating was the casual depiction of certain teams or players as 'mentally weak'. I mean, how offensive is that? The idea that someone who quite probably never held a hurley in their lives, sitting in a press box, casually rubbishing the character of a player pretty much emptying themselves on the field below?

I couldn't ever accept that as justifiable.

As the GAA 'message' becomes more controlled, so too the gap between those who do and those who write about it grows to a chasm.

That became my mindset. If someone in the media was remotely critical of my performance, I personalised my reaction. I took the view that the same person probably couldn't put a ball over the bar from 21 yards out and straight in front of goal.

Now I can accept the fundamental flaw in this kind of reasoning.

The best hurlers don't always make the best managers; so it stands to reason that the best writers don't necessarily have to have played the game. But maybe I'm talking first and foremost about an absence of empathy here. Sometimes I'd find myself reading match reports with rising indignation as the journalist in question broke everything down to some kind of soulless computer game. The thing is, you don't break bones or end up needing stitches sitting at a computer console.

My own unease with media has softened a little now – without quite disappearing. To this day, my interaction with specific journalists is instinctively wary. I sense they're almost trying to catch me out, using me for a cheap headline.

This summer I was doing a Bord Gáis event when one asked me: 'Should Henry Shefflin be under pressure to keep his job if Galway don't win the Leinster Championship?'

My immediate reply was, 'Well, if I ever heard a headline-chasing question, that's one right there.'

The other journalists erupted in laughter. I mean, this wasn't even a subtle attempt to use me for the perfect back-page story: 'Canning says Shefflin's head on the block'. I didn't appreciate the question; although, I could accept his right to ask it.

Fair enough, I'm paid to meet the media in that environment, so why shouldn't he try using me to get that line? But on some level, that's precisely the kind of journalism that has always needled me. The kind that chases a line rather than asks a genuine question.

My eventual answer was something along the lines that everybody was under pressure for results. Something suitably neutral and bland. To me, it was a dickhead question, an attempt to pin my name on something that everybody could deduce for themselves anyway.

Trouble is, him asking it affected my engagement with the other journalists from that moment. Because he now had my back up, and instinctively, I didn't want to give him anything worth using. But he would have access to my answers to everyone else's questions too, meaning he'd get precisely the same material for the following day's paper as all the others present.

This is why I always preferred one-to-one interactions with journalists rather than what amounts essentially to the pursuit of sound bites. When I was being interviewed as a player, I always wanted it to work from both sides. I wanted to be an interesting interviewee. But I always hoped too that the interviewer would ask interesting questions. That way, it would be mutually rewarding.

The group interview feels entirely different. Over time, you realise that everything just gets pooled between the journalists so that even writers who haven't been present for the interview will still get access to what you've said. I get that this has become a matter of expediency for the media. They can't be everywhere at once, and with newspapers cutting back, this ensures that they're not missing out on a story. But for me, this means that the engagement lacks a certain level of sincerity. It feels like ticking a box, with the same quotes going everywhere.

All fine, really. But it's harder to be enthusiastic about engaging with that kind of process.

I absolutely understand how people might read this and see something fundamentally hypocritical in me being a part of the media myself now. But as I see it, all I'm doing on RTÉ or in the *Irish Times* is delivering an opinion or what passes for a former player's insight. The eye-opener for me has been in realising the heckles you can raise by simply doing that. There's a knee-jerk aspect to how so many people react.

That incident in Adare was the most openly confrontational aspect of this that I've encountered so far. But it's almost impossible to escape the comments on social media. You get tagged on something, and instantly, it's got your attention. I find it amusing that some lads who'd be nice as pie to your face can say something derogatory about you in a forum they simply presume you don't have access to.

Maybe I'm my own worst enemy here. On some level, I'm still inclined to seek out the negative stuff to give me that contrary energy.

Often, the media itself seeks to do this anyway. The appetite is to take a single line and give it a status it doesn't necessarily deserve. The idea is that you fan the flames of controversy.

I wrote in my column this year that I never feared playing Cork teams, no matter the grade. The reason? They always allowed you hurl. My debut season (2008) as a senior inter-county player produced my one and only loss to Cork in championship, running right through under-14s, -15s, -16s, minor, under-21s and senior. Did that comment make me anti-Cork, even though I also remarked in the column that I suspected other teams felt much the same about playing against Galway in my time?

The week that column appeared, Anthony Nash appeared on Newstalk's *Off The Ball* and was invited by presenter Ger Gilroy to address my comment that I always found it easy to play against Cork. Needless to say his invitation didn't reference the fact that

I believed others almost certainly felt the same about my own county. Basically, as I read it, Ger was teeing Anthony up to have a pop back at me. And he duly did, observing: 'I'd say Kilkenny would have said the same about Galway.' So it becomes this kind of Punch and Judy show on the back of me making what I felt was a perfectly reasonable observation.

So everything is parochial. If my punditry isn't complimentary of a county, that county's supporters instantly have a bone to pick with me.

The funny thing is that I'm nearly more critical of my own county than I am of any other. Anyone reading this book certainly won't come away accusing me of any pro-Galway agenda. But I try to be honest and call things as I see them.

And I like to think that my experience in the game has armed me with an ability to see things that might not be instantly apparent to everybody. I was doing a Wexford game in Thurles last year when I spotted Diarmuid O'Keeffe taking up an ostensibly curious position on the right side of the pitch. I knew instinctively what his role there would be – for the simple reason we'd done exactly the same against Clare during the 2018 championship. They were inclined to vacate the left corner forward position to leave big space in that area for John Conlon – then hurling brilliantly at full forward – to run into. Clare hit oceans of ball into that corner for Conlon to gather with his left hand, so our stats people were able to tell Daithí Burke to take an early step in anticipation of that pass for our All-Ireland semi-final replay. It worked too, Conlon restricted to just a single point from play that day after delivering a big performance in the drawn game.

I reckon it's far easier for a player or ex-player to recognise this stuff than it is for someone who has never played the game.

I'm not that interested in stats because, on some level, I feel you can prove just about anything by manipulating them. There's an expression that's crept into GAA writing in recent years of someone having so many 'plays' in a game. What does that actually mean? Surely a 'play' can be virtually anything, good or bad? It's the most meaningless of metrics in my view.

And there's another dimension to the media today that undoubtedly makes life tougher for genuine GAA journalists. I call them 'TikTok mouthpieces'. Fellas, it seems to me, who are employed by websites to deliver video rants against teams or individual players. These individuals are loud, abusive and often crude, yet have the gall to present themselves as bona fide journalists at a press conference. In reality, they're just shock jocks.

If you are a proper journalist wondering about the wooden quotes coming your way from a player at some media event in the future, it might be worth looking at the individual standing next to you. My view is that the job of the genuine reporter is becoming far more difficult because there are so many disparate strands (and standards) as to who qualifies as a member of the media today.

Put it this way: there is a profound difference between criticism and abuse.

I mean, I could see that those two chaps in Adare were proud Limerick men, but it was a really uncomfortable experience the way they rounded on me. It was also, in my opinion, unfair. Shout what you like at me when I'm on a hurling field – though, in some cases, that can go too far also. But in a private moment when I'm just out with friends? That's beyond the pale for me.

In the grand scheme of things, I suppose it wasn't that big a deal. I just felt it wasn't the time or place. Maybe being in the media changes certain rules; I'm still trying to get my head around that aspect of things. But that moment certainly left me feeling indignant.

This indignation, I don't doubt, makes me ill-suited to ever being a manager because I'm convinced I wouldn't be a good one. Someone like Davy Burke would, though, because he's far more even-tempered about all of this stuff.

I fear I'd just end up perpetually angry.

Not long ago, an article appeared on a certain website focusing on Portumna's supposed fall from grace as a club since last being crowned All-Ireland champions in 2014. The tone of the article was that everything had become a bit of a mess now as we, apparently, were relegated to intermediate status.

This was factually incorrect, given we'd won a relegation play-off and our status was actually Senior B. But what really antagonised me was how the story was personalised into an attack on my nephew, Jack. It suggested that he hadn't proved to be the 'saviour' so many anticipated after he'd been named Man of the Match in the 2017 All-Ireland minor final.

This kind of 'journalism' makes my blood boil, and I reacted accordingly, posting a link to the article on X (formerly Twitter) with the description: 'Another bullshit article by—'. The owner of the website hosting the article duly rang, pretty much begging me to take the post down and offering all kinds of incentives to do so, including €10,000 worth of advertising on their website for whatever I wanted.

I wanted nothing. To me, it was just important to make the point that this was the stuff that gives journalists a bad name. Not alone was the piece undermined by factual errors, it was trying to use Jack as some kind of scapegoat.

Phone call after phone call from the owner and other journalists from the offending site eventually led me to agree to delete my post. I'd already got thousands of likes and reposts at that stage, anyway, so was happy that I'd made my point.

The night after I deleted the post, the journalist in question tagged me in a video in which he was shadow-boxing and shout-ing to camera, 'I'll take you on, Joe!'

I immediately contacted someone I knew on the website who couldn't believe what I was telling them. But to me, his video confirmed unequivocally how this individual lacked even the most basic level of respect for the people he was writing about. We were just props to be used in pursuit of self-promotion.

To him, it was as if we weren't actually real people.

I accept absolutely that abuse comes with the territory, that huge public visibility leaves you a sitting target for the cheap shots. And you can laugh off a lot of what comes your way too.

Like when we were playing Offaly in Portlaoise in the 2010 Leinster Championship, their supporters behind the goal started chanting 'you fat bastard' at me. What could I do only smile?

And there was a genuinely funny one when we played a 2019 Walsh Cup final against Wexford in Enniscorthy. A real shitty January day weather-wise and just this narrow railing between players and supporters.

There had been a few sendings-off in the first half (Pádraic and Jarlath Mannion for us; Liam Ryan for Wexford) the same day, so we were down to 13 men as I went to take a free from near the sideline, maybe five yards outside the 21.

Just as I was going through my routine, this voice from directly behind me roared, 'Miss like you did in the All-Ireland last year, you fucking prick!'

In my own head now, I couldn't afford to miss, or this lad would really go to town on me. Anyway, I managed to put the ball over the bar, giving me licence to turn around and make eye contact with the loudmouth. And what did I see but a man, aged eighty if he was a day – definitely older than my father. He was leaning on the rail, staring back at me as if what he'd just been doing qualified as entirely rational adult behaviour. I was on the brink of saying something until I saw how old he was, stopped myself and turned away, laughing.

There were certain players, too, who you always knew could be depended upon to do their share of shit-talking. Lads like Eoin Larkin and 'Brick' Walsh invariably had something to say. Nothing sinister, just little comments they might make, hoping to put you off when taking a free.

In my very last championship game with Galway – our 2021 All-Ireland qualifier defeat to Waterford in Thurles – one of the sub-plots was me overtaking Henry Shefflin to become the all-time top scorer in championship history. Twelve points down at half-time, we scored three late goals to give the final outcome some semblance of respectability. But as I was preparing to take a free at one point, Stephen Bennett began roaring at me from the far end of the pitch about making sure not to miss, given it was for that championship record.

Just his way of trying to put me off.

To be honest, I never had any great issue with that kind of stuff, because to me, fellas like Larkin, Walsh and Bennett were at least out there in the cauldron themselves. I'd give as good as I got too, though I'd never actually start something. But if anyone started that shit with me, I was never going to be a shrinking violet either. To me, the players earned the right to have a little go. To do whatever it was they felt they needed to do.

Likewise, an eighty-year-old supporter. If that was his way of defending his county, so be it. At least it was within a match environment, not on the golf course.

But I'd always have a less benevolent perspective on media criticism.

One of the things I found very noticeable in John McIntyre's columns after he'd done his stint as Galway manager was the development of a greater sense of empathy towards those he'd left behind. I could be wrong, but I think John came to recognise just how much everybody puts into representing their county at senior level, and it changed the tone of his journalism.

Certainly, when Micheál Donoghue was getting the 'Fr Trendy' treatment off Ger Loughnane in 2016, I felt that McIntyre was quite measured in what he wrote. He had no appetite – as so many others had at the time – for dishing out cheap shots.

He understood that the words *defeat* and *disgrace* didn't always have to sit side by side. Something that, in Galway, hasn't always been too easily apparent.

ENDGAME

Galway's 2024 championship ended in May this year and there was a deep rawness to the circumstance of our eviction.

I watched the defeat to Dublin from a TV studio in RTÉ, early anxiety slowly giving way to exasperation as the team completely lost its way in Pearse Stadium. I'd said to Anthony Daly before throw-in that the game worried me, that I was struggling to identify a coherent game plan in the team this year.

They'd drawn with a depleted Kilkenny, been well beaten by a 14-man Wexford and seemed to me to be endlessly treading water.

Honestly, only the venue gave me hope that something might still ignite in them, but that hope essentially died 16 minutes in when Davy Burke got red-carded for a heavy collision with Fergal Whitely. Galway were five points up at the time. They lost the remainder by 11.

It was a terrible performance, but one undoubtedly defined by that single refereeing decision. I thought it extremely harsh and would say so on that evening's *Sunday Game*. But Galway's issues, I knew too, ran deeper that day than the loss of our All-Ireland-winning captain. That much was crystal clear.

Dublin's chief attacking threat, Dónal Burke, seemed to have the freedom of Salthill during a first half in which Galway's respectable scoring tally of 0–19 was completely undermined by the concession of two goals.

Burke got 1–4 from play during that 35 minutes, and I found it impossible to identify Galway's plan for policing him. It was as if we had none.

Every modern team – bar Limerick, who trust their system so implicitly – tends to have a specialist man-marker. Kilkenny's is Mikey Butler. Wexford's is Matthew O'Hanlon. In my time playing Kilkenny, we invariably put Daithí Burke on T.J. Reid. But all the tactical ambiguity of Galway's hurling in recent seasons seemed to be reiterated that day against Dublin. I said so on that evening's programme. It's difficult being critical of players you've hurled with, players you've even won an All-Ireland with, but that's what I signed up to.

You know that they're sickened to the very core by another lost season.

But there was nothing to sugar-coat about Galway in 2024, the season passing without a single consolation.

Dublin had ended our year with the under-20s too, and watching the huge outpouring of emotion a few weeks later as Offaly were crowned that grade's All-Ireland champions left me genuinely conflicted. Like just about everybody else, you couldn't but be pleased for that exceptional group of young Offaly hurlers.

But Galway are getting plenty of things right of late themselves, albeit results this year mightn't have communicated it. People keep asking whatever happened to the four All-Ireland-winning minor teams (2017, 2018, 2019 and 2020), and the straight answer is that it's taken time to have a county board in place committed to sensible physical transitioning of young hurlers for readiness to play senior.

Micheál Donoghue always pushed this idea of a natural strength and conditioning pathway from minor up through to senior, which is pretty much why he brought Lukasz Kirszenstein into the Galway set-up. But certain people reckoned they knew better – specifically board officials and one particular underage manager. They just went on solo runs, meaning that Donoghue, Shane O'Neill and eventually Henry Shefflin ended up working with young hurlers not quite physically ready for the intensity of senior inter-county hurling.

In other words, the self-interest, maybe the ego, of certain individuals held Galway hurling back, meaning we're now effectively playing catch-up.

No question, the pain of Galway's early departure from championship in 2024 was compounded by the identity of the opposition's manager.

Hand on heart, the idea of Micheál Donoghue managing a Leinster opponent just didn't sit well with me from the moment he was announced as Dublin's new boss. I said as much at the time in texts I sent to himself and selectors, Franny Forde and Noel Larkin.

A single line to each of moneybag emojis.

Not the most gracious sentiment, I accept, but I didn't like it. I still don't.

Believe it or not, Davy Burke would have been one of those arguing the toss with me at the time. Though he was still playing, he seemed far less affronted by the idea of our All-Ireland-winning manager taking over a county we'd be in direct championship opposition with. Burkey's view was that Micheál probably felt a need to keep his hand in at inter-county level. In other words, to stay relevant. The game at that level moves so fast, it doesn't take long to end up being left behind. Just look at Ger Loughnane. He was out of the inter-county game for 10 years and found it had totally changed when taking over Galway in 2007.

My view was less conciliatory.

You see, the Galway players still wanted Micheál as their manager when he decided to step down in 2019, and I would have been only one of many members of that dressing room to have gone to his house in Clarinbridge a number of times, making that very case.

My belief is that the Galway players have never really stopped wanting Micheál back, but he had his reason for leaving at the time, and for all of us, the primary one was a county board with some prehistoric tendencies and attitudes.

A board that is now gone.

Seeing Micheál in a Dublin tracksuit the day they dumped us from the 2024 championship just ran against the grain for me. And it's probably no secret that the immediate reaction of Dublin's management to that sixteenth minute collision probably didn't help Burkey's case when the referee subsequently went to his linesman.

I know that the mature view would be that Micheál, Noel and Franny are with Dublin now and have a duty to be in that camp unequivocally. Any other approach would be plain wrong.

But put yourself in Davy Burke's shoes for a moment.

He'd have been Micheál's main man all through 2016 to 2019, the two of them chatting a multiple of times every week. In other words, they (and we) went to war together and came out the far side, bonded by something for the rest of our lives.

So that moment in Salthill – for me, at least – was uncomfortable.

The friendships will survive. Without Micheál Donoghue in our lives, we wouldn't have won an All-Ireland, and we all know that. But hurling sometimes brings us to the rawest of places, and often, only time allows us to make adult sense of the emotion.

Maybe that's why it has such a presence in our lives.

It's more than a game to us. Far more.

ACKNOWLEDGEMENTS

I have had the great fortune in life to be surrounded by good people and, for me, that always started at home. I'd like to thank my family, Mam and Dad, my brothers, Seamus, Frank, Davy, Ollie and Ivan, my sister, Deirdre, and all of the extended Canning clan for being the people that they are.

I'd like to thank Meg and Josie for giving my life a whole new meaning, and I'd especially like to thank Meg's family for welcoming me so warmly into their lives.

In a team sport, you are nothing without the people around you and I'd like to thank my teammates in both Portumna and Galway colours with whom I've shared some of the greatest experiences of my life. Experiences that would have been impossible without every single one of those teammates.

I'd like to think that my love of Portumna especially resonates through the pages of this book and so it's only right that I express my sincere gratitude to all of my club coaches – from under-10 up to senior – as well as everybody who gave up their free time to make Portumna GAA club what it is today. A club I am deeply proud of.

Having played hurling for Galway from under-14 up through 14 seasons at senior level, I want to say a big thank you to the players, management teams and all of the extended backroom staff who invested such immeasurable time and energy into our efforts to bring success to the county.

The decision to write this book wasn't taken lightly and one of the people I am most indebted to for persuading me to put my story between these covers was the late John Trainor. John was a hugely important presence in my life, someone whose business judgement I always knew I could trust implicitly.

To that end, I'd like to thank the various companies I've had the privilege of working with in an ambassadorial capacity, specifically Bord Gáis Energy, Adidas, Red Bull and Connolly Motor Group.

I would also like to thank my friends and colleagues in UNICEF Ireland, an organisation I remain immensely proud to be associated with.

I'd like to thank all at Gill Books for their help and encouragement in getting this book onto the shelves.

And I'd particularly like to thank Vincent Hogan for the shared experience we've had of developing this book from a simple aspiration into something I believe we can both be proud of. Vincent is someone I trust immensely, and I am forever grateful that he came out of retirement to help me write this book. I've genuinely enjoyed the process.

There are so many friends I'd like to mention here but am reluctant to do so for fear of some glaring omission, so let me finish by expressing my unequivocal gratitude to everybody who has been on this journey with me. You all know who you are. Thank you.